THE CITIES OF THE POOR

THE CITIES OF THE POOR

SETTLEMENT PLANNING IN DEVELOPING COUNTRIES

EDITED BY ALAN TURNER

ST. MARTIN'S PRESS   NEW YORK

Printed in Great Britain.
First published in the United States of America in 1980.

Library of Congress Cataloging in Publication Data

Main entry under title:

The Cities of the poor.
    Includes index.
    1. Underdeveloped areas – City planning. 2. Underdeveloped
areas – Housing. I. Turner, Alan.
HT169.5.C57 1980   361.6′09172′4   80-10501

ISBN 0-312-13947-0

CONTENTS

ILLUSTRATIONS

TABLES

FOREWORD

Otto Koenigsberger

This is a book by consultants for consultants and their clients.

The professional consultant is a British Invention – a British gift to the world. During the first half of the nineteenth century, Britain led the world in industrialisation and the development of engineering technology. This technological leadership brought great advantages, among them hitherto undreamt-of wealth, prosperity and power. It also brought entirely new problems and difficulties. Not the least of these were the increasing complexities of industrial life, the increasing scale of operations and the increasing magnitude of investments. These combined to make it more and more impractical to base decisions on common sense alone. The investor needed advice and help from technical specialists on whom he could rely to defend his interests and – most important – his interests alone. As Britain was leading the world in technological advance, the need for such technological advisers, i.e. the need for consultants, arose first in Britain. The profession of the engineering consultant was born and developed in Britain during the late eighteenth and early nineteenth centuries. Other countries followed as their technological developments reached similar levels of complexity.

The Nature and Nurture of Consultants*

To avoid misunderstandings, it is essential to define the role of the consultant and identify the difference between his functions and those of the supplier or contractor. To begin with the latter, the dominant motive of a contractor or supplier is to make money. If he is good and has a reputation to uphold, he will give 'value for money' and often also sound advice in technical and design matters. However, it lies in the nature of his business that these are secondary motives.

As long as the transactions and sums involved are small, the buyer can trust his common sense. Learning by experience is feasible as long as individual mistakes are not so expensive as to break the bank. When we come to objects as large as hydro-electric power plant, a

*With due apologies to Dr Jane Abercrombie, from whose brilliant paper on architectural education (*Transactions of the Bartlett Society*, Vol. 2, 1964/5) this subheading is borrowed.

communications system, a hospital building, a large university or a whole new town, nobody in his senses would proceed without specialist advice. As the magnitude of the investment increases, it becomes more and more necessary to engage a consultant whose job it is to ensure that one selects the right supplier, employs the best contractor and gets 'value for money'. If the client has experience of business or administration, he will readily understand that he alone and nobody else must pay the consultant for his services, and that this must be known to be so.

When the client is a public authority, this last feature of the consultancy relationship is perhaps the most important. To avoid suspicion of corruption the choice of a contractor or supplier must not only be the best in the public interest, but it must also be seen to be so and to have been arrived at in the right manner. Assistance with the choice of a supplier or contractor is among a consultant's most valuable services to a public authority and can be an important contribution to good government. If an authority has to make decisions of this nature frequently, it will employ its own specialist advisers to fill the role of consultants. The public works department of overseas governments are typical examples of this. If the need occurs less frequently or is of an unusual nature, the authority will employ independently practising consultants on an *ad hoc* basis. As a safeguard against suspicion this tends to be a more effective alternative.

Good contractors and respectable suppliers welcome the existence of consultants, bad ones dislike it. Unfortunately, the world is full of adventurers who would like to make a quick penny at the expense of inexperienced or innocent (or perhaps not quite so innocent) governments. Consultants are thorns in their flesh. Bad contractors have a vested interest in convincing their clients that consultants are redundant. This does not mean that we should assume the existence of a 'contractors' Mafia' or organised lobby. Opposing the appointment of a consultant comes naturally to a surprisingly large number of people. There will always be a large anti-consultant faction, and that is why consultancy has always been a 'tender plant'. The most frequent ploy is for the contractor to call himself a consultant on the grounds that he has all the necessary specialists in his employment. Another is the so-called 'package deal', which is alleged to save the client a great deal of trouble and money.

The Planning Consultant

The planning consultant — like the consulting engineer — is a British invention. Britain was the first country to establish, in the 1930s and 1940s, physical planning as a separate and independent profession. Most of our colleagues on the Continent and in Russia (where economic but not physical planning was born sixty years ago) consider it to this day as a sideline of architecture.

All that has been said about consulting engineers applies even more to consulting planners. Even the most tight-fisted treasury official or accountant has to admit that decisions on major engineering works or electronic installations require special expertise and that it is worth while spending a small percentage of the investment capital on hiring independent consultants. Not so with planning. The design and planning of human settlements is one of the most complex and taxing tasks that has ever confronted human ingenuity, and yet it is still widely thought of as a matter of common sense alone. Everybody likes to think of himself as a planner. There are many officials who secretly believe that the employment of a consultant might reduce their own decision-making powers. More often than not, such unspoken emotions get fortified by political resentments. Instead of being welcomed as a friend and as a much-needed adviser and advocate, the planning consultant finds himself treated as 'an outsider who presumes to tell us how to run our affairs'.

Initial Mistakes

The first generation of Western planners that went out to help the poor countries of the Third World was convinced that it had a lot to give and teach. The planners of the 1950s and 1960s believed that the concepts, methods and techniques that had been developed in the West were the social equivalents of natural laws and, as such, universally applicable. They did not realise that the ideas, methods and rules of work which they had learned in their universities were the results of the particular political, economic and social conditions of their countries of origin and therefore inapplicable to countries where these conditions did not apply. The early attempts to introduce, for instance, British development plans into India or North American regional science models into Chile did little to help India or Chile and a great deal to harm the reputation of the planning profession. The present generation of planners has a hard task to live down these initial mistakes. The planner who was received with great expectations in the early post-war years finds himself nowadays treated with suspicion or − worse − ignored by those whom he is anxious to help. This distrust, and sometimes even dislike, applies not only to the foreign expert, but also to the foreign-educated local planner.

Planning consultants who operate today in developing countries are aware of the handicap they have inherited from their predecessors. They know also that they do not possess an established body of professional knowledge of planning in developing countries which could form an intellectual base of their operations. There are few concepts and ideas that would be acceptable to the Third World without adaptation and even fewer universally applicable techniques for the diagnoses, prognoses and prescriptions that are expected from planners.

The Medical Analogy

The medical metaphor is particularly apt in this context, because it contains the clue for a way out of the planners' dilemma. Doctors faced a similar situation when they started working in tropical countries overseas. They have, over many decades, insisted that every practitioner records and publishes his experience and thereby contributes to the building up of a new body of medical knowledge. These records of experiences formed the basis of specific theories and hypotheses for the many different climates and cultures in which doctors had to operate. Over the years, these hypotheses have been tested through experiments or controlled field trials. They have been confirmed, modulated or refuted through the recording of new experiences and eventually included in a new generation of textbooks that do not claim universal applicability, but are limited to particular conditions or geographical regions.

I welcome the opportunity of introducing *The Cities of the Poor* as one of the first attempts to apply the time-honoured methods of our medical colleagues to the subject of settlement planning in developing countries. I would like to see it accepted as a prototype of a new kind of textbook for the planning of poor communities, as a textbook that does not claim to lay down an immutable gospel, but rather presents itself as a challenge to the profession to conform, modify or refute the conclusions of its authors through further observations, case studies and experiments.

The New Approach

The book by Alan Turner and his colleagues derives its special flavour and importance from the recognition that settlement planning in developing countries presents a multitude of new problems that cannot be solved by the transfer of Western methods, and from an attempt to derive new answers to such problems from detailed case studies of Third World settlements. Some of these are summarised in the appendices to

Chapter 2, for instance those of four new city foundations at Ciudad Guyana in Venezuela, Bogota in Colombia, Huambo in Angola and Pahang Tenggara in Malaysia; others are quoted in the context of specific subjects such as the editor's experiences of housing in Madras or upgrading of squatters' colonies in the Philippines, but all chapters — even those where this is not explicitly stated — should be read as advice based on the authors' personal experiences.

This advice comes at the right time. It coincides with a recent change in the nature of consultancy work in developing countries. Since the early or mid-seventies, the emphasis has shifted away from the large contract under which a complete development plan was prepared by a large team of consultant specialists and, after completion, left to local officials for implementation. Many of these development plans have remained on paper. Planning consultants, the governments that employed them and the international agencies that financed most of these operations have begun to realise that it was a mistake to separate planning from implementation. New methods are being developed to avoid this separation through a better synchronisation of plan-making with plan execution and by a more efficient feedback of implementation experiences to combined teams of planners, administrators and builders.

Under these new methods the specialist advisers work side by side with local staff for much longer periods than before. They see their plans being implemented — at least in part — and they cannot help getting closely involved with the social objectives of the operation.

The title *The Cities of the Poor* bears witness to this new relationship of the planning consultant and his client: the consultant as much as his employer is conscious of the fact that 65 to 80 per cent of the people of the fast-growing Third World cities are poor in the sense that they cannot afford even the cheapest type of shelter which a public sector agency could produce;

both know also that no government or international agency could provide enough subsidies to solve the housing problems on a welfare basis;
both realise that the most important resource at their disposal is the working power, the ingenuity and the spirit of enterprise of the poor; and
both see the development of this resource as the only way of creating new viable communities and cities.

PREFACE

During the last decade there has been a considerable growth in the provision of technical assistance in urban planning to the less developed countries of the Third World. Much of this has been funded by loans from multilateral agencies such as the World Bank, or by loans and grants as part of bilateral aid. Inevitably, advisers have tended to be drawn from the developed countries, whether their affiliation is with an academic institution, a government agency or a private consulting firm.

There have been changes in emphasis in consultancy, away from the large contract where a complete development plan was prepared by an expatriate team and left for implementation by local officials. Today the intention is, more and more, that advisers should work side by side with local staff and that assistance should be provided only at the rate at which it can be absorbed. While this approach is a great improvement, there are several implications which must be considered. In the first place, the advisers must be prepared to spend a large part of their time in a training capacity; second, the local counterpart staff need a reasonable level of understanding and technical competence before new methods and techniques can be absorbed; third, the work itself will take longer if skills have to be newly acquired rather than simply applied by experienced professionals.

This book has been written by consultants in urban development whose work is mainly in the Third World. It is based on recent experiences in many countries and attempts to bring these together in a way which will be useful to consultants, officials in development agencies, teachers and students.

No book of this kind can be comprehensive in the sense that it can cover every eventuality. However, the intention has been to present some techniques and methods which have been found to be effective in the field. Emphasis generally is on the creation of planned communities, either as expansions of smaller towns or as focal points for growth in larger cities. In the latter case sites-and-services schemes and slum-upgrading projects fall within the definition. If they are thought of as 'housing', they will be inadequate; they must be conceived as total communities, with all the supporting facilities which are essential to social health and progress.

16

ACKNOWLEDGEMENTS

A number of people have contributed to this book in addition to the authors. My colleague Brooke Riley read early drafts and offered invaluable advice from his own experience of working in developing countries. Pheri Evangelista, who worked with me on projects in the Philippines, devised and drew the examples of slum-upgrading and sites and services in Chapter 9. Lucy Wynne Turner drew many of the illustrations, except those in Chapters 4 and 7, which were produced by the authors. Faith Goldfinger typed and retyped seemingly endless drafts, and without her help the book could not have been produced. The case history of the Philippines project in Chapter 3 is based on a paper presented to a conference organised by PTRC Education and Research Services Ltd, and is reproduced with their permission.

17

Part One

PLANNING FRAMEWORK

1 THE CONTEXT

Alan Turner

One of the more important messages to come out of the 1976 United Nations Habitat Conference was the need to concentrate attention on the whole settlement pattern in the developing countries.

> This approach to the total settlements system also underlines the need to get away from rigid and misleading divisions between rural and urban regions, and to see a country's settlements as part of a continuum of national existence and movement in which the health and viability of the various parts are essential to the vigor and development of the whole. In particular the target set for the growth of Third World agriculture in the Rome World Food Conference — 5 percent a year — is clearly impossible to achieve without an end to the over-concentration of resources and skills in big cities (which tend to exercise most influence and political pressure). It requires a strong new emphasis on filling out the whole settlement system. Intermediate urban centers for marketing, cooperatives, services, and industries serving agriculture must be strengthened. Dispersed and desolate rural settlements need to be brought together. Such a policy offers some hope of lessening the pressures of large-scale migrations out of agriculture directly into the biggest cities. It can also provide alternative settlement systems designed to achieve more balanced regional development.[1]

This emphasis on intermediate settlements, rural development and agriculture is vital, but unfortunately has tended to be neglected in the face of the pressure on the major cities. There is little doubt that the problems of the cities must take priority and that the mixture of human suffering and opportunity which they embody must continue to absorb a large part of the efforts of governments and international agencies.

The World Bank has drawn attention to the magnitude of growth in the cities:

> We are concerned by the lack of awareness among government officials, politicians, intellectuals and others of the nature and magnitude of the task that lies ahead. Between 1950 and 1975 the

21

cities of the developing world absorbed more than 40% of the increase in population. Between 1975 and 2000 they will have to absorb at least 70% of the increase — 1.3 billion people. By any measures this is a gargantuan task. The thought of gigantic megalopolises full of poor people is an appalling prospect that has not yet induced an all-out search for a solution to future urban problems.[2]

The emphasis on *urban problems* is understandable, but a vast number will not be absorbed by the large cities. Reasonable predictions put this figure at about 800 million people.

Table 1.1 is based on the UN population projections and predicts rural increases in the less developed countries of 864 million. (This projection assumes that only about 60 per cent of the increase will be absorbed by the cities.) In absolute terms there will still be a majority of people living in the villages of the Third World. What will their lives be like? How will they be fed and clothed? What will be their share of the benefits of 'development'?

Table 1.1: Rural and Urban Populations 1950-2000 (in millions):
Less Developed Countries

	1975		2000
Urban	819	+1,334	2,153
Rural	1,382	+ 864	2,939
Total	2,894	2,198	5,092

Source: UN Population Projections, medium tempo, medium variant.

1.1 Types of Developing Countries

Even if we accept (as the authors of this book do) that the tide of migration into the cities cannot be reversed and that there is no hope of devising and implementing policies which would, for instance, rehouse the squatters of Jakarta or Lagos in new and 'sanitary' towns, there is still the daunting prospect of trying to manipulate at least a proportion of resources to the best advantage of the really poor who will remain in the countryside. At first sight it might be thought that this is beyond the capabilities of Third World governments and the international agencies and that after trying to cope with the cities, there will simply be no resources left for these less obvious rural needs. There are, however, indications that this is not the case, at least not in all countries. The World Bank has produced a paper which puts forward a useful typology of developing countries which shows that there is more scope for the creation of intermediate settlements in some countries than in others.

Type I. Those countries in which the process of urbanization is well underway. The population is already more than half urban, incomes are relatively high and there is little pressure of population on arable land and natural resources. The end of the urbanization process will occur before the turn of the century when most of the population will be in urban areas and rural areas will begin to experience absolute declines.

Type II. In these countries the urbanization experience is more recent. Over half the population is still in rural areas. Population pressures exist on the land and incomes are at relatively low levels. If population pressures can be eased and resource constraints overcome, this group of countries by the turn of the century should obtain levels of urbanization similar to those found in the Type I countries today.

Type III. This group of countries is predominately rural but urbanizing rapidly. Even so, by the year 2000 they will still be predominately rural with high rates of growth of the rural population. The outcome of the race between population growth and resources (and resulting growth of per capita income) is uncertain.

Type IV. These countries are dominated by severe pressures on the land in largely rural, subsistence-level-income societies. If the projected population growth rates are sustainable they will still be characterized in the year 2000 by large and growing rural populations living in absolute poverty.[3]

The first group includes most of the Latin American countries, while the second comprises the semi-industrialised countries of Asia and North Africa. Group III is found in Africa south of the Sahara while group IV is composed of the large countries of Asia. The paper goes on to say that there is the possibility of diverting growth to smaller urban settlements in those countries which are still predominantly rural. For instance: 'The African states have the opportunity to determine the basic pattern of urban growth likely to emerge in the next decade through policies affecting the location and costs of employment and services.'[4] Or in Type III countries: 'the potential rural-urban push will depend on the success or lack of success of rural development'.[5]

It is at this point in history in such countries that it is essential to take the opportunity to influence settlement patterns. The arithmetic leaves no alternative; if there are going to be 800 million more people in the rural areas in less than thirty years' time, there can be little doubt that most of them will live in small towns and villages. There will be isolated houses and farms, but on the whole the pattern will be composed of a multitude of settlements varying in size from a few families to a few thousand people. E.F. Schumacher has described this pattern graphically:

> The heart of the matter, as I see it, is the stark fact that world poverty is primarily a problem of two million villages and thus a problem of two thousand million villagers. The solution cannot be found in the cities of the poor countries. Unless life in the hinterland can be made more tolerable the problem of world poverty is insoluble and will inevitably get worse.[6]

1.2 Intermediate Cities

A good example of this pattern can be found in central Angola where, in a densely populated region of 800,000 people, there is only one town of more than 30,000. The rest are settlements varying in size from several families up to about 180 families, often only a few miles apart but each too small to support any but the most rudimentary facilities. How can adequate social services, let alone physical infrastructure, be supplied to such dispersed populations? In spite of mobile clinics, school buses and improvements in rural transportation, there is a pressing need for an intermediate layer of service centres between these settlements and the larger cities. This lack is well recognised and has been referred to by many recent observers, but little is done in practice as there seems to be no level of government in most developing countries which could easily implement such new centres. Raul Basaldua has pointed to the gap: 'There is a lack of small and middle-sized towns that can serve as a link between urban and rural society and which could facilitate the development and an integrated participation of the private sector.'[7] James Osborn claims that intermediate cities have been practically ignored in the literature of urban growth because of a concentration on the largest cities in the world. He uses the term 'middle city' and feels that although population size is not the most important factor, such cities could be as small as 10,000 people. In his view middle cities are way stations in rural-urban migration, communication centres between government and people, outposts of central authority and centres where population growth, economic growth and administrative authority may occur.[8]

There is now a consensus of informed opinion that intermediate cities are both necessary and viable. Barbara Ward sums this up well:

> What is certain is that medium cities are perfectly viable entities. Economically they do not offer acute difficulty. In terms of community, of access to nature, of pace of life they clearly offer considerable attractions. . .strategies for a balanced population can hardly afford to disregard such a balance sheet.[9]

She argues persuasively for careful planning to provide groups of villages with markets, banks, small-scale industry and social facilities:

> In Israel where very careful spatial organization has been devoted to the placing and servicing of agricultural communities, regional centres serve six villages. In Denmark the figure is eleven. But in countries where the spatial integration of the nation has played little or no part in economic strategy, the deadening isolation of the villages can be measured by such figures as 185 villages to each urban centre in India, 269 in Iran, a remarkable 355 in Indonesia.[10]

Attempts to define ideal size are pointless, as the conditions in each country will vary so much and 'viability' in Africa may be very different from that in Malaysia. However, there are undoubtedly certain relationships between size and the range of facilities which can be supported. (This is dealt with in some detail in Chapter 8.) Barbara Ward, writing about city quarters rather than the intermediate city, thinks that communities of 50,000 to 100,000 are necessary for wider activities and decision-making and that both schools and health require wide catchment areas.[11] The World Bank questions whether there is an ultimate size for cities 'where diseconomies of scale engender internal collapse', but concludes that there is no reason to believe that this is so. However, it refers to a recent study showing significant economies of scale for cities of 150,000 in India.[12] However, Osborn's low figure of 10,000 is also meaningful; in a region of tiny villages a town of 10,000 is a metropolis and can be an important service centre.

1.3 New or Expanded Towns?

I would emphasise that in this book we are not advocating an alternative to the large cities. Polarised arguments of this kind have little value in the real world; they are best left to the armchair philosopher. However, planned communities can and should help to provide employment and services for the millions who will not live in the major cities and these communities will be an adjunct, a complementary strategy to metropolitan development. References in various chapters are made to new towns or new communities which have a role to play, although their concept and form may be very different from European or American models.[13] Although a great deal can be learned from the thirty years of effort put into the British new towns programme and from the many research projects which have been carried out in relation to it, we must not assume that they are necessarily relevant in, say, Africa or Asia. However, while avoiding the arrogance of some Western experts, it is equally necessary to avoid the inverted arrogance which would claim that none of the experience of the West is useful to the developing countries. This is not the case; the lessons of development in the West are vital, and although concepts cannot necessarily be transferred, such experience can be helpful in devising appropriate policies.

There is a mystique about the term 'new town' which is perhaps unfortunate. Use of the term conjures up images of large development corporations and high standards of environment and amenity. There are familiar photographs of some of them that have often been reproduced in the world's technical press. But these are only a part of the story and new towns are certainly not 'new' — for instance, during the reign of Edward I in England there were nearly forty new town foundations.[14] New towns have been built for centuries and will no doubt go on being built for many more, whether they are planned or not. As Charles Abrams has said:

> The decision of an industry to locate a plant on a vacant site would gradually attract another factory nearby. . .the settlements would soon begin to spread. . .an unplanned new town would result. Planning new towns should be part of the growth process but the motivations and principles that applied to Britain and Europe were too often irrelevant for other parts of the world. As Otto Koenigsberger noted in the report of the mission to Singapore, the planning of British and European new towns presupposed a steady rate of social and economic change. . .In contrast the less developed nations are experiencing sudden population inflows. . .[and]. . .are acting more directly to spur production and investment.[15]

It is also usually true that whether the process is planned or not, growth of this kind is more often based on a small existing community than on a virgin site. Most of the British new towns were in fact large expansions of existing towns and villages — for instance, the population of the designated area of Milton Keynes in 1969 was 44,000; its planned population is 250,000. The World Bank indicates that location plays an important part in this question:

> The rapid growth of the world's urban population is unlikely to generate many new cities. Most of the growth will occur through the growth of existing centres. This is because urban centres already exist at most choice locations and the expansion of these centres is a less costly alternative than the creation of new centres.[16]

1.4 New Towns Within Cities

However, the planning and building of new or expanded communities in rural areas is not the whole story by any means. In the sprawling cities of the Third World, there is a great need for the creation of new towns within the urban fabric. This concept, which was first mooted in the 1960s,[17] describes a process which is highly appropriate to cities such as Lagos, Bogota or Madras, where there are large undeveloped areas within the spread-out urbanised area. There is a need in such cities for community-building in the best sense and not just the creation of new and inaccessible housing projects. A key feature of the Bogota Development Plan is the concept of new cities within the city. The proposed urban structure 'combines the scale and convenience of medium sized cities with access to the range of opportunities and special resources that can only be found in a metropolis'[18] (see Appendix 3, Chapter 3).

There are therefore two strategies which emerge to which the ideas and techniques described in this book are directly applicable. These are:

(1) the expansion of small central villages or moderate-sized towns to form service centres for large rural areas;
(2) the creation of planned communities within the dispersed fabric of major cities.

1.5 Rural Development and Agriculture

As part of the continuing debate about the growth of the less developed countries, polarised arguments take place between those who advocate modern industry at all costs and those who try to turn back the tide and rely almost entirely on low-technology, craft-based industries and farming. In practical terms, the most realistic policies are those which seek to combine a number of approaches in order to secure reasonable balance. Some measure of industrialisation is undoubtedly necessary in most developing countries if they are to compete in international markets, although the industries concerned may need to be labour-intensive and different in character from Western models.

At the same time, if the huge populations of the future are to eat, every means must be taken to ensure that the yield from each hectare of agricultural land is as high as possible, and that new development for either industry or housing does not consume valuable fertile land. Although this may seem obvious, it is all too often overlooked, even in those countries where the planning system is sophisticated and well managed. Barbara Ward has pointed out that in Rumania, a country with highly developed planning strategies, some of the richest farmland has been inadvertently assigned to factories and towns.[19]

Even though planners, politicians and administrators are aware of the value of agricultural land, errors of this kind continue to occur.

Bureaucratic systems are insensitive and where pressure for development is great, it is almost inevitable that they will lose sight of longer-term needs for the sake of expediency. It is essential, therefore, to develop national and regional policies which combine increased agricultural production with dispersed small-scale industrial estates based largely on the processing of agricultural produce and the manufacture of agriculture-related equipment.

The World Bank points out that the development of agriculture produces benefits to the urban sector and that rapid agricultural growth may not only have a decentralising effect on the pattern of urban growth, but can stimulate the growth of smaller towns to cater to local rural demands. 'It is now clearly realized by most national planners that the development of manufacturing industries does not preclude the development of agriculture but, on the contrary, that they are interdependent.'[20] This is no doubt true, but the realisation has come rather late and much too little is being done to create systems where small-scale industrial development is related carefully to the activities of the small farmers on whom the greatest share of the burden must fall. In spite of great progress in our knowledge of regional interactions, it is often the case that governments and planning bodies do not learn the lessons soon enough or well enough.[21] To quote Barbara Ward again: 'In most plans of the 50's and 60's, the spatial aspects of planning, particularly for the farm sector went largely by default.' She goes on to say that in India regulated agricultural markets were created, but no one thought of combining them with small-scale industrial estates which were being set up at the same time. No one had thought out the needs of farms or villages as essential elements in a 'local, regional and national network of productive services, each level depending on the efficiency of the rest'.[22]

She also cites figures in support of her argument to relate such new services to the small farmer. International agencies such as FAO show that one-acre plots almost doubled the yield per acre of farms of more than five acres. In India 5-acre farms produced 40 per cent more per acre than farms with more than 50 acres.[23] In the face of rising populations and food shortages these are powerful arguments for integrated urban-rural development.

1.6 Employment and Technology

It is abundantly clear that the emphasis must be on the creation of employment as a prerequisite to housing or social development. It is quite impossible except in a few small oil-rich states (and then for how long?) to house, clothe and feed huge underemployed populations by state subsidy. The primary need of the people is to earn a living and yet how often is the opportunity taken to create as many jobs as possible from every new development? In most developing countries there are examples of housing programmes where analysis would show that many of the components of the housing and infrastructure are imported. Corrugated metal roofs, electrical equipment, ironmongery, sometimes even complete housing systems — the list is endless. This is a pitiful failure which must be avoided by governments at all levels and the best way to do so is to devise policies which emphasise import substitution and appropriate technology. Both are vital and perhaps the best developed arguments in their favour can be found in E.F. Schumacher's book, *Small is Beautiful*. Schumacher argues that money is not the answer; financial aid, even if doubled or tripled, will not make an appreciable impact and 'the best aid to give is intellectual aid, a gift of useful knowledge.'[24] He illustrates this by saying that it is more important to teach a hungry man to make a rod and catch fish and thereby become self-sufficient than to give him a fish which he will quickly eat. The relationship between technology and scale of settlement is brought out by Barbara Ward, who claims that development must be concentrated in the village, the market-centre and the intermediate town: 'The over-riding need is for decentralized, labour-intensive, highly skilled, small-scale operations; and here the type and size of settlements can make the difference between success and failure.'[25]

1.7 Care for People

It is very easy for the technician or the expert on urban affairs to transfer unconsciously his attention from the primary goal to the secondary function. Like the hi-fi enthusiast who no longer listens to the music because his hearing is straining to detect imperfections of reproduction, the technician may lose sight of the people who are, at the end of the line, his 'clients'. It is quite amazing how clearly this was realised and how well expressed by Patrick Geddes, sixty years ago:

> Town planning is not mere place-planning nor even work-planning. If it is to be successful it must be folk-planning. This means that its task is not to coerce people into new places against their associations, wishes and interest — as we find bad schemes trying to do. Instead its task is to find the right places for each sort of people; places where they will really flourish. To give people in fact the same care that we give when transplanting flowers, instead of harsh evictions and arbitrary instructions to 'move on' delivered in the manner of an officious amateur policeman.[26]

Geddes's understanding of the problem so long ago throws into stark relief the current attitudes of many governments, housing authorities and other bodies in the Third World. When faced with squatters or slums, the usual reaction is to demolish the buildings and move the people to 'properly constructed' dwellings on sites far away from their employment and their families and friends. Writing, again in 1915, Geddes described a plan in an Indian city which would

> leave fewer housing sites. . .and the large population thus expelled would. . .be driven into creating worse congestion in other quarters. . .Even if. . .the new site offered is both suitable and acceptable to the people expelled, they are practically excluded by the present cost of building in favour of the more prosperous classes. Hence the result of these would-be improvements is to increase the serious depression of the poor and make this ever more difficult to relieve.[27]

This is almost an exact description of the results of slum clearance in Lagos in the 1950s, as though nothing had changed in the intervening forty years.[28] In many cities in the developing world, the lesson has still not been learned and slum clearance boards (*sic*) are, even now, trying to do what has been proved to be impossible.

In contemporary terms perhaps no writer is more eloquent on the subject of care for people than Hassan Fathy. From his experience of designing mud-brick villages in the Nile Valley, Fathy believes that the poor are better off when they have the opportunity to build for themselves. Government architects (he says) design for a statistically average family and build

> their million identical houses. The result is hideous and inhuman; a million families are bundled into these ill-fitting cells without being able to say a word about the design and however much science is applied to the grading of families and the matching of them to their dwellings, the majority are bound to be discontented.[29]

This is not to say that the poor do not need help from authorities — there is a desperate need for help of the right sort, but it is so easy to fall into the trap of creating supposedly improved environments in which people are unhappy. As Fathy says:

> In designing a village the architect has need of the greatest artistic care if he is to create a unity, character and beauty that will approach the natural beauty that the peasants create unconsciously in their villages that have grown slowly and naturally.[30]

This should not be construed as romantic idealism; it is not fashionable to use words like 'beauty' when writing about housing in the Third World, but Fathy's insight is highly relevant. Unity is the keyword; a unity of social, technical and aesthetic qualities which exists as the result of generations of trial and error tempered by climate and cultural attitudes. In Malaysia, for instance, the rural kampung is perfectly adjusted to the climate. Wood houses on stilts are set among tall palm trees; the trees give shade without obstructing the cooling wind which can blow around and under the houses; in times of torrential rain the houses stay dry as the thatch is efficient and the floor is raised above flood level; the grass is kept short by the goats who contribute to the food supply. All this combines to produce a truly beautiful environment. And yet in the same country there are examples of new housing on cleared jungle sites where corrugated metal roofs are exposed exposed to the sun and where, by the same act of clearance, the ground is turned back to red laterite which will erode and clog the rivers. In extreme cases families have left such housing to return to the shade and protection of the forest. It is vital, therefore, to understand what is happening when you look at a village or a town and to question every aspect before interfering with the processes of life. I think that Fathy has this understanding and that a great deal can be learned from his sensitive approach. He points to the social advantages for women in some villages in fetching water from the river, rather than drawing it from the tap in their kitchen. It was the only time they were seen in public and a girl who stayed in the kitchen would never find a husband. This, of course, is not an argument against supplying water to the house but it is a graphic illustration of the interdependence of social and technological elements, and evidence of the need to find new ways of closing the gap between society and technology. How do you institutionalise the principles behind the 'gotong royong' (mutual assistance) of the Malaysian village? How does a government help people to help themselves without crushing them beneath the weight of an unsympathetic and insensitive bureaucracy?

1.8 Self-help Housing

Enough studies have been made, enough projects have been evaluated and enough words have been written to convince any serious student that housing cannot be 'provided' for the population of the world any more than it can for the 'birds of the air'. Writing as long ago as 1952, Otto Koenigsberger remarked that 'planning problems of underdeveloped regions are problems of numbers. It is necessary to mobilize the people themselves for their solution'.[31] In 1964 the United Nations produced a manual for self-help projects which has not so far been updated.[32] By 1966 Charles Abrams had written what is still a seminal work on the problems and opportunities of mass housing and was wise enough to recognise the importance of security.

> In Pakistan those who were living on land left by evacuees and who were more certain of being given the ownership built good houses, while squatters on government land, expecting displacement, erected makeshifts. On land rented for short-terms in other parts of the world, houses are most often primitive huts which the occupants make no move to improve or expand. . .A country must choose between building for the few and demonstrating little, building for the many and exhausting its resources or providing for the many with a minimum outlay.[33]

The first of the alternatives in the last sentence is undoubtedly the easiest and the most immediately rewarding for the busy civil servant or the ambitious politician; the third is the only way ahead and is the immediate concern of this book.

Notes

1. From the Declaration of the Vancouver Symposium on Habitat, the United Nations Conference on Human Settlements, 1976.
2. *The Task Ahead for the Cities of the Developing Countries*, World Bank Staff Working Paper no. 209 (Washington) (July 1975), pp. i-ii (the views expressed are those of the authors and not necessarily those of the Bank).
3. Ibid., p.5.
4. Ibid., p. 10.
5. Ibid., p. 17.
6. E.F. Schumacher, *Small is Beautiful* (Sphere Books, London, 1974), p 162.
7. Raul Oscar Basaldua, *Policy and Institutional Aspects of Rural Development* (paper given at the Town and Country Planning Summer School, Nottingham University, September 1976).
8. James Osborn, *Area Development Policy and the Middle City in Malaysia* (University of Chicago Press, Chicago, 1974), p. 14.
9. Barbara Ward, *The Home of Man* (Penguin Books, Harmondsworth, 1976), p.108.
10. Ibid., p. 188.
11. Ibid., p. 136.
12. World Bank, *Task Ahead*, p. 24. The study referred to is *Costs of Urban Infrastructure for Industry as related to City Size in Developing Countries* (Indian Case Study, Menlo Park, California, 1968).
13. British new towns have been so well documented that there is no need to refer to specific books. In the case of American new towns, see James Bailey (ed.), *New Towns in America* (American Institute of Architects, Washington, 1973) or Alan Turner, 'New Communities in the United States 1968-1973', *Town Planning Review* (Liverpool) (July and October 1974).
14. Colin and Rose Bell, *City Fathers* (Praeger, New York and London, 1969), p.25.
15. Charles Abrams, *Housing in the Modern World* (Faber and Faber, London, 1966), p. 135.
16. World Bank, *Task Ahead*, p. 26.
17. Walter Bor, 'New Towns Within Cities', *Housing Review*, vol. 10, no. 506 (London, 1961), pp. 81-4; see also Harvey Perloff, 'New Towns Intown', *Journal of the American Institute of Planners*, vol. 22, no. 3 (May 1966).
18. *The Structure Plan for Bogota* (The technical report of the Bogota Urban Development Study, phase 2, Bogota, 1973), p.44.
19. Ward, *The Home of Man*, p. 92.
20. World Bank, *Task Ahead*, pp. 47-9.
21. There is a large body of literature dealing with the location of agricultural producers and consumers going back 150 years to Von Thunen, who in 1826 conceived the idea of the Isolated State. This theoretical city-region had no trade connections with any other nation and was surrounded by an uncultivated wilderness. From this model he obtained an ideal distribution of agricultural production as a series of concentric circles arranged about the central city. This and other theories of location are discussed by Michael Chisholm in *Rural*

Settlement and Land Use (Hutchinson, London, 1962).

22. Ward, *The Home of Man*, p. 188.

23. Ibid., p. 183.

24. Schumacher, *Small is Beautiful*, p. 184.

25. Barbara Ward, 'The Triple Crisis', *Journal of the Royal Institute of British Architects* (London) (December 1974).

26. Patrick Geddes, 'Report on the towns in the Madras Presidency 1915' in Jaqueline Tyrwhitt (ed.), *Patrick Geddes in India* (Lund Humphries, London, 1947), p. 22.

27. Ibid., pp. 40-1.

28. See Peter Marris, *Family and Social Change in an African City* (Routledge and Kegan Paul, London, 1961).

29. Hassan Fathy, *Architecture for the Poor* (University of Chicago Press, Chicago and London, 1973), p. 30.

30. Ibid., p. 72.

31. Otto Koenigsberger, 'New Towns in India', *Town Planning Review*, vol. 23, no. 2 (July 1952), pp. 95-132.

32. *Manual on Self-Help Housing* (United Nations, New York, 1964).

33. Abrams, *Housing in the Modern World*, p. 180.

2 COMMUNITY DEVELOPMENT

Alan Turner

One of the aims of this book has been to derive some degree of generality from various experiences in order to assemble a set of guidelines for development. The opportunities are considerable in view of the need to save time and professional manpower in situations where both are in short supply. A measure of a successful project should be that it can be repeated without an undue drain on administrative and technical resources and without the need to form a highly experienced international planning team. It is essential for new teams to be trained and for them in turn to train others so that the number of effective projects can be increased. The knowledge and experience of these teams will not always be of the highest order and they will need guidance. It should not be necessary for them to 'invent the wheel' on every project, but in practice it is common to find that a planning team feels that it is not doing its job unless it carries out a great deal of research into problems which may already have been thoroughly studied and documented and where the result of further research will be marginal. Where there are similar problems of climate, poverty, underemployment and lack of infrastructure, there are certain approaches or methods which can be useful and which are not necessarily specific to a particular country. These form a body of knowledge which can be drawn on and modified to suit the specific cultural and social background against which the project is being prepared.

Guidelines are required which are neither too proscriptive nor too prescriptive, and these can be helpful in avoiding the thoughtless reproduction of inappropriate solutions or the transfer of irrelevant technology or standards. The degree of specificity must vary considerably depending on the subject; for instance, the minimum need of a person for water does not vary much and reasonable standards can be laid down for the number of litres per day required by a household. Other elements, such as residential density, may be highly specific to a given community, or even to a group within a community. However, even with social and physical standards, there are certain guidelines which can be set down, certain minima or maxima which it would seem unwise to go beyond in almost any situation. The attempt, therefore, must be to provide an example but not a pattern book; a set of recommendations supported by useful data and references but not a recipe for instant communities.

There are many problems, or sets of problems, which occur with considerable frequency in different places and which are easily recognised by people such as officials of international organisations or consultants who spend their time travelling from one country to another. A lack of piped water, sanitation, transportation or employment may have great similarities even in countries many thousands of miles apart. The effects of intense rain in terms of erosion or damage to primitive structures can be surprisingly alike in quite different cultures and require similar solutions, or at least similar approaches to determining the solutions. The authors have tried to respond to these problems and to generalise from them, but the reader should be aware that any recommendations are no more than guidelines which must be used with discernment and caution.

2.1 Typical Conditions in Poor Countries

At this stage it may be useful to look a little more closely at some of the common characteristics of the poorer countries in order to form a brief context for the development of approaches and policies. Reference was made in Chapter 1 to a typology of developing countries indicating their progress towards predominantly urban societies. To this could be added a list of characteristics which are repeated time and again and which often create similar problems, although in different places they may call for different solutions. The following list is neither exhaustive nor applicable to every developing country, but most of them will exhibit some of the factors:

(1)   low *per capita* income; extremes of wealth and poverty;
(2)   large land area, much of which may be unusable for food production; difficult topography; extremes of climate;
(3)   extremely rapid population growth accompanied by rapid urbanisation. As a result the populations are young and the demand for services is high;
(4)   low educational standards;
(5)   inadequate infrastructure;
(6)   regional imbalance;
(7)   low level of technological development;
(8)   need for labour-intensive industry;
(9)   lack of professional and technical resources.

On the other side of the balance sheet, some countries have undeveloped natural resources and may only be poor countries as long as these resources remain undeveloped.

Almost without exception the poorest countries have the warmest climates and this is worth spelling out in some detail, as the implications are important. According to the World Bank,[1] there are 92 countries with a *per capita* GNP of less than US$500; 46 of these are in Africa, 32 in Asia, Oceania and Indonesia and 14 in Central and South America. If these are compared with world climatic zones,[2] it will be seen that most have hot humid or hot dry climates, although a few very large countries have a range of conditions. Table 2.1 shows the approximate climate type for each country; approximate because there may be local variations owing to height above sea level and it is difficult to be precise about the edges of zones. However, 70 per cent of the regions recorded fall into the tropical rain forest, tropical savannah or humid sub-tropical categories, while 22 per cent are in arid or semi-arid zones. This has a profound effect on the types of solution which can be sought, particularly with regard to agriculture, environmental control and building construction.[3]

Within such a framework of social, economic and climatic conditions a number of characteristics tend to be repeated with little regard to cultural or national backgrounds. There will, of course, be subtle variations, but by and large the characteristics will be recognisable. They are, as it were, the symptoms of the very low-income community whether it is a small town or part of a large city. During early discussions for this book, the authors tried to focus on these characteristics so that the various chapters could be directed to what may be called a hypothetical 'client community'.

Such a community would tend to have very low family incomes, high unemployment and underemployment, with the majority of jobs in the informal sector. Standards of education and health care would be poor and there would be a high proportion of children and young people in the population. Data on social and economic conditions would be unreliable and difficult to assemble. Environmental standards would be very poor, with unpaved roads, no drainage or sewerage networks and inadequate water supply, usually wells or common stand-pipes. As a result there would be a high incidence of gastro-enteric diseases, particularly among children. The houses themselves would be of traditional construction of mud, stone, brick or timber, probably with thatched roofs, or built of scrap materials, such as flattened oil drums or packing cases, with corrugated metal roofs.

Table 2.1: Countries of the World with Per Capita Income of Less than US$500 per Annum, Grouped by Climatic Zone

Country	Tropical rain forest	Tropical savannah	Humid sub-tropical	Desert	Steppe	Marine west coast	Continental	Tundra	Mediterranean
AFRICA — 46 countries									
Nigeria	•	•							
Egypt, Arab Rep. of				•					
Ethiopia				•	•	•			
Zaire	•								
Sudan				•					
Morocco									•
Tanzania		•							
Kenya		•							
Uganda		•							
Ghana		•							
Malagasy Rep.	•	•							
Mozambique		•							
Rhodesia		•							
Ivory Coast	•	•							
Angola		•							
Upper Volta					•				
Tunisia					•				
Mali					•				
Guinea		•							
Malawi		•							
Zambia		•							
Niger				•	•				
Senegal		•							
Rwanda		•							
Burundi		•							
Somalia					•				
Benin, People's Rep. of	•	•							
Sierra Leone	•								
Togo	•	•							
Central African Rep.		•							
Liberia	•								

Table 2.1 *(contd.)*

Country	Tropical rain forest	Tropical savannah	Humid sub-tropical	Desert	Steppe	Marine west coast	Continental	Tundra	Mediterranean
AFRICA *(contd.)*									
Mauritania				●	●				
Congo, People's Rep. of	●								
Lesotho						●			
Mauritius	●								
Botswana					●				
Guinea-Bissau		●							
Gambia, The		●							
Swaziland						●			
Equatorial Guinea	●								
Cape Verde Islands	●								
Comoro Islands		●							
Sao Tome and Principe	●								
Seychelles Islands	●								
Cameroon	●								
Sub-total Africa	15	22		7	6	3			1
ASIA, OCEANIA AND INDONESIA — 32 countries									
Syria, Arab Rep. of				●	●				
Jordan				●	●				
Yemen, Arab Rep. of				●	●				
Yemen, People's Dem. Rep. of				●	●				
Afghanistan				●	●				
Pakistan				●	●				
India	●	●	●		●				
Sri Lanka	●	●							
Nepal			●						
Sikkim			●						
Bhutan			●						
Bangladesh	●	●							
Burma	●	●	●						
Thailand	●	●							

Table 2.1 *(contd.)*

Country	Tropical rain forest	Tropical savannah	Humid sub-tropical	Desert	Steppe	Marine west coast	Continental	Tundra	Mediterranean
ASIA, OCEANIA AND INDONESIA *(contd.)*									
Laos	•	•							
Vietnam, Dem. Rep. of	•	•							
Cambodia		•							
China, People's Rep. of			•				•	•	
Indonesia	•								
Philippines	•								
Papua New Guinea	•								
Portuguese Timor		•							
British Solomon Islands	•								
Korea, Rep. of			•				•		
Korea, Dem. Rep. of									
Macao			•						
Maldive Islands	•								
Western Samoa	•								
Trust Ter. of the Pacific Islands	•								
Tonga	•								
New Hebrides		•							
Gilbert and Ellice Islands		•							
Sub-total Asia etc.	15	11	8	6	7		2	1	
CENTRAL AND SOUTH AMERICA — 14 countries									
Haiti		•							
El Salvador		•							
Honduras	•								
St. Lucia	•								
Grenada	•								
St. Vincent	•								
Dominica	•								
Antigua	•								
St. Kitts — Nevis Anguilla	•								

Table 2.1 *(contd.)*

Country	Tropical rain forest	Tropical savannah	Humid sub-tropical	Desert	Steppe	Marine west coast	Continental	Tundra	Mediterranean
CENTRAL AND SOUTH AMERICA *(contd.)*									
Colombia		●				●			
Ecuador	●					●			
Bolivia	●	●							
Paraguay	●	●							
Guyana	●								
Sub-total Central and South America	11	5				2			
Total all regions	41	38	8	13	13	5	2	1	1
Percentage all regions	33.6	31.1	6.5	10.7	10.7	4.1	1.7	.8	.8

Note: some countries fall into more than one climatic zone. The totals are, therefore, major regions rather than countries.

Sources: *World Bank Atlas*, 1975; *Times Atlas of the World*, 1974.

Quite probably there would be a government housing project built of modern materials which, equally probably, would be inappropriate to the climate and too expensive for the poorest people to afford. Land ownership or tenure would be difficult to resolve and the high incidence of squatting, coupled with the lack of cadastral maps or aerial photographs, would compound the situation.

Social and institutional facilities would be poor or non-existent and there would be little open space for recreation. Climatic conditions would be extreme, with serious water shortages during the dry season or danger from floods during the monsoons; in hot dry climates there would be dust storms and erosion. Typically, urban management would not have developed to a point where any of these problems could be mitigated to any appreciable extent. However, the existence of these conditions may in some cases point to a considerable potential for improvement. The people, who often have an almost infallible instinct for such things, may have chosen to locate where they are because of proximity to employment opportunities or transport routes, or to a natural resource, which with sensitive government intervention could be developed to their advantage.

2.2 Development Goals

The goals and objectives of a new development, whether it is the improvement of an existing community or the formation of a new one, will be many and varied and some of them will probably be mutually incompatible. The goals of the local people may be quite different from those of the local authority, which in turn may be at variance with those of the central government department lending the money for the project. For our present purposes, however, let us assume that the goals under consideration are those which will most effectively relate to the rapid improvement of the living conditions and standards of the 'client community'. Some of these will already be known and will need little research; in a community with no piped water it is not necessary to carry out a detailed social survey just to conclude that a new supply is needed. Others will not be generally known or understood and a survey such as that described in Chapter 4 should be carried out to record the felt needs of the community and to give priority to these. Still others may only become obvious as the community develops and new problems are created or new relationships formed. In most cases the level of participation will increase as time goes on; in the case of an upgrading project, new facilities such as local meeting rooms and encouragement by social development officers will help the community to form its own opinions and give voice to them; with a new project the incoming residents will soon begin to formulate their own views about the design and implementation. However, to begin with it is often necessary for the planning team to assume a set of goals, as it were by proxy. These will serve to guide the course of the initial phases of the work, but should be kept under constant review to ensure that they do not become obsolete.

Generally, the following will be among the major goals to be considered.

2.2.1 The Creation or Augmentation of an Economic Base

There can be little doubt that this must form the first priority. In existing settlements, employment is likely to be largely in the informal sector which can often be encouraged by the provision of low-interest loan facilities to small businesses. In the case of new towns, location near to either existing employment centres or the development of new industrial estates is perhaps the most important single decision to be taken, to ensure the success of the project. In the former case there are, unfortunately, more examples of destructive intervention in an informal economy than examples of effective augmentation. The network of connections in such a situation is delicate and tenuous. A whole mini-industry can exist in bits and pieces scattered among dozens of flimsy shacks, with each component a family business carrying out a simple operation for a marginal return and keeping its accounts in the head of its senior member. Expressions of intent such as 'We must clean up this area and build proper workshops for these people' may be the death knell to a whole system that can only exist *because* it is unorganised. Any rent, let alone an economic rent for a workshop, may make the operation non-viable by reducing profits to a zero. In many instances it may be better to restrict assistance to small loans, technical advice or training and perhaps elementary accounting services, rather than large-scale renewal.

2.2.2 A Housing Programme Suited to the Needs of the Community

At the same time as both skilled and unskilled jobs are created, a whole range of housing and social facilities must be provided to suit the needs of the growing population. Normal market mechanisms will ensure that houses are constructed for those able to afford them, in the middle- and higher-income groups, but provision must also be made for the lower-income groups. It will be necessary for means to be made available for the poorest families to provide themselves with housing by self-help methods such as sites-and-services projects, depots where at-cost building materials may be obtained, small loans or other financial assistance and technical advice on building methods. With projects of this kind, infrastructure may be built in a carefully phased manner related to financial resources and upgraded as time goes by. There is now a great deal of experience of such projects and the concept of self-help housing is firmly established as one of the approaches necessary in projects throughout the developing world. The concept is receiving increasing attention by international funding bodies such as the World Bank and I believe that it must be embodied in the housing programme, in addition to conventional housing, as one of the means of providing accommodation. Most areas will contain existing slums for which upgrading programmes will need to be worked out. These will concentrate largely on utilities, access and social facilities.

2.2.3 A Social Development Programme which will Ensure the Efficient Distribution of Social Services

This aspect of the plan will be extremely important and should be given close attention in terms of physical distribution and in terms of the administrative structure which will ensure a good 'delivery' of social services to the consumer. The range will be wide, from facilities for education and health care to industrial selection and training schemes, resettlement transfer schemes and, possibly, financial help with moving expenses. Families will be young and will have many children; over the early years there will be a heavy demand for primary schools and later for secondary schools and recreational facilities for teenagers. In the case of a new community young people will be the backbone of the town and if they are to be encouraged to stay, the new development must be attractive to them and provide them with all the opportunities they need not only for earning a living, but also for enjoyment.

2.2.4 A Balanced Investment Programme

Very often publicly financed projects are regarded as being quite different from private developments where profits have to be made. Certainly a private developer will expect a higher return on his money, but the tacit assumption that public money does not have to generate a return needs to be radically altered. It is vital that new or improved community projects should have workable investment programmes which will attract private investment in industry or commerce and generate internal profits or cross-subsidies which will help to pay for the non-profitable components such as drainage and sewerage. Far too often the developing authority does not look at it in this way at all and hardly knows what has been spent on what and with what effect. A degree of rigorousness generally unknown in local government circles is needed to ensure that whatever funds are available are used in the most productive way on behalf of the client community. It would be invidious to cite examples, but in most developing countries there are abandoned projects representing an unforgivable waste of resources, lying next to families who are living below the poverty level.

2.2.5 Opportunities for Institutional Growth

In addition to the location of new employment near to planned communities, there is often an opportunity to locate a new institutional use such as a college or training establishment which can be a great help in the growth of the community. However, this presupposes a degree of co-ordination at national and regional levels of government that may be difficult to achieve. The experience of Britain after the Second World War is often cited, where about 30 new towns were built and also a comparable number of new universities. Even with the high standard of co-ordination which exists in Britain (in comparison with most developing countries) the opportunity to combine a number of these was lost and it was not until the development of Milton Keynes that a university was planned as an integral part of a new town. However, whenever integration of departmental policies can be achieved, the result should be of great benefit to the community.

2.2.6 Creation of an Attractive Physical Environment

Within the constraints of topography and climate, the project will require a comfortable environment which makes the best use of the relationships between buildings, spaces and vegetation. Historically this has proved to be easier to achieve slowly and incrementally (such as the Malaysian example referred to in Chapter 1) than when a project is constructed using modern methods. The components of a large project will be provided by different organisations, both public and private, at different times and with varying degrees of quality and consistency. They will include buildings, roads and footpaths, utilities, planting and a great deal of equipment such as street lighting, direction signs and so on. The developing authority will have a difficult co-ordinating role and the skill with which this activity is carried out will largely determine the environmental quality of the new development.

2.2.7 A Positive Approach to Innovation

Finally a project can be seen as an opportunity for innovation in social, administrative or technical terms. In some ways, subject to public acceptance, a community can be a laboratory where new ways of dealing with old problems can be tried out and provide feedback for the benefit of other projects. New ways of providing contact between people and government officials need to be sought; new systems need to be created to ensure that social services reach the people they are intended for and that the funds for their provision are not absorbed before the delivery of the service; energy is always a problem and it is ironic that the poorest places have almost unlimited sunshine but hardly any innovation in using solar energy, not for heating as in the West but for electricity, cooking or cooling; the most pressing need for innovation is in environmental sanitation, where inadequate methods of disposal are responsible for serious health risks. The list, of course, is almost endless — construction technology, tenure and ownership, food production come to mind — and a project is only likely to be innovative in a very limited way, but even a small change may contribute a great deal.

2.3 New Communities

These general goals, together with other more specific objectives, can be said to apply to either the upgrading of an existing community or the development of a new area. Over the last few decades it has become very fashionable to use the term 'new town' for almost any large new residential project whether or not it is a town in the proper sense. Although, as suggested in Chapter 1, new towns have always been built, the modern concept is usually regarded as having been introduced in Britain in 1898 by Ebenezer Howard, whose book *Tomorrow: a Peaceful Path to Social Reform*[4] summarised his revulsion against the unhealthy conditions of the industrial cities. Howard wanted the government of the day to build a hundred garden cities to solve the housing problem and to give people the opportunity to live in conditions which combined the best of both town and country. He formed the Garden Cities Association to promote these ideas and two early new towns were built at Welwyn and Letchworth, near to London.

The success of these early efforts laid the foundation for planning in Britain after the Second World War, when a ring of 'satellite' towns was planned for London. The British new towns programme fulfilled a major role during the 1950s and 1960s and by 1971 there were nearly 1.5 million people living in the first 27 new towns.[5] By 1978 the total population had risen to almost 2 million, of which about 950,000 were originally resident in the designated areas.[6] In other words, just over 1 million people had been housed in new towns between 1947 and 1978. The population of Great Britain in 1947 was 49 million and in 1978 about 55.8 million — an increase of 6.8 million, so that as a result of the new towns legislation 14.7 per cent of the total population growth during that period was housed in new towns.

This is considered by many to be an achievement of great significance and the British new towns are often held up as models for others to follow. There is no doubt that the programme has been an extraordinarily effective concerted operation, backed by successive administrations over 30 years, and that its place in the history of planning as a process is secure. The way in which funds were made available (at market interest rates) to the development corporations, who acquired land, improved it and made profits from so doing is, perhaps, a unique illustration of the way in which public bodies can act as successful entrepreneurs, given the right conditions.

The physical and social results are a little more arguable. Some of the new towns are architecturally attractive and popular with the residents. Others have been castigated for their lack of urbanity and poor social and recreational facilities which have led to discontent among younger residents. Many of the criticisms of the new towns may be premature, as it takes at least a generation for a town to establish continuity and local traditions. Towns which suffered from 'new town blues' in the 1960s may now be experiencing greatly improved social environments. However, perhaps the greatest single failure has been the inability of the combined efforts of the 'exporting' city and the new town to reach the poorest members of society. The new towns are not 'one-class' towns and, on the whole, social balance is similar to the national average, but at the lower end of the income scale people have found it difficult to obtain a house and a job in a new town.[7]

In some ways the British new towns can be said to have worked too well. They were intended to provide alternative accommodation and employment for families from the inner areas of the major cities and this policy of decentralisation (coupled with other factors) is now giving cause for alarm as the inner areas are depopulating and industries are moving out. As a consequence it is unlikely that any more new towns will be designated and the population targets of those in development have been reduced. The emphasis is on aid to the inner-city areas.

If we look at the American experience, the record is rather gloomy. Early attempts to build 'Greenbelt Towns' in the 1930s were not completed and their contribution to new housing was minimal. In the 1930s and 1960s a large number of private new communities were commenced, but most of these were speculative ventures intended exclusively for middle-income families. The most important step forward was the Housing and Urban Development Act of 1968 (revised in 1970) which laid the ground rules for a comprehensive new towns programme aimed at social and racial balance.[8] The Act referred to new communities rather than new towns, as it was realised that most would not be towns in the sense of having their own local governments, and that many would be located within the areas governed by larger cities. The programme was a good example of the financial ingenuity which Americans often bring to development problems. Whereas the British system empowered central government to lend money to the new town development corporations, the Americans assumed that the funds for development would have to come from private sources. However, it was realised that developers would find it extremely difficult to borrow large sums for developments which typically do not produce a return on investment for a number of years. The idea, therefore, was that, having approved a project put forward by a private developer, the federal government would guarantee developers' loans and would step in where defaults occurred. In this way the government could foster new communities without tying up large amounts of public money.

In the early 1970s this formula seemed to offer a pragmatic approach to the problem of combining public and private interests and providing new environments for low- and middle-income families. Unfortunately this did not prove to be the case and by 1975 only four projects were still seeking to participate in the federal programme. Project after project had run into financial difficulty as sales from industrial and residential sites failed to meet the heavy 'front end' investments. Only seven years after the initial legislation of 1968 the new communities programme had virtually ground to a halt.[9]

Can any lessons be learned from these two examples which may be of value in the very different context of developing countries, in situations of burgeoning population growth, where cities may increase by several hundred thousand people each year and where poverty is so widespread? The answer is probably a qualified yes, with the emphasis on conceptual planning and financial management. The British new towns have been very profitable financially as the development corporations have had full powers to act as developers, to buy land, construct buildings and infrastructure and to sell or lease the results. But they have been able to do this so successfully only because they have been part of a comprehensively planned and managed system at national level, which made funds available when they were required and which determined the location of each town in relation to national and regional growth. This latter point was one of the great failings of the American programme, which left location to the activities of the market place. In 1970 I wrote:

> the location of new communities is left to an ad hoc decision by a developer. In one area an imaginative developer may see an opportunity for a new town; in another area there may have been no one with his vision, but an equal need. . .It would be better, for instance, if HUD (the Federal Department of Housing and Urban Development) were to commission regional studies determining

where new cities could be located and then to advertise for developers to submit proposals or applications to develop these sites.[10]

These points are important because if new towns are not well located and able to respond to market pressures they are unlikely to succeed (at least in mixed economies − the situation would be different in a centrally planned economy). It has often been thought that the British new towns were entirely funded by the public sector, whereas they secured considerable private investment in commercial and industrial areas. If the American communities had succeeded they would have attracted a number of federal and state grants which would have contributed to the less profitable infrastructure and low-income housing.

A valuable contribution of the American legislation was the way in which several different types of new community were defined. These were as follows:

(1) economically balanced new communities within metropolitan areas as alternatives to urban sprawl;
(2) expansion of smaller towns and cities to become growth centres;
(3) new-town-in-town developments within or adjacent to existing cities;
(4) free-standing and self-sufficient new communities away from existing urban centres (where there is a clear showing of economic feasibility).[11]

These were specifically tailored to the American situation and the most effective use of the programme would probably have been to rationalise land use in the sprawling suburbs (Type 1) and to bring balanced development into existing city areas (Type 3).

If the same reasoning is applied to a typical developing country the list would be somewhat different and would reflect the stage of urbanisation reached. The following paragraphs describe a possible hierarchy which would be relevant in many countries; it does not, of course, apply universally. Several examples have been used to illustrate the various categories and these are included as appendices to this chapter.

2.3.1 Large, Free-standing New City

The opportunities for locating and developing a large new city are very limited. Clearly the new capital city is at the top of the hierarchy and there have been a number of examples during the last decades including Brasilia, Chandigarh and several projected capitals in African countries. In a country which has an existing capital, the new capital is usually symbolic; it may be more geographically central, or better situated in relation to cultural groups whose differing values must be welded together to form a new nation. When a new country is formed from others there is obviously a need to develop a new capital, although this may well be an expansion of an existing town, where housing, facilities, infrastructure and the existing community may form a better starting-point than a virgin site. Even where the opportunity occurs, a new capital is unlikely to provide a great deal of help to poor people, except in the construction industry for a number of years. Regrettably, recent examples have tended to generate an adjacent squatter settlement for these workers, which in most cases will develop into the poor quarter of the future city.

A more likely candidate is the resource-based city, whose geographical location is determined by the existence of a marketable mineral resource, hitherto unused, which requires plant, labour force and transport; an opportunity for a new city is presented. Given these conditions, funds for development and reasonably good management, such a project can hardly fail to generate a secure economic base for a wide cross-section of income groups with varied skills. *Example*: Ciudad Guayana, Venezuela. Appendix 2.1.

2.3.2 Expansion of Small Town to Form New Industrial Centre

Where no overriding locational criterion, such as mineral extraction, is present the question of location is obviously much more difficult and will require a regional evaluation study. In many countries, the main city may be dominant and the regional cities may be underdeveloped, very often dependent on agricultural produce. An opportunity may exist, which, with some diversion of financial and technical resources, would enable an existing town to be upgraded or expanded, with new industry, housing and infrastructure. An industrial estate can be developed, largely related to agriculture but, perhaps, also making provision for supportive manufacturing or service industry.

In this case, the development and management problems are likely to be greater; whereas the resource-based city may 'take off' of its own accord, and, after reaching a critical size, may well require more control than stimulus, the new industrial town will require very careful development policies which will enable it to assume its place in the region's economy. *Example*: Huambo, Angola. Appendix 2.2.

2.3.3 New Community within the Urbanised Area of an Existing City

Many cities in the Third World can be best described by comparing them with a sponge; in other words they are full of 'holes'. As the city grew from many different starting-points rather than from a single core, gaps were left in the fabric which may now be waste land, agriculture or private holdings being kept for speculative reasons. These 'holes' are where the city will expand; much as the sponge can absorb large quantities of water, the city can absorb large numbers of people without enlarging its periphery. In many cases, these areas can be exceptionally large so that an observer may feel he is in a rural area rather than in a large city. Figure 2.1 is a photograph of a 'rural' squatter settlement a few minutes from the downtown area of Cebu, the second-largest city in the Philippines.

In such cases there is a powerful argument in favour of developing new communities with housing, industry and social facilities within the urban area. The development may not be within the city proper (in most cases the city boundary will enclose a smaller area than the urban area) and it may not be a town in the sense of having separate local government. However, if the city authorities can muster the necessary funds, land acquisition powers and administrative capability, the process can help to rationalise the use of land and infrastructure and can provide housing for low-income groups within reach of their existing employment in the city. *Example*: Bogota, Colombia. Appendix 2.3.

2.3.4 Development of Small Resource-based New Communities

The resource in this case is usually agriculture or fishery and the communities are dependent on the single employment source, have few facilities and are small in population (although not necessarily in land area). As with the larger new towns, it may be sound policy to expand an existing village where possible and in this case the new development could also serve as a service centre for surrounding villages. In other cases, where the settlement needs to be fairly central to a large area of crops a completely new start may be necessary. *Example*: Pahang Tenggara, Malaysia. Appendix 2.4.

These four types of planned community can, in appropriate

Figure 2.1: A Rural Area Within A City

situations, contribute to the totality of provision for new population. They do not provide an alternative to upgrading and improvement in existing towns or in the densely developed areas of cities. Whenever discussions on policy reach the point of asking whether to build new communities *or* to concentrate on improvement projects, the answer must be that both are needed. There may be questions of priority in resource allocation, but in the end neither alone will provide a 'solution'.

2.3.5 Satellite Towns

There is one further category which is, perhaps, more doubtful in terms of Third World cities; this is the satellite town such as those surrounding London. The concept was (and still is) that 'self-contained' towns would provide accommodation for overspill population from the central city and that around the towns there would be a 'green belt' where development would be severely restricted. Immediately a number of questions must be asked in our context of the poor in developing cities:

(1) is the city compact enough to require a leap over a green belt to separate towns?

(2) if such a green belt existed, would development control be strong enough to prevent the town's being engulfed by the spread of the city?

(3) (a) would the economics of development make it possible to provide a place for the poor?

　　(b) or would the new populations be more highly skilled and have higher incomes?

(4) would the new towns provide employment and other counter-attractions to migrants seeking work in the city?

(5) would the development of new towns divert essential resources from the parent city?

(6) if the new towns are considered to be relocation areas, will new migrants move into the vacated city areas?

The answers (except to (3)(b) and (6)) tend to be negative and there is little evidence to support the concept in any general way with regard to dealing with the problem of the poorest people. New towns of this kind could have uses, particularly where cities are densely developed, but the advantages may accrue more to industry, commerce, skilled workers and managers rather than to labourers or casual workers.

New towns, new communities, planned unit developments, or whatever they are called must be subjected to the most rigorous analysis in social and financial terms. The evaluation criteria must be pragmatic and directed towards realistic and achievable objectives; projects which pass such scrutiny may have much to contribute to overall urban development.

Appendix 2.1: Ciudad Guayana, Venezuela

Ciudad Guayana was planned in 1960 by the Corporacion Venezolana de Guayana (CVG) to be the major growth pole of the Guayana region of Venezuela. The location is at the confluence of the Orinoco and the Caroni rivers in an area rich with iron ore and other minerals. The rivers provide both navigation and abundant hydro-electric potential, and there are few physical development constraints. All the factors for successful growth were present, including adequate public and private funding, and by 1969 the population had reached 120,000.

In 1961 CVG obtained technical assistance from the Joint Center for Urban Studies of the Massachusetts Institute of Technology and Harvard University and planning studies were commenced. As part of those studies a physical development strategy was produced which had, as one of its goals, the integration of two existing towns, San Felix and Puerto Ordaz. Three strategies were originally considered; a single-city strategy, development to the west, and concentration of most business and administrative facilities in a major city centre.

The project has been extensively reviewed in various publications, the most important of which are: Lloyd Rodwin and Associates, *Planning Urban Growth and Regional Development* (MIT Press, Cambridge, Massachusetts, 1969); Lloyd Rodwin, 'Ciudad Guayana: a New City', *Scientific American*, vol. 213, no. 3 (September 1965) (reprinted in *Cities* (Alfred A. Knopf, New York, 1965)); Anthony Penfold, 'Ciudad Guayana: Planning a New City in Venezuela', *The Town Planning Review* (Liverpool), vol. 36, no. 4 (January 1966).

Appendix 2.2: Huambo, Angola

The Huambo district is in the central plateau of Angola, a heavily populated area with (in 1974) over 800,000 people living in hundreds of small villages. Most of them are subsistence farmers, although there have been a number of programmes of agricultural expansion teaching villagers to grow cash crops. Improvements in yield have meant that fewer people are needed on the land and there has been an urgent need for new employment for many years. In 1974 a group of consultants

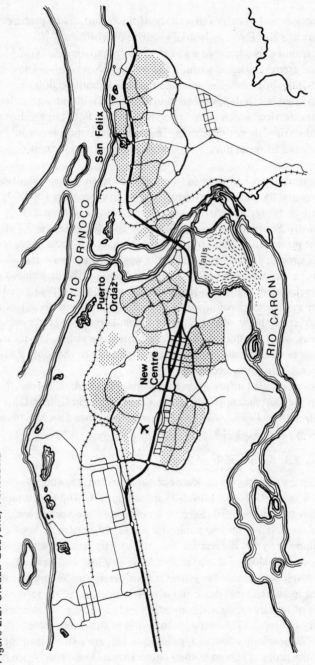

Figure 2.2: Ciudad Guayana, Venezuela

RIO ORINOCO

San Felix

Puerto Ordaz

falls

RIO CARONI

New Centre

residential areas

was commissioned to carry out a study of the region and to prepare development plans for an industrial estate and new town.[12]

A location study suggested a site at Caala (population 8,000) 25 kilometres from the largest town in the region — Nova Lisboa (now renamed Huambo) — which had a population of about 60,000.

It was intended to develop two industrial areas with infrastructure and central services which would provide space for both large industrial firms and small-scale entrepreneurs. The industries concerned would be largely related to agriculture — processing, canning, agricultural machinery, etc.

The physical configuration of the expanded town (whose population could vary greatly and could eventually grow to more than 100,000) was based on a careful assessment of the relatively fragile natural environment. Seasonal streams and fairly steep-sided valleys in a flat landscape presented difficult problems of drainage and erosion control. Over this a rough grid of roads and paths was projected, with the emphasis on goods transport, bicycling and walking. The map shows the broad development plan, with residential areas and footpaths related to the valley system. Expansion would begin from Caala and Zone 1 of the industrial estate and would be phased to include the projected new centre only when the demand had proved this to be viable. The location of the new centre permits a considerable expansion to the south and east if this should prove necessary.

For more detailed information on this project see Alan Turner, 'New Towns in the Developing World: Three Case Studies' in Gideon Golany (ed.), *International Urban Growth Policies: New Town Contributions* (John Wiley, New York, 1978).

Appendix 2.3: Bogota, Colombia

In 1972 Bogota had a population of about 3 million, growing by 250,000 a year, of which almost half are migrants. Owing to this rapid population growth some 70,000 new housing units are needed each year, and, as government and public agencies only construct about 15,000 units per year, the rest are built illegally by families who have no other choice. Most of these families have very low incomes and — as in most developing countries — there is considerable underemployment. Organised industrial areas occur in only two places; there are severe problems of overcrowding and congestion and the historic development of the city has resulted in over-concentration in the main centre.

In 1972 consultants[13] were appointed to prepare a structure plan for the city; the project, known as the Bogota Urban Development Study, was funded by the United Nations Development Programme and administered by the World Bank. Recommendations were made for various sectors including employment, transport, housing, social services, administration and financial management, together with a policy for an overall growth strategy. An important aspect of this was that development should be concentrated in three areas contiguous to the city. These growth points were intended to develop into new cities within the city and recommendations were made for the creation of appropriate agencies to manage their implementation.

A more detailed account of this project, and the planning of Bogota generally, may be found in Walter Bor, 'The Planning of Bogota', *Habitat International*, vol. 3, no. 1/2 (Pergamon Press, London, 1978); Alan Gilbert, 'Bogota: Policies, Planning and Crisis of Lost Opportunities' in Wayne A. Cornelius and Robert V. Kemper (eds.), *Metropolitan Latin America: the Challenge and the Response*, Latin American Urban Research, vol. 6 (Sage Publications, Beverly Hills, 1978), pp. 87-126.

Appendix 2.4: Pahang Tenggara, Malaysia

Regional development in Malaysia has received a great deal of attention during the last decade and authorities have been set up to promote agriculture, forestry, industry and urbanisation. In 1972 a regional plan was prepared for Pahang Tenggara which recommended the development of 36 new towns in an unpopulated area of tropical forests.[14] The new towns were to have a hierarchy as follows:

(1)   resource-based settlements of less than 5,000 people;
(2)   processing and basic service communities (10,000 population);
(3)   service and supply towns (15,000 to 30,000 population);
(4)   district centres (30,000-50,000 population);
(5)   a regional centre of over 50,000 people.

The first category (which illustrates this example) comprised small settlements of timber houses built at fairly low densities (allowing space to grow food) surrounded by oil-palm plantations. Social facilities included schools, clinics, recreational areas, shops and religious buildings. Development plans for the first of these new towns were announced in 1974 and in 1975 consultants were appointed to prepare detailed projects for six towns.[15]

The plan illustrated is for one of these towns but is a representative example. Topography and climate presented great difficulties; owing to

Figure 2.3: Huambo, Angola

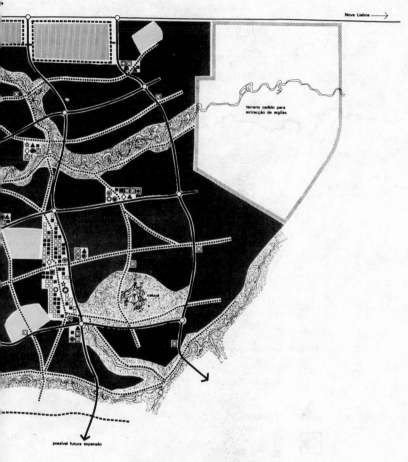

Nova Lisboa ⟶

terreno cedido para
extracção de argilas

possível futura expansão

Long term development plan showing expansion up
to a population of 130,000. The industrial estate
is in two zones to provide some distribution of
employment.

500 m   0   ½   1 km

Figure 2.4: Bogota, Colombia

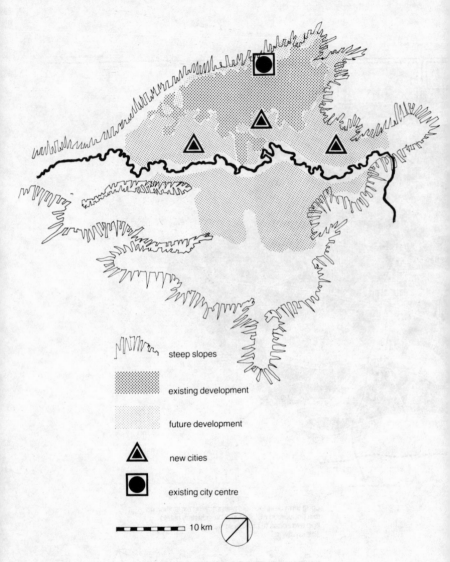

Figure 2.5: Pahang Tenggara, Malaysia

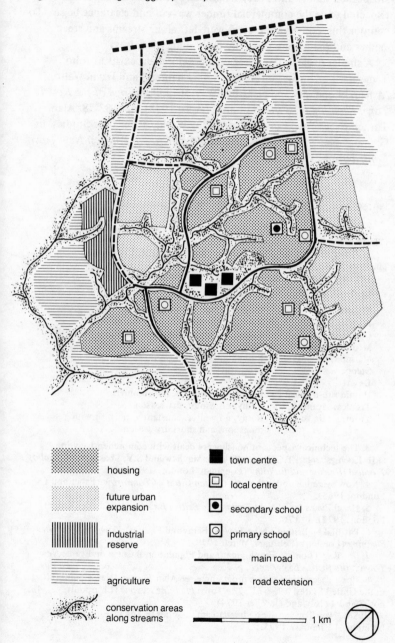

housing

future urban
expansion

industrial
reserve

agriculture

conservation areas
along streams

■ town centre

☐ local centre

⊙ secondary school

◎ primary school

——— main road

- - - - road extension

1 km

steep-sided valleys and heavy rains severe problems of erosion were expected once the commercial timber was cut and clearance began. To counter this, conservation areas were left along streams and steep valleys and roads were generally built along the ridges.

A similar programme of regional development exists in Johor Tenggara. For further information see Chapter 4 and David Walton, 'A Rural Economy and an Urban Way of Life', *Journal of the Royal Town Planning Institute* (London) (April 1975), pp. 133-38; Alan Turner, 'New Towns in the Developing World: Three Case Studies' in Gideon Golany (ed.), *International Urban Growth Policies: New Town Contributions* (John Wiley, New York, 1978).

Notes

1. *World Bank Atlas – Population, Per Capita Product and Growth Rates* (World Bank, Washington, 1975).

2. *Times Atlas of the World* (Times Newspapers Ltd, London, 1974), pp. xxvi-xxvii.

The categories used in this source are (excluding sub-arctic)

Type of Climate	Characteristics
Tundra	Polar climates, no warm season
Humid	Rainy, severe winters, cool summers
Continental	Rainy, severe winters, warm summers
Mediterranean	Rainy, mild winters, dry hot summers
Marine West Coast	Rainy, mild winters, warm summers
Steppe	Semi-arid
Desert	Arid
Humid sub-tropical	Rainy, mild winters, hot summers
Tropical savannah	Rainy, no winter, dry season
Tropical rain forest	Rainy, no winter, constantly moist or with monsoons and short dry season

3. The technical aspects of housing are dealt with comprehensively in O.H. Koenigsberger, T.G. Ingersoll, Alan Mayhew and S.V. Szokolay, *Manual of Tropical Housing and Building* (Longman, London, 1974).

4. Now available under the title *Garden Cities of Tomorrow* (Faber and Faber, London, 1965).

5. Hazel Evans (ed.), *New Towns: the British Experience* (Charles Knight, London, 1972), p. 176.

6. Pat Blake, 'Britain's New Towns: Facts and Figures', *Town and Country Planning* (London) (February/March 1979).

7. See Ray Thomas, 'Employment and Population Balance' in Evans, *New Towns: the British Experience*, p. 73.

8. For a description of this programme see Alan Turner, 'New Communities in the United States: 1968-73', *The Town Planning Review* (Liverpool), vol. 45, nos. 3 and 4 (July and October 1974).

9. See 'New Towns: the Fading Dream', a series in *The Washington Post*, beginning 12 January 1975.

10. Alan Turner, 'A Case for New Towns', *American Institute of Architects Journal* (Washington) (November 1970).

11. *Title VII Housing and Urban Development Act* (Washington, 1970), paragraph 32.7.

12. Ward Ashcroft and Parkman, L.H. Manderstam & Partners, Inbucon International and Alan Turner and Associates.

13. Llewelyn-Davies Weeks Forestier-Walker & Bor, Kates Peat Marwick & Co., Coopers & Lybrand.

14. *Pahang Tenggara Master Planning Study* (Foundation of Canada Engineering Corporation Ltd, Van Ginkel Associates Ltd, S.G. Gardner Engineering Services Ltd, Charrell International Consultants Ltd, June 1972).

15. Freeman Fox and Associates, Akitek Bersekutu Malaysia, Tahir Wong Sdn. Bhd, Roger Tym and Associates and Alan Turner and Associates.

Selected Bibliography: New Towns in Developing Countries

Most of the literature on new communities concerns the more developed countries of the world, particularly the UK, the USA, the USSR, and a number of European countries. The following selected list refers specifically to the developing countries of Asia, Africa and Latin America.

Doxiadis Associates, 'Industrial Development in Islamabad', *Ekistics*, vol. 13, no. 78 (1962), pp. 349-60.
——, 'Islamabad: the Scale of the City and its Central Area', *Ekistics*, vol. 14, no. 83 (October 1962), pp. 148-60.
——, 'The Spirit of Islamabad', *Ekistics*, vol. 12, no. 72 (November 1961), pp. 315-35.
Evenson, Norma, *New Towns – India: Chandigarh* (University of California Press, Berkeley, 1966).
Fahim, Hussein M. 'Nubian Resettlement in the Sudan', *Ekistics*, vol. 36, no. 212 (July 1973), pp. 41-9.
Golany, Gideon, *International Urban Growth Policies: New Town Contributions* (John Wiley, New York, 1978). Contributions to this book dealing specifically with developing countries are Debayoti Aichbhaumik, 'Indian Policy on Industrialization and Industrial New Town Developments' (Chapter 16); Alan Turner, 'New Towns in the Developing World: Three Case Studies' (Chapter 17).
Gomez, Benjamin F., 'Urbanization in the Philippines: the Need for an Integrated Policy in Urbanization and Development of New Towns', (United Nations Interregional Seminar on New Towns, London 4-19 June 1973).
Hardoy, Jorge E., 'The Planning of New Capital Cities and Argentina's Nineteenth Century New Town' in *Planning of Metropolitan Areas and New Towns* (United Nations, New York, 1967), pp. 176-7, 232-49.
——, 'Two New Capital Cities: Brasilia and Islamabad. The Planning of New Capital Cities', *Ekistics*, vol. 18, no. 108 (November 1964), pp. 320-5.
Koenigsberger, Otto H., 'New Towns in India', *Town Planning Review*, vol. 23, no. 2 (1952), pp. 95-132.
——, and Safier Michael, 'Urban Growth and Planning the Developing Countries of the Commonwealth: a review of Experience from the Past 25 Years' (United Nations Interregional Seminar on New Towns, London, 4-19 June 1973).
Prakash, Ved, *New Towns in India*. Monograph and Occasional Papers Series,

Monograph no. 8 (Duke University, Durham, North Carolina, Program in Comparative Studies on Southern Asia, 1969).

Rodwin, Lloyd (ed.), *Planning Urban Growth and Regional Development: the Experience of the Guayana Program of Venezuela* (MIT Press, Cambridge, Massachusetts, 1969).

Turner, Alan and Smulian, Jonathan, 'New Cities in Venezuela', *Town Planning Review*, vol. 42, no. 1 (1971), pp. 3-27; reprinted in D.J. Dwyer (ed.), *The City in the Third World* (Macmillan, London, 1974).

United Nations, *Comprehensive Report on the Planning and Development of New Towns* (New York, 1964).

——, Center for Housing, Building and Planning, 'Selected Conclusions and Recommendations on Regional and Metropolitan Planning: New Towns and Land Policy', *Ekistics*, vol. 23, no. 135 (February 1967), pp. 87-91.

——, Economic Commission for Asia and the Far East, *A Case Study for the Dodomar Valley Corporation and its Projects*. Flood Control Series no. 16 (Bangkok, 1960).

——, World Health Organization, *Health and Sanitation Factors in the Planning and Development of New Towns*. United Nations Conference Document no. 12 (United Nations, New York, 1964).

3 PROJECT PLANNING

Alan Turner

In all development projects the emphasis should be on efficient and
timely delivery – the end of the process when the benefits become
available to the groups for whom they are intended. In the nature of
the process there is often a considerable wastage of resources along the
way, so that the eventual goods or services fall short of expectations.
Equally often there is a discrepancy between the needs of the potential
beneficiaries and the components of the project owing to poor
evaluation and analysis of the needs. To avoid this, it is essential to
create a framework within which appropriate analysis and plan or
programme formulation can take place – in other words, to design for
design. This chapter examines this process and concentrates on the
technical study period during which projects and programmes are
created.[1] It has been assumed that the study is for a specific
development project involving low-income housing and related facilities.
In the second part of the chapter a case study is used to illustrate the
process.

3.1 The Planning Process

Many attempts have been made to chart the process of planning with
varying levels of sophistication and complexity. It is certain that
procedures exist which tend to be followed by most study teams; it is
also certain that no attempt to represent them by means of charts or
diagrams can be more than a very crude approximation. However, it is
useful to make such approximations in order to conceptualise the work,
which must be achieved during a particular period – time and budget
usually being all-important. Figure 3.1 is an illustration of the major
steps which need to be taken to reach the delivery or implementation
stage. A number of closed loops are shown, to suggest the cyclic nature
of the process, where it may, for instance, be necessary to go back over
previous analysis or to redefine objectives owing to factors which were
unknown at the previous stage. The process, then, is not linear, nor is it
necessarily as sequential as suggested by the diagram. Some of the
activities may be carried out in parallel and there may be considerable
overlap. An immediate action project may commence early in the
process so that implementation is not necessarily restricted to the final

stage, but is an ongoing process which can contribute to the definition of perceived needs and objectives. Figure 3.1 is a rough sketch of a sequence of operations which subsume many more detailed activities. These, too, cannot be laid down with precision; once again there are overlaps and blurred edges. Some activities may be relevant to one project but not to another and a great deal of subjective judgement is necessary to decide just what has to be done to achieve a particular result. Appendix 3.1 contains a check-list of activities which are common in planning studies and there are cases in which all of them would need to be carried out. However, if the list is used as a guide, each item should be carefully evaluated to determine whether its inclusion would materially affect the outcome of the study.

3.2 Technical Assistance

Professional advice or technical assistance in urban and rural development has increased considerably during the last decade. It would be difficult, if not impossible, to quantify this, but it amounts to a major field of activity involving multilateral and bilateral aid, a large number of national and international organisations, major institutions such as universities or research establishments, private consulting firms and individual advisers.

At some point in the future it is to be hoped that the need will decline, or even disappear altogether, as the developing countries acquire professional and technical skills, but for the foreseeable future, technical assistance is certain to form an important component of development studies. However, once a project has been defined and a study has been set up, it should be an objective to enable the local team to carry out the project (and other similar ones) without further assistance. It is axiomatic that the best kind of technical assistance is that which seeks to transfer skills, thereby reducing or eliminating the need. The process of providing appropriate assistance is complex and involves many people in government departments in two or more countries before a particular programme can be established. It is not surprising, therefore, that this process, which includes the definition of projects, the allocation of funds and the selection of technical advisers, is both time-consuming and subject to a number of inefficiencies. Whether the advisers are individuals or members of a public body or private firm, the international rules and regulations covering the movement of people, equipment and money often seem to conspire almost to prevent the work from being carried out at all. However, assuming that all the usual bureaucratic obstacles can be overcome and,

Figure 3.1: Flow Chart of Planning Progress

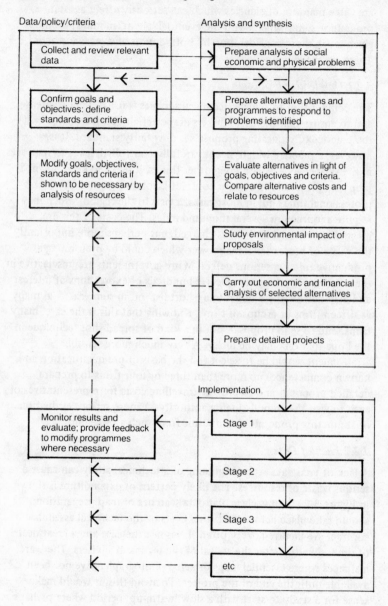

leaving aside for the moment the question of counterpart staff, there are three major inefficiencies which can seriously affect assistance programmes and which (with the eventual 'client' in mind) should be given much more consideration by both donors and receivers of aid. These are listed below.

3.2.1 Unselective Proposals

The competition to provide technical services is usually fairly intense and to ensure that the best advisers are selected (at a reasonable cost) the practice of requesting proposals is now fairly standard. It is, however, a practice which, if not carefully controlled, leads to increases in the very costs which, among other things, it seeks to keep down. To prepare a proposal for a major contract involves a great deal of professional time and, in most cases, a visit to the region, which may require a journey of several thousand miles. The costs of this are inevitably reflected in the fees charged, but perhaps more importantly the waste of professional manpower which could be preforming a productive role is a serious defect. Many governments are unselective in their first approaches, may receive hundreds of expressions of interest and may narrow these down to a 'short list' of, in some cases, as many as fifteen firms or groups of firms. Knowing that this is the case, many firms tend to send proposals out in a kind of spread-shot technique in the hope that one may be lucky. A very much more sensible arrangement would be to select (on the basis of pre-qualification and known competence) no more than three or four firms to prepare detailed proposals and to provide travelling costs for representatives of each to visit the commissioning authority. A more serious evaluation of competing proposals would result from such a procedure.

3.2.2 Lack of Data

A lack of vital data at the beginning of a technical study can cause a serious waste of resources. The likely pattern of expenditure is shown in Figure 3.2 and it is clear that data searches or map preparation should take place before the higher costs of the technical assistance contract are incurred. Very often this is not the case and a great deal of time is wasted after the arrival of the technical advisers. There are instances where essential maps or aerial photographs have not been available until the end of the project. To avoid this, it would make sense for a study to start with a slow 'warm-up' period where perhaps one or two short visits are made by specialists several months before the expatriate team is installed, to make sure that data are obtainable

Figure 3.2: Technical Assistance; Increased Costs and Productive Capacity

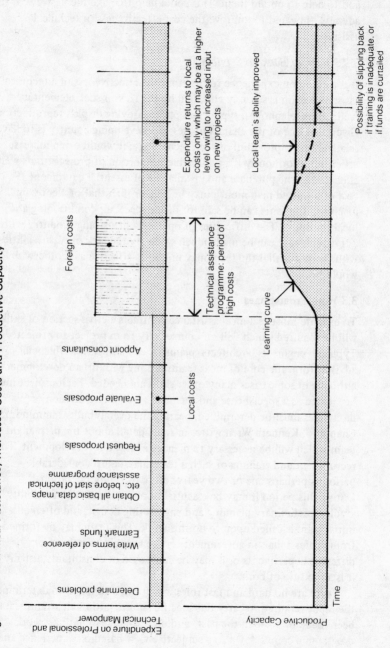

and to help to obtain them. This could help to make the best use of the advisers' time and to improve the cost-effectiveness of technical assistance.

3.2.3 Lack of Back-up Services

It is a common experience to find that the effectiveness of a technical assistance team is severely curtailed by the lack of such elementary facilities as telephones, typing and photo-copying or plan reproduction. Given that one of the characteristics of a developing country is to have relatively poor provision of such technology, it would often increase efficiency enormously if a reasonable proportion of project funds were allocated to the purchase and installation of essential equipment. The cost of a wasted man-month may be greater than that of a copying machine. The same can be said for office space, air-conditioning and local transport. The difficulties of operating in a strange country with a trying climate can be made much worse by the lack of such facilities, with the result that the team may not be as effective as it otherwise would be.

3.3 Work Programmes

To execute most technical assistance contracts a cross-section of skills will be required which will, of course, vary from project to project. Typically engineers, architects, planners, economists and financial advisers form the core of most teams dealing with urban development, although in some cases many other skills are needed. Each project must be treated as a special case and the most appropriate division of disciplines must be determined, bearing the overall budget in mind. In Chapter 6, Kenneth Wren writes in some detail about the permanent team which will be necessary to manage a large new development. The recruitment and training of such a team may take a considerable period — perhaps one or two years before it is fully operational. During this period it may be essential to move ahead with feasibility studies, preliminary planning and engineering design, and often an initial team is called upon to do this work. This team may be formed from professionals in government service brought together from different departments or it may be composed of consultants; usually it is a mixture of both.

There are no hard and fast rules which can be applied to determine the input required to carry out specific studies (although attempts have been made to do so in the past) and, in the end, estimating a work programme comes down to a subjective view based on experience and an understanding of the particular problems to be faced. Two examples are given as illustrations of the varying professional inputs in two actual projects.

Figure 3.3 shows the manpower schedule for a project which falls into the category of an expanded town; the existing population was about 8,000 and it was intended to increase this to perhaps 80,000 to 100,000 by developing a large industrial estate. As it was necessary to devise new industries, the team included a number of experts (for short periods) on highly specialised industrial processes.

Figure 3.4 shows, by contrast, a manpower schedule for the design of several small resource-based new towns. Although fewer people were involved (20 as against 24), they were working for longer periods and the work programme was much more intensive. In the first instance, 118 man-months are spread out over 15 months, a full-time equivalent team of nearly eight. In the second case, 155 man-months are used in ten months, a full-time equivalent team of 15.5. The number of people in the team and the period over which they work are not only related to the size of the project and the amount of the investment, but respond fairly directly to the time pressures which are imposed by the authority which is commissioning the work.

It must be emphasised that these charts represent only the consultants' time (both local and expatriate) needed to prepare the basic studies and to formulate proposals which were in the form of general strategies with more detailed plans for the first stages. In addition to specially constituted teams of this kind, there will inevitably be a considerable input of counterpart staff time in the client department. This is essential for a number of reasons; not only will the local staff have a much better understanding of government procedures, cultural attitudes and local customs, but they should also form the nucleus of the team which will subsequently manage the development. Most projects of this kind (especially those funded by bilateral or multilateral aid programmes) include an element of training on the job for the counterpart staff who are expected to benefit from the greater experience of the consultant members of the team. In theory this is excellent, in practice often less so. One of the goals of a conscientious consultant should be to leave behind a viable organisation which can carry on with the project with little or no outside assistance. Although there may be a genuine desire on the part of the consultants to pass on their knowledge and skills and, in effect, to 'teach themselves out of a job', there are usually considerable difficulties and the training programme may suffer. In the first place, counterpart staff may be

Figure 3.3: Technical Assistance: Example of Manpower Chart, 1

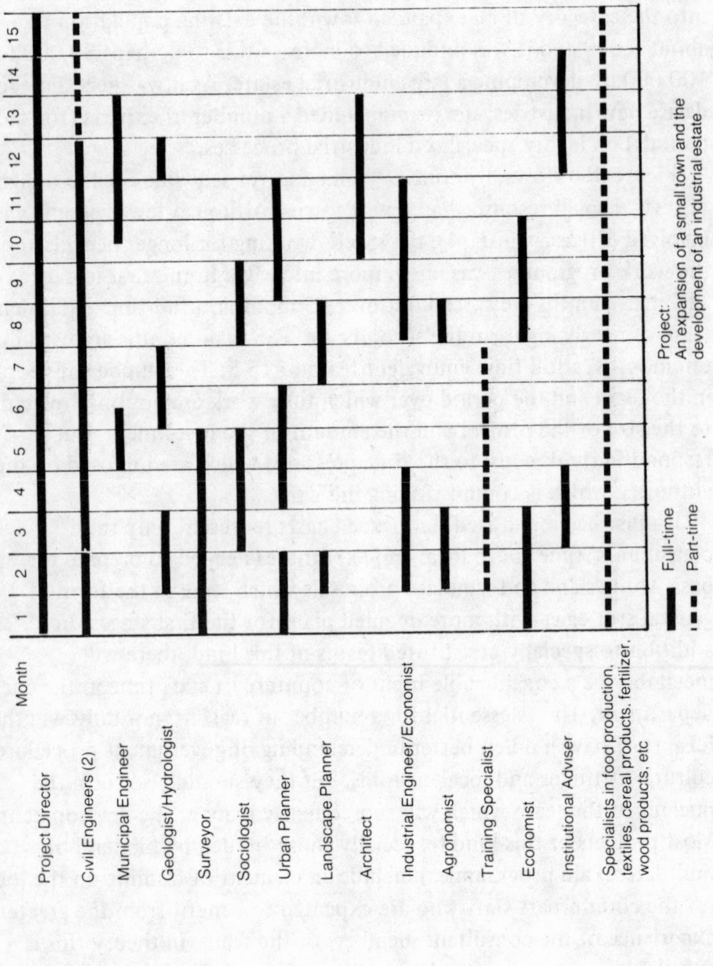

Month	1	2	3	4	5	6	7	8	9	10	11	12	13	14	15
Project Director															
Civil Engineers (2)															
Municipal Engineer															
Geologist/Hydrologist															
Surveyor															
Sociologist															
Urban Planner															
Landscape Planner															
Architect															
Industrial Engineer/Economist															
Agronomist															
Training Specialist															
Economist															
Institutional Adviser															
Specialists in food production, textiles, cereal products, fertilizer, wood products, etc															

Full-time
Part-time

Project:
An expansion of a small town and the development of an industrial estate

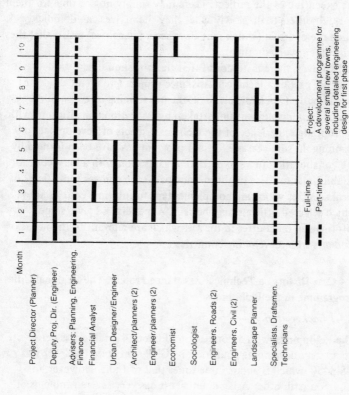

Figure 3.4: Technical Assistance; Example of Manpower Chart, 2

Month

Project Director (Planner)
Deputy Proj. Dir. (Engineer)
Advisers: Planning, Engineering, Finance
Financial Analyst
Urban Designer/Engineer
Architect/planners (2)
Engineer/planners (2)
Economist
Sociologist
Engineers, Roads (2)
Engineers, Civil (2)
Landscape Planner
Specialists, Draftsmen, Technicians

Full-time
Part-time

Project:
A development programme for several small new towns, including detailed engineering design for first phase

poorly selected and inadequately educated to take full advantage of their opportunities. They may have other duties which they cannot fully relinquish so that their participation in the programme may be limited. In some cases counterpart staff hardly appear at all and contribute little to the work. Second, the consultants' team may be good professional technicians but poor teachers and in any case their time will be constrained by the urgency of the programme and the multitude of delays and inefficiencies which are bound to creep into the execution of the project. There may simply not be time for them to teach others to do slowly what they themselves can do quickly, when the contract (which may have severe penalties) insists that they finish their work on time.

However, there is no doubt that training should be regarded as an essential part of a technical assistance project and included in the overall budget. In addition to on-the-job training, there should be a formal training element undertaken by educational institutions with appropriate experience of the technical aspects of development planning. In some cases excellent programmes have been formed by the collaboration of an expatriate organisation with a local educational establishment. These might provide part-time courses for officers of the local agencies which are complementary to full-time courses abroad, to which selected officials may be sent. Appendix 3.2 gives some information on courses in the UK which are relevant to the needs of students from developing countries.

3.4 Case History: a Technical Assistance Project. The Regional Cities Programme in the Philippines

3.4.1 Background

The Philippines, with a population of about 42 million, is better off than many developing countries; its GNP *per capita* for 1977 was US $450, which is about three times that of India. However, in common with other Asian countries it has very severe problems of poverty, not only in the rural areas where 70 per cent of the population lives in villages of less than 1,500 population, but also in the seven or eight major cities. The population in urban centres is expected to reach 46 per cent, or about 35 million, by the end of the century.

Metro-Manila is by far the largest city with a population of about 5 million, or 13 per cent of the national total. If present trends continue, the Manila urban region could have as many as 20 million people by the year 2000. The gap between Manila and the second-rank cities is large; Metro-Cebu has a population of approximately 1 million, while Davao has only about 500,000. Of the current urban population of 13 million, nearly one-third is estimated to be living at or below the minimum subsistence level (as defined by FAO/WHO). This population of approximately 4 million is living in squatter settlements and slums with very limited access to water, often with no sanitary facilities and, in many cases, considerable danger from floods during the rainy season.

In the past, public action to improve conditions has had very little effect on the problem. Attempts have been made to clear areas and rehouse the residents elsewhere but these have failed for a number of reasons, often because the relocation sites chosen have been too far away from existing employment and families have tended to drift back to their original sites in the centres of cities. In 1977 a new approach to the problem was initiated as part of a World Bank funded project whose official title was 'The Second Feasibility Study of Dagat-Dagatan and Regional Centres'. Dagat-Dagatan is a very large reclaimed area in Manila which is currently being developed for sites-and-services housing, industry and ancillary facilities; the Regional Centres are three cities in the centre and the south of the Philippines — Cebu, Davao and Cagayan de Oro.

Both projects were under the aegis of the National Housing Authority (NHA), but are quite different in organisational aspects. In the case of Dagat-Dagatan, NHA was responsible for detailed design and implementation whereas in the Regional Cities programme, it was the intention that the local authorities should design and implement the projects under the guidance of NHA, which would provide loans to each city. A group of consulting firms was appointed by NHA to work with its own staff on both projects.[2]

As in the case of NHA the consultants played different roles in each project; in Dagat-Dagatan they were heavily involved in detailed engineering design and supervision, whereas in the Regional Cities programme they were helping to build up local teams in each city and the consultants' function was more advisory and educational. The intention was to reach a situation where the local teams could carry out their work with little or no consultancy support.

The main requirements of the consultancy contract regarding the Regional Cities were as follows:

(1)   to provide guidance and assistance in the conduct of studies in regional centres for sites-and-services and slum upgrading;
(2)   to ensure that the work was carried out in accordance with

NHA guidelines;
(3) to recommend an organisational structure for implementation;
(4) to train the local counterpart staff;
(5) to provide guidance and assistance in particular for: social, economic and financial studies; layouts and engineering; overall housing strategy; land tenure.

3.4.2 Goals and Policies

A very significant step forward in Filipino housing policy was made in June 1977 by the issuance of Presidential Letter of Instruction (LOI) 555. This document, signed by President Marcos, instituted a nation-wide Slum Improvement and Resettlement Programme (SIR) and ushered in a new opportunity for millions of squatters to become legal tenants (and eventually owners) of their lots. It was a radical piece of legislation which could serve as a model to other countries.

Among other things, LOI 555 required local governments to:

institute an SIR programme;
define slums;
form a local staff of professionals;
create short- and long-term slum improvement programmes;
acquire land by expropriation;
make the land and improvements available to the bona fide residents under long-term leases with options to purchase;
collect rents or mortgage payments from the beneficiaries.

Agreements were reached with the three cities and the policies of NHA were stated to be:

(1) housing is not simply physical shelter but includes water, sanitary facilities, social facilities and employment opportunities;
(2) housing must be affordable by the target income groups with minimum subsidy from public funds (cross-subsidy from complementary development is to be encouraged);
(3) long-term solutions to the housing problem require high levels of cost recovery and the creation of revolving funds;
(4) housing is not only the responsibility of central government but must include local governments and the private sector.

The third point above is vital, not only in the Philippines but generally in developing countries (and some would argue, in developed countries as well). If costs (or a large part of them) are not recovered, the level of subsidy from general taxation is so high that only a very small percentage of the total low-income population can be helped. The Philippines could not possibly provide the present slum population of 4 million with highly subsidised housing nor keep pace with the enormous rate of increase in low-income households — possibly 11 or 12 million by the end of the century. The emphasis, therefore, is on two main concerns:

(1) repeatable projects ('replicable' in the current jargon) made possible by cost recovery;
(2) standards of development appropriate to the incomes of the potential residents.

3.4.3 The Technical Project

The following section is a composite of the experience of all three cities and covers most of the common problems and opportunities; it is written in a generalised manner and the statements in it do not necessarily apply in each city.

Site Selection: Upgrading. The first problem to be encountered was the definition and location of slums in the city. What constitutes a slum? Are the criteria simply physical or should tenure be included? Most definitions of this kind are fallible and there are always exceptions to the rule. For instance, in an area defined as a slum, it is not unusual to find one or two 'affluent squatters' with well built modern houses with their own water and sanitary facilities. However, it was accepted that, in general, a slum would consist of areas of houses varying in physical quality but without main services, or properly constructed roads or paths and where the majority of residents were squatters. The area would be defined regardless of whether it was publicly or privately owned. The latter was most important as, owing to a conceptual misunderstanding, many officials had defined slums as simply those on government land, so that the extent of slums in these cases was grossly underestimated.

Location was equally difficult owing to what must be a problem common to all rapidly growing cities — the lack of up-to-date maps. Existing maps were inaccurate and usually several years out of date, so that the true extent of urban areas was not known. It was essential to solve this by having aerial photographs taken, from which the location of slums could be defined. (The pattern of informally built squatter housing is easily distinguishable from the more orderly pattern of conventional housing.) When this was done, the total area and the number of houses were found to be greater than the figures usually quoted by local officials. The proportion of the total population living in slums was between 25 and 30 per cent.

When the various sites had been defined, an attempt was made to collect similar data for each so that priorities could be established. It was not always possible to obtain reliable answers to all the questions but the following check-list was used:

(1)   Number of houses, households: house condition
(2)   Topography
(3)   Dominant ground conditions
(4)   Shape of site
(5)   Environment
(6)   Ownership and acquisition costs
(7)   Zoning and planning proposals
(8)   Infrastructure
(9)   Transportation and employment
(10) Quality of existing facilities
(11) Availability of land for additional facilities
(12) Community attitude to improvement
(13) Existence of local organisations
(14) Possible sources of cross-subsidy

Site Selection: Sites-and-Services Areas. The concept of sites and services, although well understood now by most professionals in the international community, is still prone to all kinds of misinterpretations and misconceptions among housing officials in many countries. Thus we hear slum-upgrading referred to as 'the upgrading of sites and services' or fully constructed housing schemes (minus a few doors and windows) masquerading under the title. At the very lowest level, which is where the pressure is, the concept must be what the name implies; a piece of land with security and very basic services, which may be no more than a common water-point and pit latrines with unmade roads and footpaths.

Essentially we were looking for space for two different groups, although these could (and should) be on the same site. The first group were the small percentage of households who would inevitably be relocated from upgraded areas by road construction or other public works. (It was intended to keep this figure down to 10 per cent of any slum site.) The second group were the new migrants and the new households being created by natural growth. For such households, it was necessary to plan and develop areas where they could build a house legally rather than swell the numbers of squatters. Although this may seem rather obvious, it is not a concept which has received much attention in the Philippines, or elsewhere in my experience. Usually the approach is to build a few conventional housing units and to conveniently forget that the city's housing is growing by leaps and bounds in an unplanned and informal manner unreflected in any statistics of applications for permission to build.

Most of the locations put forward by local authorities were a long way from the city, badly served by public transport and distant from employment suitable to the residents' skills. Their sole criterion was to find government-owned land or private land which could be acquired at the lowest possible price, even if this meant that the land was unsuitable in terms of location, topography or soil conditions. It is not surprising that officials should make choices of this kind given the constraints of completely inadequate funding and lack of powers to acquire suitable land by compulsory purchase or expropriation. However, with the advent of the new programme these impediments were removed and sites within a few kilometres of the city centre were selected. The criteria were similar to those for upgrading sites except that numbers (1), (11) and (12) would probably not apply and the emphasis was laid heavily on proximity to transportation routes and areas of employment.

Feasibility Studies. After sites had been selected in each city, feasibility studies were made by teams consisting of members of NHA, the local SIR staff and the consultants. Social surveys were carried out to determine the priorities for action and to give a profile of the different communities. In addition these surveys had the effect of informing all the residents about the intentions of the programme and gauging their reactions.

Typical findings were:

45 per cent of the population were below 15 years of age;
fertility was high but so was infant mortality, particularly from gastro-enteric diseases;
household size was 6 but there were about 8 or 9 people per house;
unemployment was high among women and young people and

underemployment was common among heads of households (usually men);

educational and skills standards were low;

the majority of households owned their house (but not the land) and a small proportion were renters;

only a very small proportion of houses had sanitary facilities or water supply;

about 30 per cent of families had monthly incomes lower than 350 pesos (£23) but most expressed a willingness to pay reasonable rent for security of tenure.

Engineering studies were vital at this stage as many sites were waterlogged and in some cases tidal, with the houses built on stilts. A number of different types of slums were defined, including:

(1)   high density on low-lying land subject to frequent inundation;
(2)   low density but rapidly developing rural-urban settlements;
(3)   groups of houses built over the sea on timber piles — usually fishermen's houses.

In most cases the engineering problems required fairly expensive solutions, including levees to keep out the sea and extensive drainage works. Reclamation and land costs were high, with the result that standards of improvement had to be low to ensure financial feasibility.

The limits of feasibility clearly are very elastic. Given adequate funds almost anything can be done in engineering terms, but if the concept includes measuring the ability of the potential residents to pay for the improvements (or a large part of them), then feasibility must be a compromise between desirable standards and affordable costs. In these particular studies, financial calculations were made, assuming certain interest rates on loans and repayment periods, which aimed at a very high level of cost recovery from the residents. This does not imply that there are no subsidies at all; no community, even in high-income districts, is expected to pay directly for all its services. Roads are paved and streets are lit and paid for from property taxes generally. The assumption was made that the actual costs of the improvement of the site should be recoverable (for example reclamation, on-site infrastructure, etc.) and that those elements which would normally be supplied by an agency (major roads, street lights, etc.) should not be recoverable. This provides a reasonable compromise; the basic project funds can revolve, enabling future projects to be carried out, but the residents receive a level of subsidy common to other residents of the city. The last point is important, as it is quite possible to structure a project of this kind, in which poor people are expected to contribute proportionately more to general environment than people in wealthier areas. The extremes of unsupportable subsidy and no subsidy are unrealistic and, as usual with problems of this kind, there is a fairly wide band within which projects can be said to be financially sound.

Decision-making and Community Relations. It is possible (although not desirable) to acquire land and prepare a sites-and-services layout without community participation, but it is quite impossible to upgrade an existing slum without the active co-operation of the residents. This means that they must be involved in basic decisions and that they must be allowed to choose between different options in terms of standards and costs. However, this is not to imply that they should (or could) be involved in all aspects of the technical work. For instance, at the outset the engineering choices may be extremely complex and some work will have to be done before anything can be explained to non-technical people. But if the alternatives can be presented simply, with costs expressed as so much rent per month most residents can respond. The question will be not 'Do you want water on tap in each house?' (everyone will say yes) but 'Do you want water in each house at a cost of so much per month or a common point for a group of houses at so much less per month?' Although this may seem obvious to the reader, it is by no means always done in practice. Biased questions are sometimes asked which will produce answers the officials want to hear. It is fairly easy to lead a community into a decision to move all their houses into a 'better' layout (i.e. with straight roads and paths) only for them to find out, too late, that the disruption and costs are too great.

The emphasis in community meetings was, therefore, to give a simple and truthful account of the choices and to try to explain the links between one action and another. For instance, in some cases the only financially and technically possible solution to sanitation was for more than one house to share a toilet. If a community said they would not on any account accept this, the effect of poor sanitation on their health (and their children's health) would have to be pointed out. They can still make the choice, but at least they know the implications.

In the Philippines, as in many countries, language is a great barrier. Many of the technicians (Filipino as well as foreign) were unable to converse with residents in their own language and there was considerable scope for misunderstanding. Some concepts are difficult enough without the added 'noise level' of translation by an interpreter who does not himself fully understand the problems or the solutions. Great care is necessary to produce simple illustrated handouts that explain, in the local language, the nature of the proposals and spell out the choices which can be made. Radio, television and the local press are essential allies, but most of all it is vital to have a few dedicated people who will give up their time to explaining the same points again and again, usually at meetings in the evening when the men are home from work. Such people are, in my experience, often undervalued, but without them there can be no project.

3.4.4 Standards and Costs

Discussions of standards often generate a certain amount of heated argument. There are those who maintain that high standards must be used, that the poor should not be expected to accept second-best and that if this means heavy subsidies, so be it. This may be called the traditional view. A more radical opinion is that all standards are arbitrary and that it is not necessary to define minimum standards. Clearly such polarisation is not very useful and the word appropriate should simply be substituted for minimum and maximum.

Once again there is a range within which many things are possible. Where land costs are low, large lots and pit latrines may suffice; the lower density may enable gravel or laterite roads to be used. High land costs will mean small lots, which may in turn necessitate some more expensive form of sanitation and possibly higher investment in roads and paths. There are no absolutes and guidelines can only be generated for a particular country or region with specific cultural, technical and financial criteria. However, certain methods of approach have more general application and in the cases under discussion these methods could be described by using words such as 'judgemental' and 'iterative'. A preliminary judgement is made and then tested to see if it conforms with the desired objective. This is the way in which most things are designed and at this stage the project becomes a design problem.

It is clearly necessary to have some standards to aim for. One water-point for six people, 60 people or 100 people? Paved access to within 2 metres or 20 metres of all dwellings? Having made reasonable assumptions about appropriate standards, a design can be roughly worked out, costed, and a financial analysis prepared to determine whether it can be paid for. If it does not work (in financial terms) the standards can be manipulated until a reasonable balance is found.

Inevitably there is a compromise between what people want and what they can afford.

This is an over-simplification and there are many problems along the way, not the least of which are existing codes of practice, building regulations or planning requirements. It is probably true to say that if all the legislated standards were applied to any poor area in any city, there could be no question of improvement within people's means. The only solution would be to demolish the whole area and begin again, which is precisely what cannot be done. The expected result, when such schemes are discussed with officials responsible for building or planning control, is that the project cannot proceed because it does not comply with this or that regulation. The argument seems to be — 'Don't do anything until you can do everything'. A necessary part of sites-and-services or slum-upgrading projects is new legislation which enables reasonable standards to be used and gives local officials fairly wide scope for interpretation.

A 'reasonable range' of standards and costs must be worked out which will be carefully related to the way in which the project is paid for. Usually the following kinds of standards are necessary.

(1) *Physical planning guidelines.* These should not necessarily be expressed as absolutes, although in some cases practical minima or maxima must be specified. They should cover land use, spatial distribution, density, road and path networks and so on.

(2) *Provision of facilities.* Often the provision of schools, clinics, community meeting rooms and other social facilities is governed by a number of agencies whose goals and budgets are un-coordinated, and unrelated to very low-income housing.

(3) *Infrastructure standards.* These have to cover both provision (for example the number of houses to be served by a common stand-pipe) and constructional specification.

These all have to be thought of as levels of service which will be related to costs and affordability. The approach in the Regional Cities programme was to produce a manual which set out recommended (but not mandatory) standards and target figures for unit costs. For instance, costs per hectare or per household for different components were produced at different levels of provision (e.g. surfaced roads or unsurfaced roads). Tables were produced relating these to different income groups and different amortisation periods so that it was fairly easy to pick a preliminary 'package' of improvements which could then be used as the first rough design and subjected to specific analysis and modification in the particular project.

3.4.5 Training

Leaving aside the question of financial resources, perhaps the greatest impediment to rapid progress in programmes of this type is the lack of skilled professional manpower. One of the objectives of technical assistance is to pass on skills and the emphasis in well designed consultancy projects is more and more on this aspect. However, it is essential that the local team is at least sufficiently well trained to be able to accept and use new techniques and stable enough to have a reasonably long period to apply them in practice. Often neither of these requirements are met. This is not a reflection on the individuals, many of whom are highly motivated, but on existing educational systems and on civil service and local authority norms of employment. A department of architecture or engineering will teach a student how to design the 'best' structure using modern methods and materials. It will not necessarily teach him how to design something that will perform adequately using local materials and *ad hoc* constructional methods. The opposite may be the case and the student (now an architect or engineer) may feel that it is below his professional dignity to design such things, which are not 'good practice'.

Even if these problems are overcome and the young professional becomes a member of a slum-improvement team, the low salaries of local government may not keep him away from the call to more lucrative practice for long. Even worse, the whole team may be dispersed owing to temporary failures in the supply of funds, due either to inefficiency at the higher levels of bureaucracy or to political chicanery.

However, if we assume that a team of good well motivated local professionals can be brought together, there is a clear need for a formal training component in the programme. On-the-job training is one thing and, in my experience, counterparts can learn a great deal by working side by side with more experienced colleagues, but there is never enough time (owing to the constraints of the contract) for adequate instruction and some consultants do not make good teachers (and vice versa). It is very desirable to set up special courses for existing staff which they can attend perhaps one day a week and to create other courses, in local universities, where new recruits can be found. Added to this, it is essential for a housing authority to appoint a training

Figure 3.5: Agdao Creek, Davao, Philippines

Agdao is a high density squatter settlement built along the banks of a creek which drains part of the city. The houses interfere with natural drainage and are subject to flooding. Although upgrading policy tends to leave houses where they are, it is sometimes necessary in cases like this to relocate the houses which are actually in the creek bed.

Figure 3.6: *Bayanihan*; a House being Moved to a New Lot in an Upgrading Project in the Philippines

Figure 3.7: Tondo Foreshore, Manila

A street in the Tondo Foreshore area of Manila, the largest and most densely populated squatter area in the city. The top photograph was taken in November 1977. The bottom photograph was taken from the same viewpoint in February 1978 after roads, paths, drainage and water supply had been introduced as part of an upgrading project being carried out by the National Housing Authority. As soon as the services were improved and tenure granted, there was a remarkable increase in the amount and quality of home improvements carried out by the tenants at their own expense.

officer and to provide the necessary funds for recruitment and training. (In the Philippines, recommendations for a training programme were made to NHA by Professor Otto Koenigsberger of the Development Planning Unit, University College, London, who was a member of the consulting team.)

3.4.6 Implementation and Monitoring

At the time of writing it is too early to determine the success (or failure) of the policies and programmes put forward and the final note I would stress is that just as housing programmes require parallel funding for social support programmes and employment creation, so they also need resources for adequate monitoring. This is essential in order to make the adjustments which will be inevitable; planners cannot foresee every difficulty and cannot predict the ways in which a community may react to certain parts of a programme or project. There must be many courses being followed by authorities all over the world which, while they were appropriate when first started upon, have become irrelevant or even counter-productive, unknown to the officials who pursue them. The time-lag between cause and effect is often so great that valuable resources may be wasted for years when they could be used to greater effect. There is every reason to devote a small part of these resources to devising ways to measure the effects of policies and taking action where necessary to modify them.

Appendix 3.1: Check-list of Activities in a Typical Development Project

1 Review and Analysis of Existing Data

1.1   Review reports and data relating to the project, commissioned or carried out by government departments or private sources.

1.2   Assess future target population in terms of social and demographic characteristics, employment needs and the ability to pay for new accommodation and services.

1.3   Review existing sectoral policies and programmes, e.g. transportation, education, health, social services, industrial development, etc.

1.4   Review data on housing and infrastructure construction
   - existing investment levels
   - capacity of building industry
   - capacity of institutions connected with building industry — banks, building societies, etc.
   - availability of materials, particularly locally produced

- human resources for self-help construction

1.5 Review existing standards and costs
- infrastructure
- housing – density/type/methods of construction
  services

2 Prepare Site Analysis

2.1 Review potential development sites with particular regard to:
- ownership and availability
- location in relation to existing employment and services
- access to transport routes
- topography, soil conditions and natural drainage
- environmental aspects, vegetation, climate, etc.
- potential for expansion

2.2 Prepare sieve maps showing potential restraints and opportunities for development.

3 Confirm Goals and Objectives: Define Standards and Criteria

3.1 Review and confirm all policy guidelines established by relevant authorities.

3.2 Formulate a set of general goals and detailed objectives for the project which have the support of the implementing authority and, as far as possible, other relevant authorities.

3.3 Carry out household interview to determine the needs of the community as perceived by its members; use this to modify the goals and objectives of the authority.

3.4 Identify design standards and concepts, socio-economic criteria, construction and environmental standards closely related to 3.2 and 3.3.

3.5 Determine the need for community facilities and establish standards of provision.

4 Prepare Alternative Plans and Programmes

4.1 Develop alternative concepts and methods of providing the required development, in terms of location, land use, infrastructure and transport.

4.2 Develop alternative concepts for housing areas, recreational facilities, and access.

4.3 Develop alternative concepts for drainage, sewerage water, electricity and waste removal in relation to 4.1 and 4.2.

4.4 Develop landscape concepts for conservation areas, amelioration of climate, wind and rain exposure, land form and planting.

5 *Evaluate Alternatives: Compare Alternative Costs*

5.1   Develop an evaluation system and define criteria for the selection of plans, programmes and standards.

5.2   Evaluate the proposed alternatives using agreed criteria for performance under the following headings:
- social and economic factors
- physical planning standards
- cost
- administrative and financial feasibility

5.3   Select a preferred set of options which respond best to the criteria and make the best use of resources.

5.4   Prepare preliminary cost estimates for the development and construction of alternative plans and programmes.

6 *Study Environmental Impact of Proposals*

6.1   Describe present conditions.

6.2   Describe proposed action.

6.3   Consider the probable impact on natural systems including hydrology and drainage, local climate, vegetation and wild life.

6.4   Describe the unavoidable adverse impact of the project in both the short and long term, especially that which may be irretrievable or irreversible.

6.5   Review alternatives and decide whether modifications to policies or plans could avoid major adverse impacts.

6.6   Propose techniques to minimise damage done by any adverse impacts which are inherent in the project.

7 *Carry Out Economic and Financial Analysis of Selected Alternative*

7.1   Establish social and economic development programmes and costs.

7.2   Determine total project costs, including design and construction administrative costs and operation and maintenance.

7.3   Prepare projections of cash flow based on alternative assumptions of costs, phasing of development, sources and terms of financing mortgage factors and cross-subsidy arrangements.

7.4   Conduct sensitivity analysis of the various financial projections.

7.5   Identify sources and extent of public and private funds available for investment.

7.6   Develop and recommend financial programme.

8 Prepare Detailed Projects

8.1 Prepare a detailed phasing programme based on projections of population, employment and levels of investment.

8.2 Prepare detailed engineering and architectural designs for first phase including:
- earthworks, landscape and conservation, drainage
- distribution of services, sewage collection and treatment, waste disposal
- roads and pedestrian/bicycle routes
- construction
- sites-and-services and sanitary cores
- community facilities

8.3 Identify projects within first phase in terms of availability of land and capital for early start.

8.4 Prepare technical specifications, project by project, for all construction, including bills of quantities where necessary.

8.5 Obtain estimates for construction and evaluate within the financial programme referred to in 7.6.

9 Implement Proposals

9.1 Supervise ongoing construction and development; monitor results in terms of social and economic factors.

9.2 Recommend legal and institutional arrangements for the construction and operation of the project.

9.3 Co-ordinate support programmes including:
- health care
- education
- vocational training
- community development
- maintenance and management
- recreation

9.4 Monitor capacity of building industry, particularly in terms of labour, skills and management and investment in new plant.

9.5 Ensure good housing management with regard to client selection, tenure and cost recovery.

Appendix 3.2: Educational Institutions in the UK

A number of educational institutions in developed countries provide courses specially designed for the needs of administrators and technicians from the Third World. The following list covers courses in the United Kingdom, specifically related, at the time of publication, to the development of urban and rural areas.

University of Bath: Development Studies
University of Bradford: Planning and Appraisal of Infrastructure
    Projects
University of Edinburgh: Planning Studies (Developing Countries)
University of Glasgow: Development Policy
University of Glasgow: Public Administration (Developing Countries)
London School of Economics: Social Planning in Developing Countries
University of Technology, Loughborough: Water and Waste
    Engineering for Developing Countries
University of Newcastle upon Tyne: Housing for Developing Countries
Polytechnic of Central London: Urban Management and Policy
University College, London (Development Planning Unit):
    Development Planning and Urban Studies

A comprehensive survey under the title *Courses of Special Interest to Overseas Students* containing details of courses, entry qualifications and the addresses of the various institutions may be obtained from:

International Office
North East London Polytechnic
Longbridge Road
Dagenham, Essex RM8 2AS
England

Price £1.00 sterling surface mail or £1.50 air mail.

In overseas countries information on courses is usually available from The British Council, Embassies or Trade Development offices.

Notes

1. The word 'project' is used here to describe a particular scheme such as a building project or a project to provide a particular service, e.g. a work-training scheme. 'Programme' is used to describe a wider-ranging concept such as a development programme which may include many projects.

2. Kinhill Planners Pty Ltd (formerly Llewelyn-Davies Kinhill), Sydney, Sycip Gorres Velayo and Co., Manila, Alan Turner and Associates, London, Roger Tym and Partners, London.

Part Two

SOCIAL, ECONOMIC AND FINANCIAL CONTEXT

4 DEFINING SOCIAL NEEDS

David Walton and Graham Fowler

4.1 Social Research in Development Studies

In recent years a great deal of emphasis has been placed on the creation of a dialogue between planners and the public. In developed countries this dialogue is generally part of a public participation process which can include exhibitions, public meetings and, increasingly, attitude surveys with random samples of the population to ensure representativeness. Social research techniques are being used to provide ever-increasing amounts of information, not only on the public response to a particular plan but also at the early stages of plan-making so that the planning becomes more sensitive to the needs of the public and more acceptable when the final plan is presented to the public for comment.

Social research in planning can take many forms, ranging from the sounding of informed opinions, frequently with elected representatives of the local community but also with members of local pressure groups, through to sophisticated attitude surveys consisting of detailed one-hour interviews with a large number of households. When social research is used as part of a planning study there is a real need to ensure that the work is geared directly to the study requirements. If the study is concerned with building new communities, the aim should be a market research survey into alternative environments — 'What is going to make these communities attractive to the inhabitants?' — rather than being content to describe how people live now, which is the classic sociological/anthropological approach.

This chapter discusses some of the reasons why social research is undertaken in development studies and discusses the general benefits of this research. A study in Malaysia, concerned with designing new towns of between 5,000 and 20,000 population in the Pahang Tenggara Development Region is used to illustrate these points in more detail. The photographs and drawings that are included in this chapter are all part of the work that was undertaken during the social research programme in the Pahang Tenggara New Towns Project.[1]

The general argument that underlies many of the comments in the chapter is that social research is a necessary requisite within planning studies but social research programmes must be properly planned and restricted to be of maximum benefit and relevance. A check-list has been drawn up to serve as a guide to the operation of a social research programme.

One of the major reasons for including social research within planning studies is to provide a bridge between the client, the planner and the community in order to achieve an identity of purpose over both objectives and means of pursuing these objectives. Effective and relevant proposals are considered more likely to result from allowing the people to participate in the study from the outset.

The United Nations has stated that, in order to achieve social progress and development, attention must be given to: 'the adoption of measures to ensure the effective participation, as appropriate, of all the elements of society in the preparation and execution of national plans and programmes of economic and social development'.[2] A more practical reason arises from the nature of many planning studies in the developing world. These studies often involve the creation and improvement of settlements to aid the transition of people in deprived rural circumstances to situations where they can enjoy better opportunities in employment, incomes, education, health and shelter. If this transition is to be smooth then it is necessary for the planner to have an understanding of the rural background of the settlers. Rural people have, in general, gradually adapted their environment by their own hands and effort; slow, labour-intensive processes are inherent in the rural tradition. With the pressure towards modern development, and with the use of professional skills as well as powerful machinery and so on, there is often a demand, if not a necessity, to use techniques that are alien to the rural environment. The planner in these circumstances should be striving to provide a development framework and system which is both cost-effective and sensitive to the needs of the people; and to do this he needs to have an understanding of the people.

The emphasis in planning in developing countries has moved from long-term planning to a greater emphasis on early action to relieve the plight of the urban and rural poor, such as the concepts of sites-and-services, slum-upgrading and integrated rural projects. Thus, both for economic and practical reasons, social research has come to play a more important role.

Progressively, government effort is being directed solely to creating the necessary basic conditions to stimulate the most productive use of the skills of the people. In this situation it is of crucial importance to understand how the people are likely to react to new situations in order to define the key inputs to ensure that development will proceed.

4.1.1 Outline Approach

A number of decisions must be taken before any detailed aspects of a social research programme can be considered. The most important is to define the objectives and scope of the research. Social research is often so interesting that there is a danger of collecting masses of data that will have no relevance or will only be analysed after the relevant programmes have been devised. The objectives and scope of the research must be fully discussed by the planning team and it is essential to allow adequate time in the research programme for a dialogue between the social research staff and other members of the planning term, and, in a consultancy commission, with the client, to ensure that all relevant aspects are covered by the research and that the results will be of use to the planners. It is always useful to define problems and to formulate the objectives, in writing, prior to looking at the means available for collecting the information.

It is usually worth while to talk to as many other people with a knowledge of the community to be surveyed as possible, in order to narrow down the research and to focus more clearly on those issues that are of concern. It is also necessary at this stage to make some judgement as to the capabilities of the research staff (interviewers, etc.) and the abilities of the people among whom the research is to be conducted, so as to use research techniques that will be practical in the field and provide reliable results. To this extent it is probably wise to use techniques that are relatively straightforward, but this does not mean that the ability of rural people to talk about their present life-style and to make appropriate decisions concerned with their future hopes should be underestimated.

A timetable must be drawn up that will provide relevant information at critical times in the overall planning process and this will serve to limit the scope of the research. It is important to remember that decisions concerned with the planning philosophy will be made during the course of the study and social research will be most useful if it can influence these decisions and make them more sensitive to the needs of the people. It is sometimes necessary to produce working papers or discussion papers to provide background to these decisions before the full analysis can be undertaken. The decisions will have to be made at these points in the study regardless of whether or not social research findings are available and it is felt that providing findings based upon partial analysis is better than providing no guidance at all.

Obviously, the research techniques to be employed will be

determined by the type of information that is required to satisfy the objectives of the study. However, there is a clear distinction between regional planning where a general sociological and anthropological approach may be required to provide a broad understanding of present living patterns and a market-research-orientated approach where the aim is to provide the information to be used to answer the specific questions required at a detailed planning level. In the past, sociological research has been undertaken which, although interesting and often original, has had little bearing upon the final plans because it did not provide the planner with information he could use.

There are three types of social research that are applicable to defining social needs in developing countries. They are:

(1)   qualitative research methods where the intention is to gain some insight into the behaviour and attitudes of the target groups;

(2)   structured interview surveys which seek to quantify the particular feelings and attitudes of the target groups and therefore provide a numerical basis for interpretation;

(3)   observation, which may involve making drawings and plans of how the target group live now; although generally not a technique of social research, it is particularly applicable to planning studies in developing countries.

4.1.2 Qualitative Research

Qualitative research can be used either as the exploratory stage within a larger social research programme, or it can stand by itself if the timetable of the job prohibits any more detailed quantitative research.

Qualitative research can involve either semi-structured interviews, depth interviews or group discussions.

(1)   Semi-structured interviews consist of a questionnaire where the majority of the questions are open-ended, i.e. with no set answers but with space on the questionnaire for the interviewer to record the respondent's answers.

(2)   Depth interviews allow the interviewer to probe in more depth to ascertain the respondent's underlying feelings towards the topic in question. Interviewers follow a guideline of questions, and the answers are recorded, often by tape-recorder for transcription later, or in longhand. The interviewer, although supplied with a guideline, is allowed flexibility to explore

issues in greater depth depending on the circumstances of the particular respondent.

(3) Group discussions require from four to eight people to talk about the research issues, with the aid of the group leader who will outline the areas of research and will provide some guidance to the discussion.

The purpose of qualitative research is to understand how respondents perceive the main issues of the research, so that some insight may be gained into these issues. If qualitative research is to be used alone then it is probably wiser to undertake semi-structured interviews, while if it is to serve as an exploratory means of research to be followed by a structured survey then depth interviews will probably provide more insight into the areas of research to be explored. Group discussions can also be used in the exploratory stages, but it is felt that these will be more meaningful among educated people, i.e. where the concern is about the 'induced' sector of rural developments, rather than when the participants are typical potential migrants who may not have the necessary educational background.

4.1.3 Structured Interview Surveys

A structured survey requires interviewers to ask a series of identical questions of a sample of respondents. The main constituent of these types of surveys is, therefore, the design of suitable series of questions in the form of a questionnaire, but also of importance is the method of selecting respondents and interviewers.

The questionnaire can contain two basic types of question:

(1) structured, where the respondent is presented with alternative answers, one of which must be given. Care must be taken to ensure that the alternative answers offered cover the full range of opinions likely to be held by respondents;

(2) open-ended, where the respondent is encouraged to give the reasons for his choice which the interviewer writes on to the questionnaire as fully as possible. However, open-ended questions are difficult to analyse and should therefore be limited in number.

The questions can be conveniently divided into behavioural questions concerned with how people live now and what activities they currently pursue, attitudinal questions which are concerned with what the respondent feels towards his present situation or more hypothetically, what are his hopes and aspirations for the future, and classification questions, which are used to define the respondent and his household in terms of age, sex, etc.

The first consideration in drawing up the questionnaire (after having narrowed down to the type of information required) is the sequence of the questions. Generally, it is as well to divide the questionnaire into distinct sections concerned with each of the topics being examined, and then within each section to have a series of behavioural questions followed by a series of attitudinal questions. Generally, classification questions are put at the end of the questionnaire when the respondent is less likely to react to the personal nature of some of these questions.

Having determined the sequence of questions, the actual wording must be drawn up. The qualitative research will have given a good indication of the type of language that respondents use to talk about the topics and, as far as possible, questions should be phrased in everyday conversational terms. Questions relating to attitudes are more influenced by the form of wording used and care must be taken in phrasing these questions to ensure that the questions themselves do not bias the responses towards any one answer. If extensive or complicated information is required, it is far better to split the questions into a number of shorter questions.

Questionnaires should not be allowed to become too long, as after 45-50 minutes the respondent would be rather tired and his answers would become less reliable. As a very general rule, one question can be assumed to take about half a minute to answer and this implies that questionnaires should be limited to 90-100 separate questions at a maximum. This highlights the need for ensuring the relevance of the questions and their ongoing analysis to the important alternatives involved in the planning study as a whole.

A particular problem with structured surveys conducted in developing countries by consultants from elsewhere is the language in which the interview is conducted and the questionnaire drawn up. The alternatives are to translate the questionnaire or to allow the interviewer to translate the questions as they interview the respondent. The latter alternative is only likely to be reliable where the interviewers are completely bilingual, and even here care must be taken to avoid misunderstandings of the intent, as well as the content, of the questions.

Interviewers. Often, the most convenient method of recruiting interviewers is to approach the nearest university and arrange to use sociology students during their vacations. Not only are these students generally interested in the contents of the research, but they are likely to be sufficiently sensitive to the respondents to be able to build up some rapport. If possible, the students recruited should come from the same background as the people being interviewed, although in the more rural areas this will not always be possible.

It is relatively easy for interviewers to bias the answers given at the interview either by failing to establish a rapport with the respondent so that he gives answers that he feels are expected of him even though he may hold the opposite viewpoint, or by the interviewer feeling that the respondent had not understood the question fully and, therefore, not marking the answer given to him. These difficulties are likely to be more pronounced in research in developing countries where a larger gap exists between the educational abilities of students and the rural sections of the population. It is an essential part of the training of the interviewers to stress to them the importance of each respondent's views and that care must be taken in order for this view to be presented correctly through the medium of the questionnaire.

Sampling. Sampling is probably the most difficult aspect of social research surveys undertaken in developing countries, because there is often a lack of reliable data upon which to base the sample and there is often a necessity to sample a large population with a relatively small number of interviews.

The first point to decide is how many interviews can be conducted within the time scale of the study, remembering that one of the most important features of the survey will be to provide relevant results at the appropriate points in the overall planning study. The number of interviews will also be determined by the possible range of answers that you can expect; for a survey of squatter housing conditions within a fairly homogeneous area, then it would be sufficient to interview and observe fewer than 100 households if they were selected in an unbiased manner. However, for a study for new towns where there is no great certainty about who would be the target group, then it may be important to interview in a number of locations, selected by type, and to complete up to 500 interviews to ensure a wider range of views. Even these numbers of interviews do not ensure a very high statistical reliability to the responses given, but the time scale of planning studies generally prohibits larger numbers of interviews.

There are various types of sampling procedures and probably the easiest to undertake in surveys of this type is some form of cluster sampling, although random household samples can be more valid if there is reliable information upon which to base the sample.

Cluster Sampling. It is sometimes possible to group the total target population into groups with similar characteristics (clusters) and then to sample within these clusters to provide a sample which is to some extent typical of the total target population. For a large area of squatter housing, it may be possible to divide the housing on the basis of geographical location within the area or the relative age of the dwellings (there may be older and newer areas) and then to sample within each cluster to be able to make comparisons between the different clusters in order to build up a clearer picture of the whole.

In the case of new communities, a more complicated clustering arrangement will need to be devised, based upon the propensity of the various types of rural dwellers to migrate. It is possible, by making certain assumptions based upon the background research and intuition, to limit the social research quite closely to those people who are of most interest in planning terms and thus improve the usefulness of the results. It is of little use, and is a waste of limited time and resources, to conduct a truly random sample among a population most of whom are unlikely to be of interest in research terms.

Thus in a cluster sample there are two stages to the definition of whom to interview:

- define which types of settlements or locations the survey should cover (the clusters);
- within these settlements define which type of people should be interviewed (the target groups).

Cluster sampling is generally appropriate when there are a limited number of interviews, the divisions within the sample population are relatively clear cut and the differences of opinion and attitude are the focal points of the survey.

Random Household Sampling. This sampling procedure is more generally applicable in planning studies within developed countries where there is both reliable information upon which to base the sample (i.e. electoral registers) and each house has an address, thus making it relatively easy to sample addresses and then find them on the ground, and where the primary purpose is to find the view most common among the total population.

Random household sampling is usually undertaken by using a two-stage probability sampling procedure — the first stage involves the sampling of primary areas (possibly voting districts), which is done with probability proportional to population, and then sampling within the selected districts by use of the electoral register. A sampling interval to give a predetermined number of addresses in each district should be used.

Analysis. The major constraints upon the sophistication and the amount of analysis undertaken in social research surveys in developing countries may be the lack of access to a computer and the lack of time. The main constraint on the analysis, whether by computer or by hand, is the need to provide results within the timetable of the overall planning study. It has been emphasised throughout this chapter that although social research is interesting for its own sake, it is not of any value to the planning study unless the results are available at the time that the major decisions are being made and this is usually in the initial stages of the study.

The mechanics of hand analysis serve to limit the amount of analysis that can be undertaken within the time available, but it is possible to do a partial hand analysis of the data and to use this both to come to preliminary conclusions and to decide on the full analysis. Hand analysis is limited to simple cross-tabulation, which is generally most easily done by the various locations in which the interviews were conducted. Only very limited analysis can be undertaken to look at different responses by the type of respondent (age, occupation, etc.) outside these location categories.

If card-punching and computer facilities are available, in terms of time-saving, accuracy and sophistication of analysis it is worth while punching the survey responses on to cards and analysing by computer. A decision to use computer facilities should be taken during the planning stages of the social research, as it affects the design of the questionnaire in terms of the layout of responses and the requirement for serial numbers and card numbers to identify separate parts of the questionnaire. Because the analysis has to be specified prior to the computer tabulation of the responses, there is a danger of the analysis being either too stereotyped, simply looking at the various answers by the obvious breakdowns, or too detailed, looking at each answer analysed by each possible breakdown. It is more practical to take an initially narrow approach and, if possible, allow time for further tabulations to examine in detail the questions which provide the more interesting answers.

4.1.4 Observations

In order to relate the verbal data and tabulated results to the physical environment in which people live, it is often extremely informative to undertake some observations of present living conditions. This is most usefully done by making plans and drawings of the villages and houses in which the social research is being undertaken.

It is a fairly easy matter to employ a small number of architectural and planning students to accompany the social research teams and to undertake drawings of the layout and use patterns of villages, groups of houses, and of the houses themselves. Often, urban designers relate more easily to these drawings than to the tabulated results and can find information guidelines and even inspiration from them when they are designing new layouts or house types. It is useful to examine closely the types of house design that have evolved in the rural areas in response to the climatic and social needs and to use these as a basis in examining new house designs. For exampie, in a recent study, an analysis of rural housing indicated that the size and location of the kitchen was based on the premiss that over time the house would be expanded, while in equivalent government-designed housing, the location of the kitchen hindered the process of adding extra rooms to the house as the family increased in number.

The uses to which various parts of the house are put can also be shown clearly by the drawings. This understanding of how rural people use and view their settlement, surroundings and housing is difficult to show clearly in survey responses, but is essential in order to design new areas that will be attractive to settlers.

There is a most important side-effect to the use of planning students in the social research. When these students return to the study office to make their drawings, they help to create an office environment which is alive with an appreciation of the realities of life in the rural areas; the effect of having student planners drawing up village plans alongside professional expatriate planners drawing layouts of new residential areas is rich in cross-fertilisation of ideas and leads to a more sensitive final product than might otherwise be the case.

4.1.5 The Benefits of Social Research

Numerical Results. It must be said that, generally, the value of the specific numerical aspects of the type of social research discussed in this chapter is severely limited. The statistical reliability of the analysis, based usually on a limited number of interviews, is too low to give great confidence in individual results. The results are primarily important in that they build up a picture of how people live at present and what they aspire to in the future. Within this picture, individual results should not be treated with too much confidence.

The Interpretation of the Results. The results from the social research provide an awareness of the people. This awareness should provide the foundation for a meaningful interpretation of present behaviour and future aspirations and from this should flow the design philosophy upon which the planning decisions will be made. Interpretation of results is sometimes dangerous in that researchers can impose their own ideas on to a set of figures and produce a misleading interpretation.

Numerical Support for Appropriate Standards. In developing countries, there is a tendency for development often to be seen as the creation of many of the artefacts of more affluent societies. Similarly, development can involve the use of inappropriately high standards of infrastructure and building. The costs and/or relevance of these tendencies are often not appreciated at the political and administrative levels of development agencies. It is sometimes difficult for consultants and advisers to convince government that these standards are neither relevant nor affordable and that a low-key approach that stimulates the inherent abilities of the likely residents is more suitable. The acceptance of these ideas is sometimes complicated by the lack of technically trained staff who would have the ability and experience to understand the choices involved. It may be possible for planners to use the results from the social research to demonstrate the benefits of their ideas and to show how their approach would be more in sympathy with the feelings of the likely residents towards development.

Education of Planning Staff. As well as using the social research to educate development agencies, a programme of social research also tends to educate planners within the study team. If planners are involved in the early stages of questionnaire design they tend to gain a deeper understanding of the people for whom they are planning, they begin to think in social terms before the design process begins, and the designs become more sensitive to the needs of the people.

Influence of Local Interviewers in the Study Office. It is possible to use the students employed as interviewers as a sounding-board for new ideas. The hot-house atmosphere for ideas that can occur when a group of generally aware and committed sociology students are encouraged to help in the exploration of new ideas concerning the development of their country is extremely fruitful. In many cases, it is the only opportunity that planning staff have of talking so frankly with local people; the client/professional relationship of the formal government agency and study team is often not conducive to the exploration of ideas, but students tend not to be overawed by any professional mystique when it is clear that the planners are turning to them for help.

4.2 A Case Study — Pahang Tenggara, Malaysia

The results of the social research for the new towns programme ran contrary to many expectations of the government administrators and the professional staff of the client and the consultant. The priorities, as expressed by the potential settlers included in the research, showed differences from the hitherto accepted priorities for infrastructure and amenity provision and gave a very different picture of the types of towns that would be attractive to the settlers.

Some of the more important examples of the differing priorities which influenced the design of the towns are given below.

4.2.1 Infrastructure

The overwhelming preference, in respect to amenities, was for a water tap in the house (69 per cent of potential settlers) followed by the provision of electric power. This conflicted with past programmes, which had supplied water to stand-pipes situated outside the house and shared between groups of five to ten families, and provided only evening lighting, but not permanent power.

Conversely, government standards for new development insisted upon a 40-foot reserve width for all roads, yet the social research results showed that there was no desire upon the part of the potential settlers for this level of infrastructure provision. The potential settlers desired that each house have easy access but there was no necessity for this to be any more than a track.

4.2.2 Commercial and Social Services

The research confirmed the government's priorities in respect of giving educational facilities the highest importance amongst the social services, followed by better health facilities. However, within shopping, the priorities were for large markets in town centres, both to satisfy basic food needs and to sell produce, and at a local level frequent small groups and individual shops were preferred, some set up by settlers themselves. This contrasted with expectations that it would be facilities such as cinemas, sports grounds and more specialised shops that would be important attractions in the new towns.

4.2.3 Housing

Sixty-eight per cent of the potential settlers preferred to live in a timber-built house. This result conflicted with the confidently held belief that these rural people aspired towards the brick-built housing found in most new urban developments in Malaysia. Similarly, it was considered important to have plots large enough to keep chickens and grow fruit and vegetables to supply some of the basic needs, as well as providing space to set up a small enterprise on the plot. The settlers took a far more rounded economic view of housing than the typical public authority attitudes in which an economic rent or rental equivalent for a given house or plot and its services was seen as the limits of economic appraisal. The settlers saw the security of home ownership and the flexibility for additional economic activities as very important.

A similar proportion of the potential settlers expressed a wish to be able to build their own houses. This conflicted with the official view that although there was a tradition of house-building in the rural areas of Malaysia, sites and services was not an acceptable concept for the new towns because settlers would not move unless they had the opportunity to live in a finished house.

The overall picture that emerged from these, and many other, results of the social research was that expensive levels of infrastructure provision would not attract sufficient numbers of settlers to the new towns but that certain factors, such as individual water supply, would be attractive if allied to an environment that allowed the settler to bring with him many of the aspects of rural life that he valued and created a framework for him to put his own skills and resources to their most productive use.

The results confirmed many of the intuitive feelings of the planners, architects and economists who had had experience in other parts of the world and who in general saw appropriate forms of development as minimum-cost infrastructure and self-help housing which would stimulate the inherent abilities of the likely residents. It was clear that likely settlers had no great wish to change their way of life, and if economic forces meant moving to a new area then they preferred this to incorporate many features of their present houses and environments —

hardly a surprising finding but one which needed to be understood in some detail in order to produce a strong commitment to proceeding in this manner.

The social research also served a major function by providing a framework of choices where conflicting viewpoints would be articulated. The discussions between the development agency and its consultants concerning the translation of the social research findings into planning guidelines allowed the development of an urbanisation programme and policy supported by all concerned.

Interpretation of the social research results gave the planning team a very firm and clear brief for the design and development of the settlements, especially when combined with other aspects of project research. In essence, a brief was developed which allowed the continuance and development of many of the traditional characteristics of Malay rural life within an urban pattern of physical and social infrastructure services, as well as providing opportunities for commercial, industrial and social development. The aim became one of creating the essential basis and stimulus for the extensive abilities of the rural settlers in terms of building their own housing, community and employment structures.

4.2.4 An Illustrated Check-list

The purpose of this section is to provide a simple and easy-to-read check-list of the steps in a programme of social research. The check-list is accompanied by the most salient points from the Pahang Tenggara project. The case study is used to illustrate the check-list rather than to provide a full and factual record of what the research entailed, and in particular the concern is to present the techniques of social research rather than the results of this particular study.

Background to the social research in Pahang Tenggara, Malaysia: The consultants were engaged to plan six new towns for the Pahang Tenggara region and to provide guidelines for a further 30 new towns that were planned for the region. The towns ranged in size from 5,000 population to 20,000 and were based mainly upon employment in oil palm estates.

Malaysia is the world's major producer of oil palm. Owing to the soil and slope characteristics, and to the climate of the country, large areas are suitable for its cultivation. In response to high world prices in recent years, vast areas have been and are being given over to the crop. Palm oil is used in varying degrees of refinement in the production of soaps, cosmetics, margarine, confectionery, tin-plating and other commodities.

The concept of new urban development as a means of settlement within a land development region has both economic and social implications within Malaysia. The settlements were seen as offering people better access to a wider range of employment, housing, educational, commercial and other opportunities, thus providing a basis for greater growth in secondary service and industrial activities, and a framework to assist rural migrants in making a transition to a modern economy and urban way of life.

Figure 4.1: Social Research Work Programme

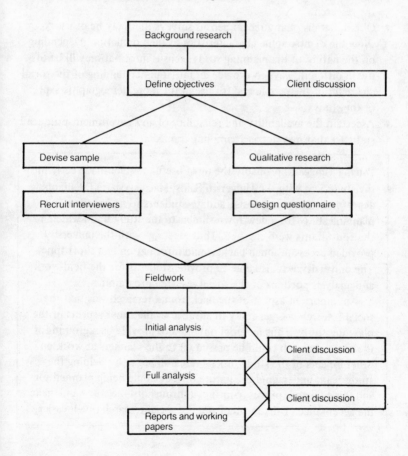

Background Research

- Contact government departments with responsibility for planning and social welfare to ascertain reports or other documents with any bearing upon the type of research envisaged.
- Contact universities and other institutions having an interest in the subject both with regard to obtaining information and to ascertaining the availability of students to undertake field-work.
- Obtain any relevant research and establish contact with others working in the same field of research. There are very few places which have not been subject to some anthropological research and this type of general background information is very useful in understanding the nature of the people who are to be the subject of the research.
- Obtain details of any recent census surveys that may be of use to show the demographic characteristics of the population. Depending on the nature of the planning study, census information will be of use in different ways to provide an initial understanding of the social character of the people and for use in the more demographic aspects of the study.
- Ascertain the availability and reliability of any government-produced statistics that may act as a sampling frame.

Pahang Tenggara: probably the most useful contact made early in the study was with the Universiti Sains, Malaysia; here the planning department was using post-graduate students to undertake a planning study for a new town similar to the study upon which the consultants were engaged. Thus meetings with the university provided access to much background information in a short time. The university was also able to provide students for the field-work and analysis portions of the social research programme.

An important aspect of the background research was that the social research was generally in advance of the other aspects of the planning study. Thus material obtained to provide background for the social research could be passed on to the planners at work on other aspects of the study. Social research began by helping the study team understand the nature of the people being planned for and this educative process continued throughout the study and made the acceptance of the results from the social research much easier.

Define Objectives

- This is probably the most important aspect of the research programme. It is essential that the research is restricted to those points of information that are relevant to the planning study.
- Discuss the objectives as fully as possible with the planners and the client, and decide how these objectives can most easily be translated into research techniques.
- The background research will have provided some guidance on the sample population and this should be borne in mind when devising the contents of the research programme.

Pahang Tenggara: As the study involved district and local planning there was a need to look closely at the present life-styles of potential migrants, not only in respect of housing but also employment, shopping, transport, etc. One of the major purposes of the new towns would be to attract migrants, and it was essential to determine what they would find attractive. As it was expected that the new towns would be competing with other types of settlements to attract migrants, then it was felt to be helpful to examine these alternatives from the viewpoint of both the potential migrant and the recent migrant to these settlements.

The objectives of the research were therefore:

(1) to analyse and describe the current environment and life-style of the people defined as potential migrants;

(2) to examine the attitudes of the potential migrants towards their present living patterns;

(3) to examine their hopes, expectations and aspirations in relation to a new environment;

(4) to contrast the views of potential migrants with those people from similar backgrounds who have recently migrated to other areas.

Devise Timetable

- Define the crucial points in the timetable when research findings are required.
- Determine the availability of students to undertake field-work.
- Devise a research timetable to produce the results at the appropriate times.

- The timetable will indicate whether there is sufficient time to conduct a structured survey or whether the research is best limited to more qualitative research techniques. It is best not to attempt to undertake too much data collection in a short period; the initial collection of data can be time-consuming and should not be allowed to swamp the analysis and interpretation of the data.

Design Questionnaire

- Discuss the contents of the research with the planners involved on the study and then draw up an outline of the information to be collected and discuss this further with the planners. Use the revised outline as the basis for depth interviews.
- Recruit a small number of students (preferably sociologists) to conduct the depth interviews. The students should write up the depth interviews as soon as possible. This, however, is a very time-consuming job and in the short term much can be learned from an intensive debriefing session with the students. A round-table session with the students and the study team can be most informative, both with regard to questionnaire design and educating the study team.
- Draw up a questionnaire and discuss this with the students who undertook the depth interviews. Circulate among the planners for comment, and then finalise a questionnaire for piloting.
- A pilot survey should be conducted to point up the parts of the questionnaire that are not working and the questions that are open to misinterpretation, as well as showing the overall length that the interview will take. The pilot survey should be conducted in advance of the main survey with sufficient time allowed to make any necessary changes to the wording of questions.
- The questionnaire should be designed to provide quantified data where possible, but it is often difficult to define the answers that will be made to all questions. Therefore a certain number of questions should allow more qualitative, open-ended answers that will provide some insight into why particular preferences are held.

Pahang Tenggara: the questionnaire contained 100 questions in sections dealing with:

the household including age, sex of each member, race and family history;
attitudes to migration, including knowledge and consideration of migration alternatives;

Figure 4.2: Timetable, Pahang Tenggara

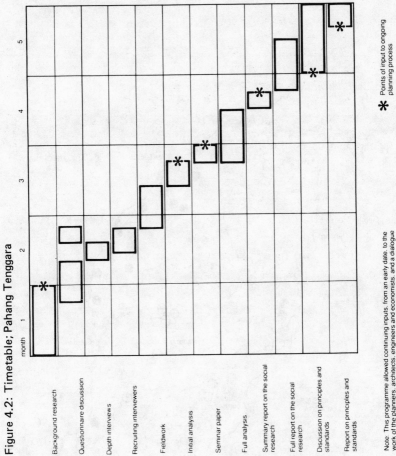

month

Background research

Questionnaire discussion

Depth interviews

Recruiting interviewers

Fieldwork

Initial analysis

Seminar paper

Full analysis

Summary report on the social research

Full report on the social research

Discussion on principles and standards

Report on principles and standards

* Points of input to ongoing planning process

Note This programme allowed continuing inputs, from an early date. to the work of the planners. architects. engineers and economists. and a dialogue between the professionals. the client. and the social researchers.

Figure 4.3: Social Research Interview Locations; Pahang Tenggara

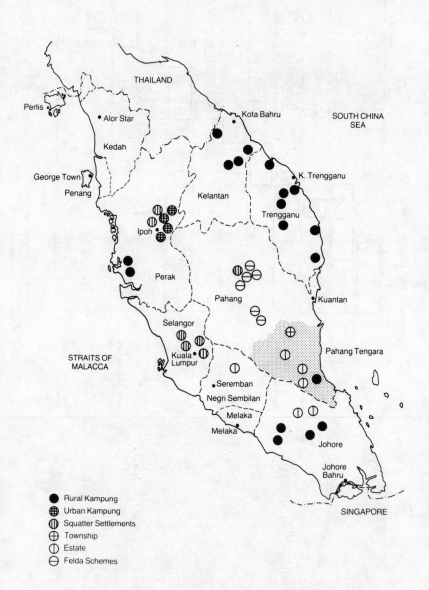

- ● Rural Kampung
- ⊛ Urban Kampung
- ◍ Squatter Settlements
- ⊕ Township
- ◐ Estate
- ⊖ Felda Schemes

Figure 4.4: Typical Survey Areas; Pahang Tenggara

A squatter settlement in Kuala Lumpur

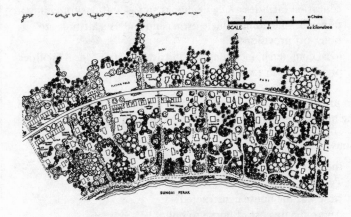

A kampung in Perak

the house, including the materials of which constructed,
condition, cost, number and use made of rooms, satisfaction
with house type and size, and preferences for new housing;
the house plot, including size and use, problems and
importance of house plots;
amenities in the house, including details of amenities available
and priorities for the future;
visits to towns, including details of visits and preferences for
town facilities;
social visiting, including frequency of visiting, details of social
and sports facilities available and social problems involved in
moving to a new area:
employment, including details of paid employment and
ownership of land and attitudes to alternative employment
opportunities;
education, including details of education, history of family,
education facilities available, hopes and aspirations for children;
transport, including vehicle ownership and use, attitudes to
transport provision;
local commerce, including use and availability of local facilities,
preferences for facilities.

To provide an illustration of the type of questions that were asked,
the housing section consisted of the following questions:

House Classification

Indicate material that house is constructed of
Type of house
How was the house constructed?
Approximate cost of house to build
When it was built (i.e. the original house)?
Have any extensions been built on to the original house?
If so, describe:
Total floor space of the complete house?
Interviewer assessment of the condition of the house.

Attitudes to Housing

How happy are you about living in a house of this type?
What do you like about living in a house of this type?*
What do you dislike about living in a house of this type?*
How happy are you with the size of your house?

What extra rooms would you like to add to your house?
Would you like to live nearer or further away from your
neighbours?
Why do you say this?*
What type of house would you like to live in?
Would you still prefer this type of house if you had to pay
$ . . .a month
If you were to move to a new area, would you like to be able
to build your own house?
Why do you say this?*
If you were to move to a new area, would you prefer to rent
your house, buy your house for cash, buy your house over a
period of years, have your house provided with your job?
Why do you say this?*

*Open-ended questions with a space on the questionnaire for the
interviewer to write in the responses given.

Devise Sampling Procedures

- The background research will have indicated whether there is a
  reliable sampling frame available. However, if the survey is to be
  spread over a wide area with only a relatively small number of
  interviews (less than 1,000) then it is likely that there will be a need
  to devise a simpler sampling method.
- Define in broad terms who are the people who are likely to be of
  most interest to the research. Devise a method of clustering these
  people either by settlement type, economic base, geographical
  location or some other factor.
- Determine the number of interviews that are required in each
  cluster and therefore the number of different locations in which to
  conduct interviews.
- Decide how to go out and select the areas where the interviews will
  be conducted. In most surveys, the areas will be contiguous with
  the study area; however, in the case of settlers to new areas then the
  survey is likely to be more widespread.

Pahang Tenggara: the objectives of the social research required that
the survey be carried out among potential migrants and recent
migrants. There was no readily available information that would
effectively define potential migrants and therefore a convenient

definition had to be drawn up. The first stage was to devise a scale of settlement types identifying the economic activity, income, type of housing and amenities, and the migration potential of each type of settlement in the area. The scale of settlement types indicated that the potential migrants were likely to come from rural kampungs.

Some analysis was then obtained from the 1970 census, which showed migration patterns to the study area between 1950 and 1970, and this was used to indicate those states from which migrants to the new towns were most likely to originate. A cluster sample was used which simply involved the selection of broadly typical kampungs of the type shown to have migration potential, within the states shown to have previously supplied migrants. The selection was done on a subjective basis by a member of the social research team accompanying each of the interviewing teams. Within each selected kampung, potential migrants were defined as persons under 40 years of age and generally it was the head of the household who was interviewed.

Recent migrants were selected in a similar manner — they were defined as people who had migrated in the previous four years to either government land settlement schemes, the squatter areas of large towns, traditional estates, new estates, or to Bukit Ibam, the only existing township within the study area.

Recruitment and Organisation of Fieldwork

- The background research will have established contacts with the local universities and the timetable will have been tied into the university vacations, if at all possible.
- Decide how many interviewers will be required. This is most effectively done by dividing the total number of interviewers by a nominal number of interviews per person per day and the number of days available. It is as well to deliberately take a low number of interviews per day (i.e. about 4 one-hour interviews in an eight-hour working day) to allow for travelling time and the time to find suitable respondents.
- The payment of the interviewers will obviously vary with local conditions, but it should include a daily rate and a subsistence allowance for overnight accommodation. Transport arrangements will have to be made, either by hiring a minibus, or obtaining the use of such a vehicle from the client.

- A full day should be set aside for the briefing of the interviewers both with regard to the overall aims of the social research and where it fits into the planning study, and the more detailed aspects of the questionnaire.
- A further two or three days should be used to train the interviewers. This is most efficiently done by beginning the required interviews at a location where all the interviewers can be kept together and the interviews can be checked for consistency at the end of each day and comments transmitted immediately to the interviewers.
- It is always easier to divide the interviewers into teams of five or six, with one interviewer appointed to be supervisor. In this manner instructions can be passed from the social researcher to the supervisors through to the interviewers. It is extremely difficult to control more than eight interviewers without dividing them into teams.
- The interviews should be conducted during the late afternoon and the early evening to ensure an adequate representation of heads of household who are away from the house during most of the day.

Pahang Tenggara: the first stage of recruitment was to find three people to conduct the initial depth interviews. This was achieved by simply approaching the University of Malaysia at Kuala Lumpur and advertising on their notice-boards for sociology students.

The main body of interviewers were recruited from the Universiti Sains, because the background research had involved the university and the staff were keen to involve some of their sociology and planning students. A further twelve interviewers were recruited along with two post-graduate planning students to undertake plan drawings of the houses and kampung layouts in which the survey was being conducted.

The first few days of field-work were used to train the interviewers in the use of the questionnaire to ensure that where interpretation by the interviewers was necessary, it was done consistently and correctly. Following this, the interviewers were split into two teams, each under the supervision of a study team member. One team travelled along the west coast of Malaysia while the other concentrated on the east coast. Each day the teams selected an area for survey which they felt to be broadly typical of the type of settlement they were to interview in. When the settlement had been selected, the interviewers proceeded to find potential migrants or recent migrants by asking from door to door, using the predetermined requirements of what constituted a potential migrant, etc. Each interviewer was required to complete four interviews per day. Field-work lasted 3 weeks and there were no great problems either in the selection of typical kampungs or respondents or in the supervision of the work of the interviewers.

Analysis

- Decide the type of analysis to be undertaken. If there are card-punching and computer facilities available, then the questionnaire can be designed so that the information can be punched directly on to cards. Although computer analysis is less flexible than hand analysis, it is invariably quicker and more accurate and the amount of cross-tabulation that can be undertaken make it worth while.

- However, if there are no computer facilities available, then the questionnaires must be analysed by hand. This generally involves sorting the questionnaires by the main characteristic of the respondents, be it type of settlement, economic activity or physical location, and analysing each question by this breakdown.

- Hand analysis has a flexibility because a small subsample of questionnaires can be analysed initially to point up the most important results. Therefore, taking, say, one-quarter of the questionnaires, decide on the questions to be analysed and proceed. This initial analysis should be the basis of discussions among the study team and with the client.

- On the basis of the discussions, the full analysis can be completed. The major constraint, with regard to analysis, is to ensure that the most important results are available in time to influence the course of the planning study.

- Most questions are relatively easy to analyse, but care must be taken with open-ended questions where the interviewer simply writes down what the respondent has said in reply to the question. These answers must be categorised, on the basis of an initial look at the types of answers being obtained, and the categories must be wide enough to encompass most of the answers and yet narrow enough to allow sufficient grouping of responses to make analysis useful.

Pahang Tenggara: the analysis of the questionnaires was limited by both time and lack of punching and computer facilities to a relatively simple hand analysis of the responses, subdivided into the seven settlement types in which interviews were conducted.

The first stage of analysis involved one-quarter of the questionnaires from each settlement type, which allowed for some initial conclusions to be reached that formed the basis of a discussion paper and a seminar with the development authority. This analysis also concentrated on the more numerical aspects rather than an analysis of the open-ended questions.

The full analysis was completed in 5 weeks and eventually consisted of 100 tables cross-analysed by the seven settlement types in which interviews were conducted. Some difficulty was experienced in analysing open-ended questions, and it is likely that the constraints of hand analysis forced the grouping of answers into a relatively small number of categories with some distortion of the data.

Reports

- The main emphasis must be to produce reports at relevant points in the planning study; these reports need be no more than working papers and need not be based on more than a partial analysis. It is often more important to provide guidance to the planning team than to wait until all the results have been analysed.
- Although the analysis of the responses is important, it is equally important to interpret the responses and translate them into guidelines for the planning study. The numerical value of most social research in development planning is limited because generally a small number of interviews are used to represent a large number of people.

Pahang Tenggara: the reports produced from the social research were timed to provide information at the relevant points within the planning study. This meant that some reports were produced, and conclusions reached, on the basis of incomplete analysis, although as analysis was completed the opportunity arose to go back and amend.

The reports produced are listed below.

(1) A *Seminar Paper*, based upon an analysis of one-quarter of the questionnaires, that provided a basis of discussion among the study team and with the development

authority.

(2) A *Summary Report*, which consisted of the conclusions and implications for planning that resulted from the social research. The conclusions were prepared for incorporation into the concept plans being prepared at this time. The Summary Report was then fully discussed with the client: it was felt to be important to provide results and conclusions at this stage because this was a point where major decisions for the future execution of the project were taken.

(3) The full *Report on the Social Research* was then produced. This report was intended for distribution to the client and to other government bodies and to provide a record of the methodology and results of the social research, and, as such, it was of some influence on other research being undertaken in Malaysia into related and similar topics.

(4) The full Report on the Social Research provided major inputs to the *Development Reports* for the six specific towns and also to the *Project Summary Report* which described the various aspects of policy research undertaken as part of the study.

(5) In addition, three working papers were produced:
    (a)   a paper consisting of the edited depth interviews;
    (b)   a paper consisting of details of the social research methodology and the full tabulations;
    (c)   a paper consisting of the drawings and layout plans of the kampungs where interviews were undertaken.

Notes

1. Freeman Fox and Associates, Akitek Bersekutu, Tahir Wong, Alan Turner and Associates and Roger Tym and Associates, *Summary Report: Six New Towns in Pahang Tenggara*, and associated reports and working papers (November 1976).

2. *Declaration of Social Progress and Development*, General Assembly Resolution 2542 (XXIV), United Nations (December 1969).

5 THE CREATION OF NEW EMPLOYMENT

John Butler

5.1 Development Problems

Of the many problems of development, the most difficult to resolve, but nevertheless fundamental to the economic well-being of any country, is that of job creation. The World Bank figures quoted in Chapter 1 indicate that the population of the developing countries will increase by over two billion by the year 2000 and that more than half of these will be inhabitants of urban centres, either born there or immigrants drifting into towns from smaller settlements and rural areas. Since the larger the centre, the greater the potential opportunities for employment, either of a formal or informal nature, the big cities will attract the bulk of those without work. Smaller centres, however, will tend to have the same effect on a lesser scale, with the added factor that they attract the seasonally unemployed often to a somewhat greater extent than large towns. These are typically rural labourers who only find work at harvesting time, e.g. cane-cutters and fruit-pickers.

In a perfect world the desirable solution for the smaller centre with a need for new employment would be to establish a manufacturing or processing factory which would become the principal source of employment. In turn, the wages earned would create a demand for other goods and services, while secondary activities would develop to serve the factory itself, e.g. a transport facility. Investment in such a factory would have a very considerable multiplier effect on the community. Unfortunately the greatest problem in developing countries is to find the capital, know-how and markets required before such an investment can be made.

Although these considerations are negative, they merit examination because they are fundamental barriers to achieving an even spread of industrial investment; many of the same conditions apply equally to developed countries. The first type of activity that might arise naturally out of the economy of the centre and its hinterland would be processing a locally grown crop. This activity might range in scale from, say, drying cocoa beans and curing tobacco to milling sugar or decorticating cashew nuts. Obviously not all types of crop-processing require factory conditions, but for many cash crops bulk handling and processing become inevitable at some stage in the progress from field to market-place.

The problems posed by processing primary cash crops in the areas where they are grown are many and varied:

(1)   most cash crops, e.g. rubber, cocoa, tea are primarily grown for export, and are thus not in demand in the area in which they are produced, and therefore need not be processed locally;

(2)   most cash crops that require some immediate processing tend to require very simple treatment — often only sun-drying — which can be carried out by the grower before the crop leaves his hands;

(3)   the next stage is generally one which offers very substantial economies of scale, e.g. a sugar factory which will serve an extensive plantation area;

(4)   there are economies of scale to be achieved by handling a single crop in bulk at rail-head or port, e.g. the ground-nuts grown throughout the northern part of Nigeria are graded at a single centre, Kano, which is also the rail-head for evacuation to Lagos;

(5)   the final-stage processing, e.g. sugar-refining or chocolate manufacture, is generally much more economic in the large industrialised centres, often because crops from many producing countries are used.

Thus in most developing countries there is little scope, in a secondary urban centre, for processing primary crops, or minerals, for export. If the community had any natural advantages as a processing centre, it would almost certainly have already become an important town.

A similar type of activity which can be based on agricultural produce is processing crops for domestic consumption. There are a range of such crops from palm kernels, which need crushing to extract the oil, to tobacco, which can be made up locally into cigarettes or cigars. Some of these activities, such as oil-seed crushing, will take place in a small centre; an area of a few thousand inhabitants will usually support a simple press, but the output will generally be no more than can be consumed within the community's own catchment area. At some stages of development palm oil can be traded to other centres where it is not available and so becomes an element contributing to the economic viability of the centre. In some instances, such as the Federal Land

Development Authority (FELDA) projects in Malaysia, the locally pressed oil will contribute to exports and become a vital part of the economy.

Similar activities in this category include hand-weaving and dyeing, pottery and bread-making. All are small-scale and do not necessarily employ men; some, such as weaving and dyeing, traditionally employ women in almost all parts of the world.

In order to generate employment in larger-scale projects, it is necessary to examine the possibilities for processing a crop for sale to a wide, possibly country-wide or export, market. The case of cigarette manufacture is a relevant example. Tobacco is processed at the first stage in the area where it is grown by drying. It is then collected and taken to a factory for final manufacture, possibly but not necessarily via a market at which it is graded and sold. There is no reason why cigarettes should not be made in a plant near to the tobacco-growing area and the final product delivered to the market by truck, but there are no advantages in siting a factory in the growing area unless it is geographically central so that costs of collection of the leaf can be optimised. In this case the small community will have a special advantage which could be exploited. In practice, however, this advantage is a relatively minor one. Not only do cigarette factories require tobacco, they also need paper, wrapping materials and fuel, as well as the capital equipment. The cost of delivering all of these items to a point distant from their point of origin must be added to the distribution costs of delivering the finished products back to the main cities which will inevitably tend to be the distribution points for the country as a whole. Since it is generally the grower who bears the cost of delivering his leaf to the factory, either directly or in terms of a lower end-price, there is a positive disincentive in terms of physical transportation costs to a manufacturing concern to base itself in an area where the raw materials are grown.

This argument, of course, applies even more forcibly to situations in which a plant might be set up to process or manufacture goods for sale in the country as a whole, based on raw materials which are not indigenous to the area. In this case the transportation costs would represent a crippling increment to the base costs.

These are some of the simple but almost insurmountable barriers to achieving industrial development in small centres. The difficulties are not new, but are common to countries at all levels of economic development. In industrialised countries the problems can be overcome by a shift of the working population away from centres of low employment to those with a shortage of labour. In Europe this has resulted in the movement of the economically active from southern Europe and the Asiatic and African shores of the Mediterranean northwards to the industrial heartland of Europe. In developing countries similar effects can be seen in the concentration of Yemeni labour in Saudi Arabia and the Gulf States, or in the attraction of the copper mines at Ndola for Africans from outside Zambia. But such opportunities are rare in the Third World. Instead, there is often a great deal of movement away from the rural areas to towns as conditions of rapid population increase create a situation of rural poverty which drives the dispossessed and workless younger sons of peasant farmers away from agriculture. In this phenomenon, work is not the pull factor which attracts movement to urban centres, but, on the contrary, the complete absence of opportunity in the rural environment is a powerfully compulsive push factor serving to create an exodus from the country.

5.2 Intervention at the National Level

Governments are often powerless to create employment opportunities in economically viable occupations, because of lack of resources in terms of money, skilled personnel and technical know-how. The general means of intervention is by means of national planning and over the last twenty years many a national plan has been prepared which has among its other goals that of increasing employment opportunities. There is no doubt that the governments of developing countries are thoroughly committed to the concept of job creation. In a democratic country the increase in the number of workers in employment is the proudest boast of any successful administration — a failure to increase employment is generally reflected in defeat when seeking re-election to office. In one-party systems, or even military dictatorships, the governments prefer to see their populations actively employed, if only to minimise causes of unrest. Therefore there can be little doubt of the genuine desire of governments to provide employment, and of the fact that every effort is made in almost every corner of the world to increase job opportunities.

Although generally governments have been unsuccessful in stimulating the kind of increase in productive employment that is required to provide for the needs of the burgeoning armies of unemployed, they have had some success in spreading administrative and, to some extent, industrial employment to centres other than the capital cities and main ports. This, however, tends to be a function of national income. Nigeria and the Federation of Malaysia and, for that matter, the People's Republic of China have stimulated regional development because of administrative structures which devolve a considerable degree of autonomy on the states or provinces within the country. This theory of subregional development is one that Saudi Arabia has adopted as a method of spreading the benefits of oil revenue as widely as possible across the country and its population.

Certainly the employment opportunities created by the governmental administrative machine cannot be neglected; although the benefits are not always spread wisely, administration employs many who would not otherwise be in work. In most developing countries, the agricultural sector accounts for at least 70 per cent of gross national product, and government plays a large role in the organisation, regulation and encouragement of agricultural output. Such activities produce their obvious benefits, but even non-productive jobs in government have an economic function. At the very least employment in the public sector is a means of redistributing income derived from taxes. The expenditure of these civil servants has its own multiplier effect and serves to stimulate employment in service activities.

Therefore, overall government strategy should take account of the benefits of spreading administrative office, agricultural extension services and education establishments as widely as possible. The more decentralised the country's system of government, the easier this becomes. Nevertheless it runs counter to the natural tendency of bureaucrats to concentrate in the capital city and for educators, for example, to flock together in university towns. It must be recognised that employment in the public sector entails some assumption of wider responsibility rather than being a secure and highly paid sinecure in the comfort of an air-conditioned capital city far away from the rigours of village life. Certainly the presence of a secondary school or government office in a small community will not stimulate manufacturing, but it does provide an inflow of funds from outside which will generate forms of employment from domestic service to clerical and secretarial jobs. The other means that governments use to direct investment or create economic activity tend to be less successful.

Generally, when preparing national plans there is a stated objective of spreading employment as widely as possible in the country. In the last resort, however, it is the means that a government has at its disposal which finally determines success in implementing such an intention. In most developing countries capital is a scarce resource, and for industrial and commerical enterprises it tends to come from foreign sources, both public and private. The great difficulty in dealing with private and foreign capital, from the point of view of the national planner, is that it is virtually impervious to direction and organisation. Private capital will clearly be invested in enterprises which show at least as good a rate of return as can be obtained from bank deposits. It can be argued in developing countries that the yardstick should be the return from owning property for rent, since sometimes this is almost the most attractive investment in fast-expanding towns where the demand for accommodation exceeds the supply. Even official foreign funds which are channelled through aid institutions such as the East African Development Bank, or bilateral operation such as the UK's Commonwealth Development Corporation must be invested in enterprises that will provide a profit, since the EADB has to cover the cost of its operations and pay interest on its own capital, and the CDC also uses profitability as justification for investment.

Once investors, whether they are entrepreneurs or institutions, need to consider the return on their funds, they are making comparisons between a particular opportunity and one or more alternatives. The private capitalist is looking for the highest return on his investment with the minimum of risk and, often, the minimum of effort. In a small centre there will be very few capitalists; those who do exist will have put their money into the few modern houses, or into trading ventures. Clearly these activities generate some employment, but they are not sufficient sources of work to meet the needs of a growing number of able-bodied men and women. The capital required to start a small factory is not available in the town. Therefore an investment opportunity must exist which will attract capital from the nearest large city. The chances of doing this successfully in competition with the investment opportunities available in the large city itself, in a period of scarcity of capital, are virtually nil. If only because the operation might be many miles from the capitalist's base, it is extremely improbable that a private investor will be prepared to invest here rather than closer to home.

5.3 Investment in Smaller Centres

It is clear that providing employment in small centres is by no means easy, and that the principal obstacle is that larger towns are in competition for the same scarce resources. It is probably desirable that such resources that are devoted to industrialisation in the form of large-scale activities in a developing country should be concentrated in a few main centres. In a large centre there is no doubt that the need is greater; the number of unemployed is higher and the concentration of poverty can create far more serious problems, particularly in terms of health, than poverty in a small community; for the individual the conditions may not be significantly different since the marginal employment opportunities in a large town may offset some of the physical penalties of the overcrowded urban poor, but for the community as a whole urban poverty is a considerably more serious burden. The financial and economic benefits to be derived from large-scale industrial investment are likely to be greater in a city than in a small town for a variety of reasons. Nevertheless there is still a tendency among governments to encourage diverse investment patterns.

The arguments that can be proposed to resolve the difficulties in promoting investment in industrial and commercial activities in small centres simply reflect the ideology or politics of the government in power. Broadly the choices are:

(1) that the state will invest, since private capital is not attracted. The result may be that there is no investment because capital is scarce and other projects in bigger places will have a larger economic impact, or they will be more visible.

(2) that the state will try to direct private capital by means of financial assistance, such as loans from an industrial investment bank or equivalent institution. The degree of pump-priming possible will depend on the resources of the industrial development bank, which it can be assumed are scarce. If capital is short, then the process of selection of projects will be exacting, and a small centre will be in competition with all other industrial investment projects in the country.

(3) the state will offer incentives other than capital in the form of tax allowances etc., on the lines of pioneer legislation devised to encourage foreign private investment. The difficulty is in devising sufficiently attractive incentives which would specifically encourage activity in small centres. In its overall programme the government would undoubtedly be offering encouragement to investors generally, in the hope of attracting any new or foreign capital. To devise further tax inducements for particular places is an act of economic sophistication several stages beyond that of a country desperately attempting to embark on a switch from agriculture to industry.

(4) the state will provide the basic infrastructure for industrial

estates in all communities of a certain size as an automatic public facility. This need consist of little more than a designated area with road access, main services of electricity and water available for connection by tenants, possibly a light covering structure and available at low rents. The costs are minimal but can be inflated by elaborate central administrative bodies. This system will tend to encourage small-scale local activities, but will not be a decisive factor in influencing investment by an outside capitalist in a major industrial activity. These facilities would be available at other locations, so that again the centre is in competition with all comers.

This consideration of the scope for intervention by central government has ignored a number of the secondary services that are required to support any medium-sized business venture. These include such facilities as banks, telecommunications, stationery supplies, etc. These facilities are in the chicken or egg category — which comes first? The service or the customer? Clearly, if such services exist, they will tend to act as a minor incentive to invest; their absence can act as a rather more severe deterrent, since there is no guarantee in most developing countries that public services, such as telecommunications, will follow the establishment of an enterprise that needs them. Often, due to the general pressure of demand on scarce resources, there will be a considerable time-lag between a requirement for telecommunications and their provision. Therefore, in the absence of such facilities it is worth examining the economic activities which tend to develop naturally.

5.3.1 Trading

In most places the first formal economic activity other than agriculture is trading. In all communities there are facilities for the exchange of goods; in parts of West Africa a market sometimes exists without a community. There are examples of Yoruba periodic markets (e.g. held every five days) taking place at points between villages where there is no habitation and a typical small settlement may have quite an important market operating on a daily basis. Associated with it will be a form of transportation service to other centres, and to the rural hinterland to enable produce to be brought to market. This may be a local bus or truck service. In turn this will require a vehicle park which generates repair services, a petrol pump and a retail store offering that most common item of failure in tropical countries, tyres. In this way a small community first encounters engineering and metal-working skills — through maintaining and repairing the internal combustion engine and all the machines it powers from irrigation or water-supply pumps to generators. Metal-working in a small community is a vital service which extends into building, furniture, etc., and has a real multiplier effect in that it enables a whole range of new activities to develop.

5.3.2 Construction

Parallel with trading is the growth of that other fundamental human activity, building, which cannot be ignored when considering employment creation. In small communities construction becomes an economic activity in two ways; the first is the obvious development of specialisation of skills when a building is first constructed for cash, i.e. not built by its occupant; the second is in the manufacture of building materials. Even in small villages there tend to be craftsmen who make doors; sometimes there are specialist roof-makers, etc. In a larger community bricks may be made commercially as well as fittings. Construction and the manufacture of building components tend to encourage wood-working skills which are also applied to general carpentry, such as making furniture and wood-turning.

5.3.3 Clothing

The third strand of basic activity is related to clothing in all its forms. Weaving and dyeing is a common village activity; in a larger community the possession of a sewing-machine can be the foundation of a family fortune. In the post-colonial period there has been a steady swing to local or traditional clothing, away from European styles, which were, and are, often imported. In any community, even a relatively small one, there is a significant demand for clothing, sometimes for ritual purposes, e.g. veils for women and head coverings for men in Arab countries. There may be little that government can do to actively promote the small-scale manufacture of clothing, but it can avoid discouraging local producers. The policy towards imports should be to prevent cheap clothes made overseas competing with a developing local industry. On the other hand, imports of raw materials should be allowed free of duty if they are not available in sufficient quantities from domestic sources. Free import of sewing-machines and similar equipment is again a positive step. In parallel to this small-scale cottage industry it is probable that most developing countries, particularly those which grow cotton in any quantity, will have their own textile industry manufacturing cloth and certain items of clothing such as shirts. As a stimulus to small-scale tailoring it is important to produce material in dress lengths, etc. Often tailoring is an activity undertaken only by women, acting as individuals; once it becomes organised on any basis, say half a dozen employees and an entrepreneur who designs and markets the output, then it tends to employ men. This scale of making up clothing is one which suits the production of traditional dress rather than European styles, which are more cheaply and efficiently produced in larger volume.

5.3.4 Metal-working

As an example of the second stage of development of manufacturing, it is worth returning to metal-working. As indicated above, the prime incentive to undertake such activity is provided by the demand to service and repair bicycles, motor cycles, cars, trucks and pumps. In carrying out these tasks the artisans will need to acquire the skills of beating metal panels and making joints, etc. This immediately opens up a range of simple activities from modifying vehicles, e.g. converting closed vans to buses by providing windows and seats, to making water-tanks, metal structures and beds. Given the possession of certain basic skills, even a relatively small community will have a range of metal-working activities, probably specialist in nature. In general these survive and flourish because the transport costs associated with buying water-tanks or bed-frames from another town are high enough to afford some measure of protection to local craftsmen from competition from outside. For some items the raw materials are already available in the form of waste materials, e.g. funnels for filling petrol tanks of cars or motor cycles are made out of old oil cans; wrecked vehicles provide a source for spare parts and sheet metal.

5.4 Population Growth

The uses to which such materials are put depend on the skills, ingenuity and basic entrepreneurial drives of the community. On the whole, in a well-balanced society, the social structure, customs and law tend to reflect the needs and habits of the population, and in developing countries such constraints are far less severe than the shortage of capital, and of skills. The problem of creating employment is exacerbated by rapid increases in population allied to a revolution in economic expectations. While there are very severe limits as to what can be done to create employment when resources are scarce, governments can at least avoid following policies which will simply increase the problem.

As a first step, very obviously, anything that can be done to restrict the birth rate is a move in the right direction. Second, the maximum of emphasis should be given to the encouragement of agricultural employment; schemes which tend to depopulate rural areas must be avoided, since it is difficult to envisage any financial return large enough to balance the social cost of unemployed farmers drifting into cities. It seems desirable to avoid disruption of social practices which contribute to a balanced system of dependence. For example, in some Arab countries there has been a custom that women should only carry out certain functions in society, such as teaching or nursing. Unless there are alternative employment opportunities for women as well as all the male labour force, there would appear to be little merit in changing such customs at the cost of increasing the competition for employment. Education is a two-edged weapon in that many jobs require some literacy but more emphasis on applied skills. Often, however, education is provided without close regard to the employment opportunities available to school-leavers, in that it concentrates on literacy but ignores practical training.

5.5 Guidelines for Educational Policy

Education can be geared to be more responsive to the needs of a small community in a number of ways. The traps of an academic education have been widely discussed, and the dangers of creating a class with high educational qualifications but no practical skills are well documented. One of the effects of this educational system is that typically in developing countries there is an immense over-supply of applicants for clerical jobs, but a shortage of qualified agricultural extension staff. Therefore the deduction is clearly that the educational system should be aimed at producing agricultural workers rather than clerks. This is not to deny the benefits of literacy. In a rural community the evidence strongly suggests that it is the literate who are the innovators in their society; the first to use fertiliser, or the first to use corrugated metal roofing in preference to thatch. On the other hand a State Commissioner in Nigeria responsible for road traffic claimed that illiterates make the best drivers, particularly in contrast to the highly educated — 'the elite'.

There seems to be a good case for teaching a basic level of literacy, if only to ensure that opportunities for further education are as open as possible, but there could be considerably more emphasis on imparting agricultural and mechanical skills. In view, however, of the real shortages of qualified teachers capable of giving an adequate training in mechanical skills, there is a strong argument in favour of running both child and adult programmes together. If a school can give a training in wood-working or textiles or metal-working, for example, then this should be offered as widely as possible. The overall aim in providing education in small centres should be to equip the members of these communities with a reasonable level of literacy and a practical training in at least one specialised activity which can be pursued in that centre, and is not of a nature that can only be a qualification for employment in a large city.

Thus there is scope for designing an educational system which is capable of producing the kind of people who can find work in a small centre, and who, because of the nature of their skills, can contribute to the economic development of the community. This will not demand an excessively high level of teaching, but rather a process of training in the use and maintenance of tools, and a rudimentary introduction to methods of work. Again, it is important to match the system to the availability of teachers, which will be severely restricted, and to the realities of the employment available. There would be little point in aiming at producing highly skilled precision engineers who could only find work in a heavily capitalised machining plant. In practice, some technical teaching could be provided by practitioners such as the local carpenters.

The benefits of such education might be greater in their negative — rather than positive — effect, in that it would not produce people who feel compelled to go to the large cities to seek the clerical jobs for which their training fits them, since such jobs are not available in small centres. This would serve to reduce the push factor towards large cities. By itself it would not create employment in a small community, but it might encourage employment by making it possible to establish activities which would utilise semi-skilled but appropriately trained labourers.

5.6 Appropriate Technology

Part of any discussion of employment in developing countries is always devoted to consideration of the 'appropriate technology'. There are numerous arguments seeking to show that the appropriate technology is something less than a capital-intensive manufacturing plant, but this issue may be largely predetermined in communities which are too small to attract major investment in employment-creating activities and, therefore, extremely unlikely to be in a position in which they can afford to choose between one technology and another. Almost all activities which create employment in such a community will be relatively low in technological rating in terms of capital investment, but need not necessarily be unsophisticated. Indeed it is probable that the tasks undertaken to maintain and repair internal combustion engines, for example, might well be considerably more elaborate than would be carried out in a large centre where parts might be thrown away and replaced, since in the absence of adequate spare parts the broken component must be repaired. This is a pattern which is not unknown in the developed countries.

There are implications arising from this situation which might well have a bearing on the future prosperity of a small community. If the small centres develop altogether more rigorous conditions than large cities in terms of lack of capital and an absence of expensive facilities, then their inhabitants are likely to acquire a specialised range of skills which by their nature are unlikely to be present in large cities or small villages. It seems to be of some importance that such skills should be encouraged and supported, if only to ensure that they are not lost to the larger centres.

Unfortunately, the exact forms that this type of development might assume are almost impossible to predict, and thus to allow for in preparing plans. For example, in countries such as Egypt or India, with rigid restrictions on the import of cars, a large and wide-ranging branch of metal-working has been generated by the need to keep old vehicles on the road without a supply of factory-made spare parts. If the import restrictions were relaxed, this industry would rapidly wither away. A host of similar situations can be created by changes in a government's import policy, none of which can be foreseen accurately by planners or administrators: even if such policies could be foreseen accurately, the response is not easily predictable. Nevertheless it is of the utmost importance to ensure that small centres are planned in such a way as to ensure that any opportunities can be exploited by the industrious or the enterprising. In general this means that there should be the minimum of official restrictions, constraints and intervention, but the maximum of facilities available to those who might be able to use them. In an ideal world the facilities would consist of easy access to finance, cheap space for workshops, offices or shops, and readily available services. In fact in all developing countries the only one of these that can be provided without difficulty is space; capital and services are scarce resources.

5.7 Scarcity of Capital

The scarcity of capital is reflected in the very high cost of credit in many countries, but for small concerns in small communities there is often no formal institution from which to borrow money. Large enterprises are encouraged to expand by means of funding from industrial development banks and similar agencies, as discussed above, but no funds are available from these sources for small concerns. The World Bank has drawn attention to this problem, among others, in so far as it affects the growth of small concerns in a sector policy paper.[1] This paper points out that small-scale businesses must pay extremely high interest rates, rising to 10 per cent a day for short-term cash in some South-East Asian countries. Such rates are less a reflection of the risks involved in making loans to small retailers than of the fact that there are no alternatives to the kerbside money lender, or the rural wholesale trader. The Bank paper suggests that it is more difficult for small businesses to cover their operating expenses than their initial capital outlay since commercial banks can more readily lend funds to acquire assets in the form of plant or equipment which can in themselves be used as collateral cover. Operating expenses, however, present a more severe problem. These include such items as input materials or the stock for a retailer, and banks very rarely afford credit to cover such purchases to small businesses, generally because the business can offer no guarantee.

To overcome some of these problems the World Bank favours the creation of new credit facilities, which might include, for example, a form of undertaking by governments to commercial banks, or other credit institutions, that losses incurred in making loans to small businesses would be reimbursed. In the United States there is a system which is operated by some banks in certain cities of providing loans on a two-tier basis; large companies pay the prime interest rate, whereas small concerns are charged a slightly lower rate. Solutions to the critical shortage of credit facilities cannot be provided overnight, but it is clear that more credit at lower cost will stimulate economic activity. In planning the development of small communities access to commercial finance is a vital ingredient.

5.8 The Development of Small Communities

In devising plans for the development of small communities, there is a crucial need to identify the lines along which trade and industry will naturally grow. There may not be a great deal that the planner can do to stimulate employment, but he must be aware of the risk of stifling economic activity through insensitive planning. In general, trading activities, which include the provision of such services as banking, need to take place at the centre of a community so that the entire population has relatively easy access. Thus there will be a market-place, or soukh, at the heart of any successful community. This will almost inevitably be associated with a vehicle park for goods and passenger services, so there must be provision of adequate space for these functions, and for the secondary activities that they will generate. In terms of physical planning there is no need to view markets as fixed permanently in one place. In many African towns there is a tendency for community markets to spring up as a town expands, and for the functions of the central market to change. Such activities as the sale of live animals tend to become segregated at a relatively early stage; sometimes fruit and vegetables are also sold at a separate venue. Thus the moral is to ensure flexibility and to avoid rigid constraints.

At the institutional level the same principles apply, It is counter-productive to impose rigorous rules for licensing traders which entail substantial fees or taxes. In most cases such regulations will simply drive traders away from where they are enforced to areas where they are not enforced; rents for trading sites can easily be set at a reasonable level. It is always an advantage to central government to encourage the buying and selling of goods to take place openly so that if it becomes necessary to monitor price changes, to control buying or selling prices, or to pay subsidies, the information necessary is readily available, and the means for control or intervention are simple.

The function of trading can generate its own growth. The bigger the market, in terms of range of goods on offer, the wider will be its catchment area. If visitors from the surrounding countryside are attracted to a centre because of its market, then the goods and services will tend to expand to meet more of the needs of these visitors. As the trade of a community expands, so will the wealth of the community which will tend to be reflected in new building. As is discussed above, construction is one of the first industrial activities to take place in a small community. The first steps will be in block-making and carpentry, followed by metal-working. Neither wood- nor metal-working will be entirely directed towards building, but where they do serve as inputs to the construction industry there is no reason why they should be sited by the side of the market square. Block-making tends to require a relatively generous site, if only to store the finished product, but in many small communities it can be seen in the centre, generally because when it first started there were vacant plots. Again, depending on how the community has grown in the past, other similar activities can be found in the middle of many small towns.

There are four good reasons to encourage these industrial activities to move out of the centre of the community:

(1)   the activity can grow more readily where there is space for physical expansion;

(2)   access to adequate space to store finished products enables the manufacture to take place over the whole year, even if demand is seasonal, e.g. not much construction work is carried out in the rainy season;

(3)   those outside the community, i.e. the rural hinterland, will have easy access to sites on the outskirts, and may thus be encouraged to become customers;

(4)   the establishment of industrial activities outside the centre will itself stimulate certain secondary activities such as setting up of small shops to service those working in the industries.

One of the problems of planning in some communities is that zoning can only be achieved by changing the law or, alternatively, an industrial zone can only be set up by purchase of land. It is important that planning for industrial development takes account of the real constraints imposed by society and the laws of that society.

In general, it seems to be true that more development, resulting in employment creation, takes place by accident than as a result of any deliberate policy pursued by government. From the planners' point of view, it is most important to plan for a future which will be shaped by accident. Some of these unforeseen and unforeseeable factors have been discussed above. In terms of location, this need to take some account of the unforeseen is a further encouragement to a policy of attempting to site industrial activity in areas which have plenty of space for further expansion or for the creation of subsidiary activities.

Another aspect of industrial estate strategy is that of the funding of space for individual enterprises. The options are to provide freehold premises or to offer space to rent. In order to encourage small businesses, the latter appears to be a more desirable option and indeed offers the possibility of various levels of subsidy in the rent that might be charged, e.g. it might be desirable to permit someone to use a site at a nominal rent for a year or so before moving to a fully economic rent. In order, however, not to discourage larger enterprises from using an industrial zone, it might be desirable to permit tenants to buy long leaseholds on their sites, but the policy should be flexible enough to enable tenants to move from an annual renting agreement to a longer-term leasehold. Again, the keynote in operation should be flexibility so that users are encouraged to move into the industrial estate.

5.9 Conclusions

The recommendations for policies to be pursued in encouraging the creation of employment in small towns can be stated as follows:

(1) There should not be a conscious effort to rival large centres in attracting major industrial investment. Such effort will not usually be rewarded since large-scale investment will only be made in places which offer financial and economic benefits to the investor on a continuing basis. This might seem somewhat self-defeating, but the experience of Western countries has shown that it is very difficult to direct industrial investment to areas which may be preferred by government, but hold no attraction to the entrepreneurs. Therefore, effort can be saved if it is recognised that such policies are unproductive.

(2) It is desirable to encourage such processing of local crops as can be economically carried out in the area. A certain degree of education and government intervention might achieve some greater level of processing of local crops than at present takes place. Again, it would be misguided to break up large-scale processing plants to create a number of smaller substitutes, all operating at a higher cost, if the net effect were to increase unit export prices and to lose sales on world markets.

(3) Government policy should be directed to creating conditions which encourage economic activity. This can often be achieved by relaxing restrictive legislation and by limiting its own intervention. Where the government does have an opportunity to stimulate activity is in its location of the various elements of administration. If the government can spread its own direct employment around the country rather than concentrate it in the capital, the expenditures of the civil servants will in themselves stimulate secondary and tertiary activity. This applies not only to the machinery of government but also to other public facilities such as hospitals and schools. In cases where the government does have development money to spend, as in some Middle Eastern countries, the increase of employment in the civil service and the distribution of administrative facilities around the country has a demonstrable impact in redistributing funds which originated from central government.

(4) Governments should accept that the profit motive, whether for individual entrepreneurs or for corporate institutions, for example, is a sensible and practical means of judging employment creation. It is only in situations where the investor can see his way to making a reasonable return on his capital and effort that he will risk it by taking on labour.

(5) The availability of cheap capital, through development-orientated financial institutions, is an important factor.

(6) The provision of cheap site-and-service facilities for industrial activity will encourage enterprise.

(7) The judicious manipulation of import policy is not out of place, but may not do more than encourage domestic producers to raise prices to unacceptable levels to exploit a monopoly situation.

(8) Governments and planners must recognise that the development of industrial employment is likely to cause social change and should be prepared to accept and accommodate such change.

(9) Education can help to create future employment of the school population if it is geared to the realities of village and small town life. There should be an emphasis on training in practical skills, which includes an introduction to the use of tools and methods of work. Indeed, it is possible that local skilled craftsmen might be able to play a part in this educational system.

(10) It is assumed that in a small community the entrepreneur will select the level of technology that is most practical to the circumstances of the market, and to the skills and experience of the labour force. It seems unnecessary to adopt any theoretical stance as to recommending a particular level of technology. In reality, any investment that will create jobs will be welcome even if its level of technology is not the most appropriate to the community. At the level of the small community, it may be more important to attract investment than to be too doctrinaire about how that money is spent.

(11) Planners should ensure that there are facilities in an appropriate site or sites where the function can be related to the market both inside and outside the community. In practice it probably makes more sense to encourage the siting of new industrial activity outside the centre of any community.

(12) The provision of sites for industrial or market activities should be at costs which are related to the ability of the tenants to pay.

Note

1. *Employment and Development of Small Enterprises* (The World Bank, February 1978).

Bibliography

United Nations Publications

Reference	Title
E.72.11.A.1	*Transfer of Operative Technology at the Enterprise Level*
E.72.11.A.3	*Appropriate Technology and Research for Industrial Development*
E.72.11.A.11	*Attack on Mass Poverty and Unemployment*
E.74.11.A.4	*Industrialization for New Development Needs*
E.69.11.B.9	*Industrial Processing of Citrus Fruit*
E.71.11.B.12	*Profiles of Manufacturing Establishments Vol. III*
E.69.11.B.39	*Vol. II Problems and Prospects of Small-scale Industry in Developing Countries*
E.69.11.B.39	*Vol. 20 General Issues of Industrial Policy in Developing Countries*
E.69.11.B.28	*Selection of Projects and Production Process for Basic and Intermediate Petrochemicals in Developing Countries*
E.69.11.B.32	*No. 3 Studies in Plastics Fabrication and Application*
E.69.11.B.25	*No. 4 Studies in the Development of Plastics Industries*
E.69.11.B.27	*No. 5 Establishing Standardization of Plastics in Developing Countries*
E.68.11.B.12	*No. 1 Training of Economic Administrators for Industrial Development*
E.68.11.B.16	*No. 2 Estimation of Managerial and Technical Personnel Requirements*
E.70.11.B.6/Vol.1	*The Lodz Textile Seminars. Textile Fibres*
E.70.11.B.6/Vol.2	*Spinning*
E.70.11.B.6/Vol.3	*Knitting*
E.70.11.B.6/Vol.4	*Weaving and Associated Processes*
E.70.11.B.6/Vol.5	*Non-Conventional Methods of Fabric Production*
E.70.11.B.6/Vol.6	*Textile Finishing*
E.70.11.B.6/Vol.7	*Testing and Quality Control*
E.70.11.B.6/Vol.8	*Plant and Power Engineering*
E.66.11.B.9	*Report of Expert Group on Second-Hand Equipment for Developing*
E.66.11.B.10	*Studies in Economics of Industry. 2. Pre-Investment Data for the Aluminium Industry*
E.66.11.B.16	*Industrial Estates: Policies, Plans and Progress*
E.66.11.B.19	*Industrial Developments in Asia and the Far East Vol. I*
E.66.11.B.20	*Industrial Developments in Asia and the Far East Vol. II*
E.66.11.B.21	*Industrial Developments in Asia and the Far East Vol. III*
E.66.11.B.22	*Industrial Developments in Asia and the Far East Vol. IV*
E.66.11.B.23	*Industrial Developments in the Arab Countries (3 parts)*
E.67.11.B.3	*Technical Co-operation for the Development of Small-scale Industries*

Reference	Title
E.69.11.B.2	*Development of Metal-Working Industries in Developing Countries*
E.69.11.B.19	*The Establishment of the Brick and Tile Industry in Developing Countries*
E.69.11.B.21	*Factors Inhibiting the Indigenous Growth of the Fertilizer Industry in Developing Countries*
E.69.11.B.22	*Report of the Interregional Seminar on Industrial Location and Regional Development*
E.69.11.B.30	*Bicycles. A Case Study of Indian Experience*
E.69.11.B.36	*Report of the Second Interregional Iron and Steel Symposium*
E.69.11.B.38	*Report of the Expert Group Meeting on the Design, Manufacture and Utilization of Dies and Jigs in Developing Countries*
E.70.11.B.5	*Industrial Development Survey Vol. II*
E.72.11.B.15	*Industrial Development Survey Vol. IV*
E.73.11.B.9	*Industrial Development Survey Vol. V*
E.70.11.B.11	*Production of Distribution Transformers in Developing Countries*
E.70.11.B.12	*Processing Problems and Selection of Machinery in the Woollen and Worsted Industry*
E.70.11.B.13	*Establishment of Pharmaceutical Industries in Developing Countries*
E.70.11.B.15	*Industrial Location and Regional Development. An Annotated Bibliography*
E.70.11.B.16	*Metalworking Industries as Potential Export Industries in Developing Countries*
E.70.11.B.17	*Financial Aspects of Manufacturing Enterprises in the Public Sector*
E.70.11.B.19	*Technical Services for Small-scale Industries*
E.70.11.B.22	*Small-scale Industries in Arab Countries of the Middle East*
E.70.11.B.24	*Directory of External Sources of Financing Available for Industrial Projects in Developing Countries*
E.70.11.B.25	*Modernization and Mechanization of Salt Industries Based on Seawater in Developing Countries*
E.70.11.B.27	*Development of Plastics in Industries in Developing Countries*
E.70.11.B.29	*The Manufacture of Cement and Sulphuric Acid from Calcium Sulphate*
E.70.11.B.30	*Utilization of Non-Ferrous Scrap Metal*
E.71.11.B.20	*Organization and Administration of Industrial Services for Asia and the Middle East*
E.71.11.B.22	*Industrial Research Institutes. Guidelines for Evaluation*
E.71.11.B.24	*Clay Building Materials Industries in Africa*
E.71.11.B.25	*Extraction of Chemicals from Seawater, Inland Brines and Rock Salt Deposits*
E.72.11.B.2	*The Development of Engineering Design Capabilities in Developing Countries*
E.72.11.B.3	*Manufacture of Telecommunications Equipment and Low-Cost Receivers*
E.72.11.B.4	*Production of Panels from Agricultural Residues. Vienna,*

	14-18 December, 1970
E.72.11.B.29	*The Growth of the Leather Industry in Developing Countries: Problems and Prospects*
E.73.11.B.11	*Machine Tools in Latin America*
E.73.11.B.21	*Guidelines for the Acquisition of Foreign Technology in Developing Countries*
E.74.11.B.6	*Pre-Investment Considerations and Appropriate Industrial Planning in the Vegetable Oil Industry*
E.74.11.B.7	*The Hydrogenation of Vegetable Oils and the Production of Vegetable Ghee*
E.74.11.B.8	*Review of Comparative Analysis of Oilseed Raw Materials and Processes Suitable for the Production of Protein Products for Human Consumption*
E.74.11.B.10	*Technical and Economic Aspects of the Oil Palm Fruit Processing Industry*
E.74.11.B.11	*Castor Oil Production and Processing*
E.74.11.B.13	*Profiles of Manufacturing Establishments. Vol. IV: Three-Country Study on Export-Orientated Industries*
E.74.11.B.14	*Industrial Development Survey. Special Issue for the Second General Conference of UNIDO*
E.73.11.K.4	*Rural Organizations: Job Opportunities in Agriculture*
E.72.1V.6	*Prefabrication of Wooden Doors and Windows in Community Development*
E.74.1V.6	*Guidelines for Government Policies and Measures for the Gradual Industrialization of Building*

Other Publications

Akinrele, I.A. *Techno-Economic Feasibility of Small-Scale Distillation of Potable Spirits from Palm Wine* (paper presented at OECD, Development Centre Conference on Low Cost Technology: An Inquiry into Outstanding Policy Issues) (OECD, Paris, 1975)

Armas, Jr. A. *Implications of Legislated Minimum Wages on the Choice of Technique in the Agro-Canned Pineapple Industry in the Philippines: a micro-approach* (papers and proceedings of the Workshop on Manpower and Human Resources) (University of the Philippines, School of Economics and National Economic and Development Authority, Laguna, 1972)

Aurora, G.S. and Morehouse, W. 'Dilemma of Technological Choice: the Case of the small Tractor', *Economic and Political Weekly*, vol. 7, nos. 31-3 (Special Number, August 1972)

Austin, V. *Appropriate Technology: Agricultural Engineering* (paper presented at the University of Edinburgh Appropriate Technology Conference, September 1973)

Bhalla, A.S. 'Investment Allocation and Technological Choice: a Case of Cotton Spinning Techniques', *Economic Journal* (September 1964)

Boon, G.K. *Choice of Industrial Technology: the Case of Woodworking Industrialization and Productivity*, no. 3 (1961) (UN, New York)

——, 'Technological Choice in Metalworking with Special Reference to Mexico' in A.S. Bhalla (ed.), *Technology and Employment in Industry* (ILO, Geneva, 1975)

Boschoff, W.G. 'Development of the Uganda Small Tractor', *World Crops*, vol. 24, no. 5 (1972)

Bourke, W.O. *Basic Vehicle for South East Asia, Technology and Economics in Economic Development* (USAID, May 1972)

Cabanos, P. 'Jeepney Manufacturing in the Philippines: a Model for Developing the Agricultural Machinery Industry', *Agricultural Mechanization in Asia* (Autumn 1971)

Cooper, C., Kaplinsky, R. and Turner, R. *Second-Hand Equipment in a Developing Country: a Study of Jute-processing in Kenya* (ILO, Geneva, 1974)

——, 'Choice of Techniques for Can Making in Kenya, Tanzania and Thailand' in A.S. Bhalla (ed.), *Technology and Employment in Industry* (ILO, Geneva, 1975)

Cunningham, J.F. *The Development of Locally Manufactured Irrigation Pumps in the Republic of Vietnam* (paper presented at the Second International Seminar on Change in Agriculture, Reading, September 1974)

Date, A. *The Manufacture of Miniature Cigars* (Tropical Products Institute Report No. G.15, 1965).

Dickinson, H. and Winnington, T.L. *Ferro-Cement for Boat Building* (paper presented at the University of Edinburgh Appropriate Technology Conference, September 1973)

Edwards, D. *The Industrial Manufacture of Cassava Products: an Economic Study* (Tropical Products Institute Report, No. G.88, 1974).

Garg, M.K. 'Problems of Developing Appropriate Technologies in India', *Appropriate Technology*, vol. 1, no. 1 (Spring 1974).

German Foundation for Developing Countries 'Development and Dissemination of Appropriate Technologies in Rural Areas' in R. Kraetsch (ed.), *Proceedings of an International Workshop* (GFDC, Kumasi, Ghana, 1972)

Government of India, Ministry of Industrial Development (Appropriate Technology Cell) *Appropriate Technology for Balanced Regional Development Vol. II, Group Studies*, B. Bahari (ed.) (New Delhi, 1974)

Hall, M.N.A. *The Small-Scale Manufacture of High and Low Boiled Sweets and Toffees* (Tropical Products Institute Report No. G.77, 1973)

Hewavitharana, B. 'Choice of Techniques in Ceylon', *Economic Development in South Asia*

Howes, M. and Hislop, D. *The Transfer of Technology to the Thai Silk Industry* (Science Policy Research Unit, University of Sussex, mimeo., 1974), Part 3: 'Success and Failure in the Transfer of Technology — The Case of Thai-Japanese Sericulture Programmes'

International Labour Office *Employment, Incomes and Equality: a Strategy for Increasing Productive Employment in Kenya* (ILO, Geneva, 1972), Technical Paper No. 7, 'A Case Study of Choice of Techniques in Two Processes in the Manufacture of Cans'

——, *The Role of the Textile Industry in the Expansion of Employment in the Developing Countries* (ILO Programme of Industrial Activities, Textile Committee, Report II, 1973).

——, *The Woodworking Industries and the Creation of Employment* (ILO, Programme of Industrial Activities, Second Tripartite Meeting for the Woodworking Industries, Report II, 1975)

Johnston, P, *Appropriate Technologies for Small Developing Countries* (Smoothie Publications, Brighton, 1974)

Kamath, J. *Small-Scale Manufacture of Carbonated Beverages* (Tropical Products Institute Report No. G.65, 1971).

——, *Small-Scale Manufacture of Soluble Coffee* (Tropical Products Institute Report No. G.82, 1973)

——, Flynn, G. and Mars, P.A. *The Manufacture of Woven Sacks from Natural and Synthetic Fibre* (Tropical Products Institute Report No. G.90, 1975).

Kaplinsky, R. *Innovation in Gari Production: the Case for an Intermediate Technology* (Institute of Development Studies, Discussion Paper No. 34, 1974)

Kilby, P. *African Enterprise: the Nigerian Bread Industry* (Stanford, 1965)

——, *Industrialization in an Open Economy: Nigeria, 1946-66* (Cambridge University Press, 1969)

King, K. *New Light in Africa: Kenya's Candlemakers* (paper presented at the University of Edinburgh Appropriate Technology Conference, September 1973)

Mars, P.A. *The Manufacture of Orange Squash in Developing Countries* (Tropical Products Institute Report No. G.53, 1971)

Marsden, K. 'Progressive Technologies for Developing Countries', *International Labour Review*, vol. 101, no. 4 (May 1970)

McBain, N.S. and Pickett, J. *Low-Cost Technology in Ethiopian Footwear Production* (paper presented at OECD Development Centre Conference on Low Cost Technology: an Inquiry into Outstanding Policy Issues) (OECD, Development Centre, Paris, 1975)

McDowell, J. 'Development of High Protein/High Calorie Biscuits in Uganda Using Indigenous Protein Sources', *East African Journal of Rural Development*, vol. 6, nos. 1 and 2 (1973)

Ngoddy, P.O. *The Case for Appropriate Technology in the Mechanization of Gari Manufacture in Nigeria* (paper presented at the OECD Development Centre Conference on Low-Cost Technology: an inquiry into Outstanding Policy Issues) (OECD Development Centre, Paris, 1975)

Pack, H. 'The Choice of Techniques and Employment in the Textile Industry' in A.S. Bhalla (ed.), *Technology and Employment in Industry* (ILO, Geneva, 1975)

Palmer-Jones, R. and Halliday, D. *The Small-Scale Manufacture of Compound Animal-Feed* (TPI Report No. G.67, 1971).

Parry, J.P.M. *Review of Prospects for the Manufacture of Permanent Building Materials in the Juba Area of South Sudan* (Intermediate Technology Services/Regional Development Corporation of South Sudan, July 1975, mimeo.)

Powell, J.W. *A Review of Experience Gained from Three Projects at the Technology Consultancy Centre, University of Science and Technology, Kumasi, 1972/3* (paper presented at the University of Edinburgh Appropriate Technology Conference, September 1973), Part 2: Steel Bolt Production, Part 3: Broadloom Weaving

——, *Soap Pilot Plant – Review of the First Year's Progress* (Technology Consultancy Centre, University of Science and Technology, Kumasi, Ghana, 1973) and *Soap Pilot Plant Project – Review in Progress in 1974* (TCC, Kumasi, 1975)

Ranis, G. *Technology Choice, Employment and Growth* (Yale Economic Growth Center, Discussion Paper No. 97, 1970), p.16

Robbins, S.R.J. *The Manufacture of Dry-Cell Batteries* (Tropical Products Institute Report No. G.46, 1970)

Schwartz, S.L. 'Second-hand Machinery in Development: or How to Recognize a Bargain', *Journal of Development Studies*, vol. 9, no. 4 (1973)

SIET Institute *Employment, Technology and Development* (Clarendon Press, Oxford, 1975), Appendix D: A Study of Tractorization in India

Small Industry Development Network 'Mini Cement Plants: an Alternative Approach', *SIDN Newsletter*, vol. 1, no. 4 (1975)

Spurgeon, D. *Anyone for Instant Yams* (IDRC Reports, vol. 4, no. 2 (June 1975)

Stewart, F.J. 'Employment and Choice of Technique: Two Case Studies in
    Kenya' in D.P. Ghai and M. Godfrey (eds.), *Essays on Employment in Kenya*
    (East African Literature Bureau, 1974)
Tropical Products Institute *The Small-Scale Manufacture of Confectionery*
    (TPI Report No. 14/60, 1960)
UN Department of Economic and Social Affairs *Small Scale Power Generation:
    a Study for Pioneer Electrification Work: an Overall Review of Methods and
    Costs of Power Generation, with Particular Emphasis on Small-Scale
    Generating Plants for Pioneer Electrification Work* (UN, New York, 1967)
UN Economic Commission for Asia and the Far East *Small Industry Bulletin for
    Asia and the Far East* (UN, New York, annual)
UN Economic Commission for Latin America *Choice of Technologies in the
    Latin American Textile Industry* (UNECLA, 1966)
UN Industrial Development Organization *Boats from Ferro-Cement* (Utilization
    of Shipbuilding and Repair Facilities Series, no. 1) (UN, New York, 1972)
——, *Building Materials Industry*, UNIDO Monograph on Industrial Development
    no. 4 (UNIDO, Vienna, 1969)
——, *Report of Expert Group Meeting on the Selection of Textile Machinery
    in the Cotton Industry* (UNIDO, Vienna, 1967), ID/WG/8/1
——, *Seminar Report on the Development of the Leather and Leather Products
    Industries in Developing Countries: Regional Project for Africa* (UNIDO,
    Vienna, 1972)
Wells, Jr., L.T. 'Men and Machines in Indonesia's Light Manufacturing Industries',
    Bulletin of Indonesian Economic Studies, vol. IX, no. 3 (November 1973)

Handbooks, Manuals, Buyer's Guides and Technical Publications

Intermediate Technology Development Group, London *Appropriate Technology:*
    quarterly journal
——, *How to Make a Metal-Bending Machine* (Intermediate Technology
    Publications, London, 1973)
——, *Oil Drum Forges* (Intermediate Technology Publications, London, 1975)
——, *The Iron Foundry – an Industrial Profile* (Intermediate Technology
    Publications, London, 1975)
Volunteers in Technical Assistance, Inc. *Village Technology Handbook* (VITA,
    New York, 1970)
Watt, S.B. *A Manual on the Automatic Hydraulic Ram Pump* (Intermediate
    Technology Publications, London, 1975)

Some Relevant Bibliographies

Baranson, J. *Technology for Undeveloped Areas: an Annotated Bibliography*
    (Pergamon Press, Oxford, 1967)
Dean, G.C. *Technological Innovation in Chinese Industry* (Mansell, London, 1972)
Ganiere, N. *The Process of Industrialization of China: Primary Elements of an
    Analytical Bibliography* (OECD Development Centre, Paris, 1974)
Ganiere, N. *Transfer of Technology and Appropriate Techniques, a Bibliography*
    (OECD Development Centre, Paris, 1974)
Jackson, S. *Economically Appropriate Technologies for Developing Countries:*

a Survey (Overseas Development Council, Occasional Paper no. 3, Washington, 1972)

Bibliography – Additional

Alexander, P.C. *Industrial Estates in India* (Asia Publicity House, Bombay, 1963)

Cairncross, Alec and Puri, Mohinder (eds.) *Employment, Income Distribution and Development Strategy: Problems of the Developing Countries: Essays in Honor of Hans Singer* (Holmes and Meier, New York, 1976)

Employment and Development of Small Enterprises, Sector Policy Paper (World Bank, February 1978)

Johnston, B.F. and Kilby, Peter *Agriculture and Structural Transformation: Economic Strategies in Late-developing Countires* (Oxford University Press, Oxford, 1975)

Mellor, John W. *The New Economics of Growth* (Cornell University Press, Ithaca, 1976)

Rural Enterprise and Non-farm Employment, a World Bank paper (World Bank, January 1978)

6 ADMINISTRATION AND FINANCE

Kenneth Wren

6.1 Administration

Most, even the smallest, of the developing countries can boast a
medium-term socio-economic development plan. It provides the
strategic framework within which communities are enabled to develop.
In some cases the pace is slow and measured, but in others it must be
forced in an attempt to meet the growing pressures and demands of a
developing nation. 'Planned' development is an essential feature of any
attempt to succeed in the latter, where resources, in the sense of
organisation as well as capital investment, are focused on the
achievement of a given socio-economic objective, the goals of which
are clearly set out in a strategic plan for the country's development.

Each of the developing countries will have a view on whether these
objectives can best be achieved through central, regional and local
administrations. But these views will largely depend on the present
administrative arrangements for implementation of government policies
and most probably the degree of delegation possible from central to
more localised units of government. It is undesirable to be dogmatic as
to the emphasis to be placed at either central or local levels of
government, but it may be useful to offer some general comments on
the appropriate level, based on experience in the developing countries
to date.

It would be true to say that, save for the largest cities in the
developing world, the level of responsibility which most local
administrations are able to accept is limited. The reasons are varied,
but within the context of the need for fairly rapid expansion of the
community, generally include inadequate resources, which even though
supplemented by central agencies do not allow for the necessary
degree of expansion of services, and a lack of political direction which
tends to a more parochial rather than strategic outlook. For these
reasons, and also for the reason that so often new communities are
created where none existed previously, responsibility for achieving the
necessary objectives of the development must rest largely with either
national or regional government agencies. That is not to say the local
administrations do not have a part to play, indeed they have an

important role in satisfying the demand for local services generated by the growing community.

An essential element in any successful administrative unit is the political backing necessary to ensure the co-operation of other agencies in the provision of utilities and other components of any development. Certainly in the initial stages of the programme, both central and local political support is a prerequisite of success, to ensure an adequate supply of areas for new development and to obtain the agreement of both national and local agencies concerned in the provision of key services. This suggests that the optimum solution for planning, design and implementation of community development lies principally with national or regional government, probably through a locally based team, assisted as necessary by any local administration that might exist.

It is equally essential that any successful organisational solution must recognise the role that can be assumed by the community. Highly organised resident groups can clearly lead to reduced involvement by the public authorities and can greatly ease the latters' burden both administratively and in cost terms. This is very important where basic minimum-cost solutions are necessary, when settlers can be encouraged to organise themselves in achieving a level of services best suited to their particular requirements and their ability to pay for them.

Any administrative solution should recognise the important role of the private sector in the provision, financing and management of major elements of the development. There are examples where the private sector has not been encouraged in the earliest stages of development, only to find that when private-sector investment is required, entrenched pricing policies are a prohibiting factor against adequate returns and therefore a major deterrent against attracting the requisite amount of investment.

Finally, a major requirement of any organisational arrangement is that of flexibility and adaptability to change. During the process of implementation it may become apparent that changes of an administrative and organisational nature are called for, perhaps arising from the response of the settlers themselves, or from the growing competence of the administrative unit created for the project.

6.1.1 Size of Administrative Unit

Naturally the number of staff required in a project agency can only be determined in relationship to the scope of its activities and the size of the programme being undertaken. Bearing in mind the inherent objective of producing cost-effective development, the aim must also be to ensure that administrative costs are kept to the minimum, if the settler is not to be penalised, or the government's burden so heavy as to lead to possible abandonment of the project. Thus an administrative structure which limits activities to the key elements of development is preferable, suggesting that the agency should deal with the development of the basic infrastructure of the community and other general neighbourhood provisions, including the co-ordination of the social and welfare service provision. The private sector, where appropriate, and the residents themselves should then be encouraged to contribute towards the achievement of the new community's objectives, through the provision of commercial development in the former case and collectively in the provision of dwelling units.

A new administrative unit, created for the purpose of developing a new community, will assume responsibilities which normally belong to local government and national government line agencies, but are appropriately transferred to the new unit for ease of implementation and effective co-ordination in the provision of project components. This creates the possibility for secondment of personnel to the new unit from these key agencies, thus offering a possibility for reducing administrative costs to be recovered from the new development.

6.1.2 Organisational Aspects of Development

Despite the overall goal of limiting the duties and responsibilities of a new administrative unit, and therefore the costs, the unit's responsibilities in developing the new community will nevertheless be still considerable. This will be particularly so where new employment opportunities are to be created for the new community as part of the overall development strategy.

The management of the new unit will require the establishment of clear and relatively unchanging operational objectives within an overall policy framework. Working relationships between the management and other interested and responsible government agencies should be established, and the terms of reference for the unit's contractual relationships with private industry and developers should be decided. The management should seek to create the role of a public entrepreneur, able to initiate and develop the means of managing public financial resources in the most cost-effective way. Its guiding principle should be that funds from all sources are scarce and that their recycling is to be encouraged as far as possible. Certain key issues will require more specific attention. For example, it should be made clear from the outset of development what the policy should be with regard to land pricing. Later in this chapter a methodology is outlined which relates to land transactions likely to be experienced during the course of development and how they relate in turn to the creation of a pricing policy for land disposal, whether by freehold or leasehold. It is for these and other reasons that the new unit should be separately accountable for the investment in land and other developments. The system adopted should certainly provide for the creation of a separate land account. Land, as in reality, must be considered to be a valuable and largely irreplaceable asset. Not to take account of this and to allow the values created to benefit others will severely reduce the financial performance of the new unit.

The unit should control the rate, type, location and quality of all development. Above all, the necessary funds should be made available to enable the unit to achieve the level of capital investment required in infrastructure, roads and open spaces. The development should be seen as a partnership between the public and private sectors. Each party to the development will have a commitment of resources and will depend upon the other side fulfilling obligations to ensure that those commitments are not prejudiced or put at risk. A vital element in the success of any new community is not only the extent to which the new unit can develop its facilities at the required rate, but also the extent to which it can control and limit unplanned, unco-ordinated and disruptive developments.

It should be emphasised that the need is for management, through its powers, responsibilities and functions, to perform the foregoing tasks in the most efficient and sensitive way possible. Above all, it must be seen to be creating an organic, vital community where people are happy and relatively content.

6.1.3 Management Team

The development and subsequent management of a large new community requires considerable administrative and professional resources organised in an integrated team, and given strong and responsive direction. These executive functions will preferably become the responsibility of a managing director who, with a team of professional officers, will perform the task of planning, developing and running the new town. The managing director's responsibilities will be twofold; to give direction, in general terms, to his team of chief officers; and to represent the activities of the organisation to the outside world — government, other public agencies and private-sector interests.

Ideally, in exercising the first of these two roles, the managing director would co-ordinate the team of chief officers, each of whom would have a functional responsibility. He would require a very small staff, sufficient to ensure effective liaison between the various officers and their departments; and to deal with the outside agencies as suggested.

The following key development functions will appropriately fall to the responsibility of separate departments, each headed by a professional skilled in these aspects:

(1)   planning and design;
(2)   construction;
(3)   financial management;
(4)   promotion of housing, commerce and industry.

In addition an administrative department should be set up to deal with the operation and functioning of the new agency. Its functions would include general office administration, secretarial, office maintenance and repair and transport. Additionally it would embrace personnel administration, public relations aspects not covered by the promotion department, and a small legal section.

Finally, it will be necessary to establish a separate functional department which would be responsible for the management of all types of property, especially residential, owned by the new unit; including general maintenance. A large new development may mean weekly or monthly collection of several thousand rents and the inspection, maintenance and repair of the same number of dwellings. Defaulters will have to be pursued and changes in tenancies for one reason or another will have to be arranged. (The facilities of the banking institutions can be utilised to mitigate the burden of collection and recovery of rents and charges due from inhabitants.)

The maintenance and management of the roads, drainage, water supplies, open spaces, etc. may ultimately fall to the responsibility of a separate local government administration; but until that day arrives the new unit will be responsible, as suggested, for this function and will have the task of recovering charges from the inhabitants, sufficient to meet the costs incurred.

In order that the social and welfare need of the growing population of the town should be looked after effectively, there should be a social services department which could deal with both the welfare needs of the population as well as the co-ordination of social and recreational activities. To create a department of this kind could never, however, be an adequate substitution for the spontaneous organisation of the cultural, religious and recreational life of the town by the people themselves. But as a means of introducing these essential elements into the community in the early phases of its existence such a department could perform an invaluable service.

The transition from a collection of new housing areas to an established organic urban community is a difficult step, and as a consequence the incidence of social and family problems is often considerably higher than in established urban areas. The appointment of qualified and experienced social and welfare workers is an essential part of the management structure of a new town.

The four key development departments' responsibilities would be as follows:

(1) Planning and design: this department would encompass demographic and economic studies, engineering and general urban design. Its key task would be the preparation (or updating) of the development plan for the town, the setting of design and economic briefs to architects and engineers and the provision of guidelines for the private development agencies. It would set up a monitoring process for updating the plan to respond to changes arising during the course of development and would contribute towards the introduction of a programme and budgeting system in conjunction with other departments. Personnel to be involved would embrace many of the professions — town planners, architects, engineers (civil and structural), economists, demographers and sociologists.

(2) The construction department would also include many of the disciplines listed above but would seek the additional skills in contract negotiation (tender procedures) and supervision of works. Its main responsibility would be to ensure the implementation of the development plan at the required pace of the programme.

(3) The financial management department, apart from fulfilling the service function of the new town organisation such as payments of salaries and invoices, etc., collection of revenues, and raising of finance (public and private funds), will have a vital role to play in ensuring the viability of the various developments. It will prepare a financial plan, based on the physical plan adopted, which will incorporate the costs of the phased development (including financing charges) and the rate of recovery. It will be concerned with the viability of individual projects, developing financial performance criteria for each type of development and for monitoring the progress of the financial plan. Professional skills

required would include accountants, economists and business graduates.

(4) The department concerned with promotion and attraction of development to the town will have the vital responsibility of ensuring that the pace of development is maintained through the timely introduction of private investment interests. It will be responsible initially for promotion of industry, will negotiate the terms of disposal (freehold and leasehold) for land and buildings and will play a key role in the negotiations with private sector developers it is hoped will be attracted to the town. One of the department's key objectives will be to develop a pricing structure that will allow private interests to operate within an overall framework. Despite the fact that the main industry may often be directed to the town through central government policy, there will nevertheless be a need to 'sell' the town, and the commercial and investment opportunities within it. It cannot be assumed that retailers and other sources of jobs and services will simply be drawn to the town; it will be necessary to sell the concept of the town to them, and provide them with the appropriate site for development. To perform this function adequately, there should be a separate commercial section within this department, with sufficient resources to enable it to seek out the new investors. This section will have the responsibility for the introduction of such necessary items of the urban fabric as banks, shops, offices, insurance companies, doctors, dentists, restaurants, suppliers of all the necessary goods, services and equipment for a rapidly growing community. The personnel employed in the department will need to be skilled negotiators in real estate and general estate management.

It is not possible at this stage to specify the actual numbers of managerial, professional, technical, clerical and manual workers that would be required. This is clearly dependent on the scale of the operation and the efficiency of the existing agencies. Nevertheless a commitment to develop a large new community, including industrial areas, could also imply a commitment to a substantial number of jobs and salaries. The development of the town would move slowly from a contracts and development phase to one in which the town as an urban community was slowly establishing itself. The personnel requirements would similarly change over time to match the growing needs of the emerging urban community, though they might not necessarily diminish.

Figure 6.1 is a graphic presentation of the organisation most suited to perform the development of a new town within the context

Figure 6.1: Organisation Chart

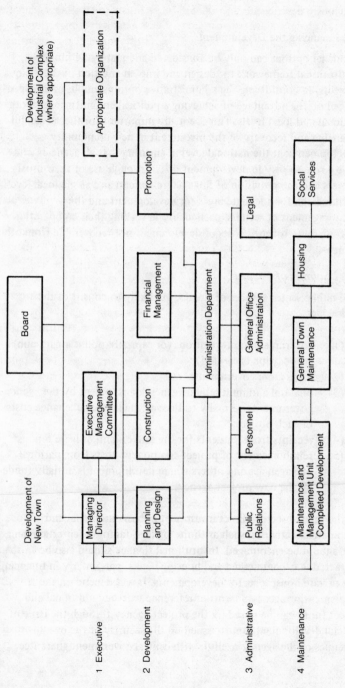

Note: All heads of department form the Executive Management Committee

previously described.

6.2 Financing the Development

Financial options can only be considered adequately within the institutional framework for design and implementation of the various projects. In considering the administrative options emphasis has been placed on the advantage of achieving a political commitment at both national and local levels. This is equally important for the successful financing and recovery of the investment in new community developments; at the national level in ensuring that all agencies who have a role to play in development do so through use of their usual powers and the provision of financial resources; and at the local level in the search for adequate areas for development and the encouragement of settlers, particularly in seeking their co-operation to contribute towards costs of development not recoverable from other sources.

6.2.1 Sources of Finance

The public sector sources of finance are likely to consist of the following:

(1) government appropriations (or capitalisation if a para-public corporation is created);
(2) loans from government;
(3) bilateral and multilateral agency loans, onlent by the government, normally to finance the foreign exchange costs of each project;
(4) receipts from residents for the sale of land or lease rentals;
(5) reimbursement of project component costs from national line agencies and others where development is initially funded by the new project agency.

In the private sector, direct investment in basic industrial and commercial activities, such as shops, offices, factories, entertainments etc. should be encouraged. Institutional finance should also be attracted, e.g. commercial and housing banks, particularly in financing the private housing sector developments. It will depend on the implementing agency's terms of reference whether additional and direct funds can be raised by the project agency through the issue of special development bonds; issued on the security of the overall revenues of the agency itself or with central government guarantee.

6.2.2 Land Transactions and Land-pricing Policy

If the private sector is to be involved in the development, a charging
policy must be evolved. The value of the land in its present state, i.e.
lacking major services, is undoubtedly very low, but once designated
as a site for a large new development, and when essential services and
infrastructure have been brought to the site, considerable increases in
value will be discernible. As the development proceeds and the
population, purchasing power and general level of demand for land and
property increase, very substantial increases in value will occur. To
allow these increases to fall into the hands of private owners or
occupiers is to lose the opportunity to return to the public sector its
investments in infrastructure and urban services. The gains or increases
are those which occur as a result not of investment or risk-taking by
the private sector, but as a result of the fact that a new urban
community with its own market values has been created. These gains
therefore should be retained as far as possible for the benefit of the
community.

Rents of dwellings and any subsidies that may be granted must
clearly be accounted for separately, but to do this effectively the unit
must know very precisely what the actual or true costs of the dwelling
are. These costs will include not only the actual dwelling superstructure
costs, but the costs of capital items of infrastructure, water reticulation,
sewerage from the dwelling to the main sewer in the street, electricity,
telephone and gas pipelines, etc., and finally an element for land costs.

Initially, the various land uses in the plan can be divided between
land having intrinsic or saleable value and land which does not. Costs
will have been calculated in respect of:

> raw land cost (acquisition cost plus legal and administrative costs);
> off-site strategic services to the site boundary (to be met by the
> executing agency);
> on-site development costs (distribution roads, water and sewerage
> network, public open spaces, gas and electricity distribution).

A series of land uses will be identified covering the following broad
categories (excluding land used for utility services, roads, etc.):

(1) residential;
(2) commercial — central and local;
(3) industrial;

(4)   public open spaces and other amenity land;

(5)   land for community development: schools, health/welfare
        centres and meeting places;

(6)   other land uses (airports, public buildings, churches,
        mosques, etc.)

An average land plus general services cost can be allocated to each
identified area of land use, thus setting the framework within which
the land-pricing policy can be determined. It should be emphasised
that the cost of services indicated above relates only to general site
development costs applicable to the whole site. There will be additional
site development costs applicable to specific land uses incurred over
and above these broad costs, e.g. residential site reticulation costs,
connecting roads and footpaths, service connections, etc. These costs
will be site-specific to land use.

First, it is important to determine the price to be attached to land
for the strictly non-commercial uses. This will follow normal national
or local practices. The items (4), (5) and (6) fall within this category.
It may be necessary to dedicate public open space to whichever local
administrative agency exists or is to be set up for the purpose, at nil
cost. Similarly, land for community development may have to be
passed over to the appropriate agency at either nil or basic cost.

If land in the categories identified above is to be dedicated at nil
cost, then it will be necessary to recalculate the average cost of land to
be attached to the remaining land uses with an intrinsic value. For the
purposes of this chapter and to demonstrate a methodology, let it be
assumed that public open space and other amenity land has been
dedicated at nil value, and that basic costs have been attached to other
items, as at (3) and (6). The following table demonstrates the possible
surpluses/deficits from generated development activity.

The figures in Table 6.1 are in 'units', as the principle remains the
same in any currency.

Since this table is prepared in absolute terms, no time element has
been attached to the costs of development and the realised values. In
practice, however, costs of development will be phased and values
realised over the normal period of development. The realisation of
values is somewhat delayed in all developments, therefore in calculating
the average allocated cost per hectare, some interest element must be
included to cover the period of delay between the creation and
realisation of values.

It will be necessary for the new unit to determine from the start of

Table 6.1: Land Uses: Costs and Realised Values

Land Use		Ha.	Allocated cost	Values realised	Surplus +	Deficit –
1 Residential	(1)	150	750	375	–	375
	(2)	300	1,500	1,500	–	–
	(3)	150	750	1,125	375	–
	(4)	50	250	500	250	–
2 Commercial		10	50	500	450	–
3 Industrial		50	250	750	500	–
4 Community development						
Schools		40	200	200	–	–
Health/welfare		10	50	50	–	–
Meeting places		5	25	25	–	–
5 Other uses		35	175	175	–	–
Sub-total		800	4,000	5,200	1,575	375
6 Land used for utilities, roads and open spaces		200	–	–	–	–
Total development area		1,000	4,000	5,200	1,575	375

Notes:
a. Assumed that area of development covers 1,000 hectares, of which 80 per cent is saleable land.
b. Assumed that allocated cost of total development is 4,000 units of currency.
c. Assumed that residential area represents 65 per cent of total development area and values realised represent 50 per cent, 100 per cent, 150 per cent and 200 per cent of basic cost ((1) to (4)).
d. Commercial areas of 10 hectares and industrial area 50 hectares are valued at 10 times and three times cost.
e. Allocated costs exclude interest charges prior to land value realisation but include overhead/design costs.

development what its policy towards land should be. Sales or long leases of land even in the early years of development should carry with them an element of price which represents the worth of the land within the new town context. The need for this approach will be greatest in the case of land which is to be used for commercial or industrial uses. These are the ones that yield the highest values and should reflect true market value at the time of sale, the levels of which will change during the development period. The higher-income residential areas are extremely likely to generate surpluses, as are the commercial and industrial areas; while the lower-income residential areas may not generate sufficient value to meet allocated costs of development.

It is therefore necessary to prepare a cash flow statement in respect of basic costs and values and to calculate the discounted value of the surpluses indicated at Table 6.1. The following cash flow statement assumed costs and values as shown in Table 6.1 which make no adjustment for the time element in terms of interest charges.

From the cash flow statement (Table 6.2) it will be seen that the

Table 6.2: Land Transactions: Cash Flow Statement

Item	Total	Year 1	Year 2	Year 3	Year 4	Year 5
Costs in Currency Units						
1 Land acquisition	400	400				
2 Strategic services provided by implementing agency	1,200	800	400			
3 General site development costs						
(a) Roads						
(b) Sewerage and sewage disposal						
(c) Water supplies	2,400	700	500	400	400	400
(d) Electricity						
(e) Gas						
(f) Open spaces						
	4,000	1,900	900	400	400	400
Values in Currency Units						
4 Residential	3,500	300	800	800	800	800
5 Commercial	500	100	100	200	50	50
6 Industrial	750	50	150	150	200	200
7 Community development	275	75	50	50	50	50
8 Other land uses	175	25	25	25	25	25
	5,200	550	1,125	1,225	1,125	1,125
Net surplus	1,200	—	225	825	725	725
(Deficit)	—	(1,350)	—	—	—	—
	1,200	(1,350)	225	825	725	725
Net present value (discounting @ 10 per cent)[a]	524	(1,227)	186	620	495	450

Note: a. The rate at which costs should be discounted will equate to the average borrowing rate on funds raised for the project.

original crude surplus of 1,200 currency units is reduced to 524 units in net present value terms.

6.2.3 Detailed Financial Viability Study and Overall Cash Flow

The foregoing analysis will have enabled a check to be made on land transactions; related to original land cost, development costs (on- and off-site) and estimated land values to be realised, based on a forecast of market price for various land uses and their rate of absorption. The fact that notional capital values have been attached to land should not be taken as an indication that a policy of freehold disposal has been adopted. The use of notional capital values is necessary to confirm the viability of the determined land-pricing policy. If leasehold disposal of land is preferred, so long as the leasehold rents are related to such notional capital values then the general effect will be the same. The arguments between freehold and leasehold disposal of land are dealt with elsewhere in Chapter 10.

The more detailed financial appraisal of the project will probably include the cost of buildings, where the implementing agency becomes involved in the building of superstructures. However, should other agencies become exclusively involved in this element of the development (e.g. private developers for housing; private/public agencies for commerce, industry and other community development), only the land transactions will be included in the more comprehensive financial appraisal undertaken.

The ultimate cash flow statement prepared will probably include the following items:

(1) Expenditure:
   (a) land acquisition costs;
   (b) off-site works;
   (c) on-site development costs (to be undertaken by the executing agency);
   (d) building construction costs (to be undertaken by the executing agency);
   (e) design costs and administrative overheads;
   (f) loan charges: principal interest;
   (g) other expenses.
(2) Income:
   (a) loans raised;
   (b) grants or capitalisation of executive agency;
   (c) sale of land: freehold/leasehold;

(d) sale of buildings: freehold/leasehold;
(e) other income.
(3) Surplus/deficit of items (1) and (2).
(4) Cumulative surpluses/deficits.
(5) Net present value/internal rate of return of transactions.

6.2.4 Apportionment of Costs and their Recovery

Having established the sources of finance for the development, certain
principles should be adopted in seeking to allocate the costs to the
different agencies. Where national line and local agencies, in the
exercise of their normal functions, would expect to provide some of
the components of development, then in so far as the project agency
in their capacity as the implementing agency do so, the costs should be
recovered from the responsible agency. In some instances it may be
appropriate for the responsible agency to provide such components
independently of the main contract, thus relieving the project agency
of the responsibility for the initial funding and ultimate recovery.

It is important to ensure that adequate and timely financing
arrangements are made by the various agencies responsible for
components of development. Formal liaison machinery between all
agencies involved in the development is of considerable advantage in
ensuring a smooth programme.

In the first instance, the preparation of a schedule of project
component costs, identifying the agency responsible for financing,
design and implementation should be undertaken as a basis for
discussions and agreement with all agencies having an involvement in
the project. This might be prepared on the basis outlined in Figure 6.2.

6.3 Inter-agency Liaison Machinery

To ensure that there is sufficient lead time for each agency to approve
the level of services necessary and make adequate budget provision,
early and effective liaison arrangements must be set up for each project.

It might be considered that there would be advantage in setting up
two formal liaison groups, one covering the provision of utilities and
infrastructure; the other covering the provision of community facilities.
Though this is not imperative, it may facilitate the discussion of two
very different types of components.

Figure 6.2: Project Components

Project Component	Agency Responsible for:		
	Financing	Design	Implementation
1 Land Acquisition			
2 Land Reclamation/Fill			
3 Flood Protection			
4 Roads			
5 Drainage			
6 Water Supply			
7 Sanitation			
8 Sewerage			
9 Street Lighting			
10 Community Facilities			
i Schools			
ii Health Centres			
iii Welfare Centres			

(These main headings can be broken down into detailed components as necessary)

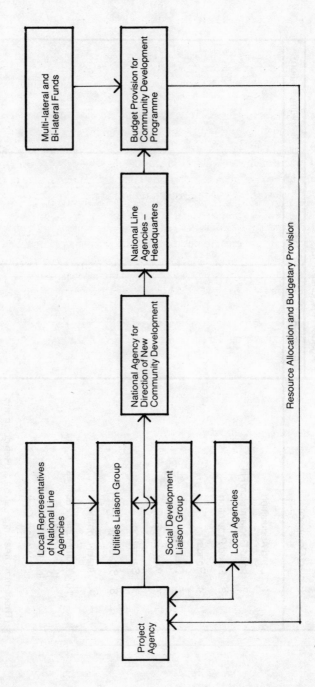

Figure 6.3: Budget Provision for New Community Development

The groups' terms of reference should broadly include:

(1)   effective arrangements for exchange of data; plans; programmes, etc.;

(2)   discussion and agreement on the level and standard of provision;

(3)   determination of responsible agency for design and implementation of components; planning the detailed phasing;

(4)   agreement on costs; level and timing of budget provision;

(5)   investigation and resolution of any difficulties arising in the timely development of each project.

It is likely that initial discussions in the liaison groups will be conducted by national agency local representatives. The machinery should allow for them to consult with the appropriate national agency headquarters if appropriate. It may also be necessary for the national agency responsible for the development of the new programme to have formal communication with these national line agencies when difficulties arise in the provision of components.

Efficient arrangements need to be agreed for draw-down funds agreed to be met through the budget agency. Forecasts of likely investment must be made by each project agency and advances made perhaps on a quarterly basis to the latter, with adjustments if necessary.

It is clear that the various agencies will be unable to agree on every conceivable occasion the precise terms of cost apportionment, and adequate arrangements therefore need to be made to settle differences to avoid delays in the programme.

6.4 Continuing Maintenance and Management of Completed Development

As the town develops, the costs of running the key services such as water supplies, roads, sewerage and drainage, plus some social and recreational services, will rapidly increase and a system of recovery of such costs from the beneficiaries will have to be introduced. It is therefore extremely important that from the outset of development a system is worked out whereby inhabitants begin to contribute immediately to the amenities from which they benefit. Delay in introducing such charges will only lead to resistance once the decision is taken to do so; the habit must therefore be encouraged from the outset.

A number of methods for recovery of such costs can be introduced, but must generally accord with local custom where possible. It would be appropriate to introduce a system of user charges where the commodity provided is capable of precise measurement, e.g. water and electricity. This is clearly the most equitable method of recovery of costs related to benefit received.

More general costs of management and maintenance that cannot be so measured must form part of a general levy, based as far as possible on degree of benefit enjoyed and ability to pay. In this respect, a tax on property, while having the merit of simplicity and stability, is very highly regressive in its impact on the inhabitants. It would therefore be more appropriate if other forms of local taxation were introduced, at least to supplement the revenues derived from a property tax − if its introduction becomes inevitable. This might take the form of a business tax or a sales tax.

It is likely that the most successful system will be a composite of user charges, real estate tax and a form of sales/business tax. In the early years of development, however, when few residents exist, the costs of maintenance etc. are unlikely to be fully recovered. It is important therefore to allow for this shortfall to be taken into account as a cost of overall development. Certainly, such losses will have to be financed initially by this method, even though, eventually, accumulated losses may be fully recovered from future surpluses on the maintenance and management account as the town develops and the volume of taxes increases.

Apart from these likely early financing difficulties, the system of recovering costs should follow the important principle that current costs should be met from current revenues, and the use of surplus funds arising from capital transactions should be avoided. Failure to introduce a viable system of taxation to cover such costs can only lead to insurmountable problems in the later stages of development.

Part Three

PHYSICAL DEVELOPMENT

7   ENVIRONMENTAL EVALUATION AND DESIGN

Richard Westmacott and Christopher Blandford

7.1 Evaluation

7.1.1 Introduction

As part of the formulation of national and regional development
policies, it is assumed that broad areas will have been identified for
development. It should be emphasised that this process must be carried
out with an understanding of the ecological implications of alternative
policies, and that the locational criteria used in assessing the suitability
of alternative sites for alternative uses should have been chosen after a
careful study of the region and its resources. The areas identified will
probably contain a number of specific sites where a new community or
settlement could be planned and built. A careful environmental
assessment of the whole of the designated area is important to ensure
the suitability of land for development and to minimise adverse impacts.
The analysis technique is summarised in Figure 7.1.

Any landscape is unique, and there can be no definite standards or
rules for site selection. However, a method can be designed which, in
principle, can be used to analyse any area. In order to demonstrate a
method hypothetical areas are described and analysed in this chapter.
The principles used in the evaluation are important here, rather than
the site itself. Thus the data given are not detailed. Indeed, in most real
cases there will be gaps in the data, particularly those dealing with the
natural environment. Suggestions are made, however, as to where data
searches can be made and where 'short cuts' can be used if data prove
to be unavailable.

Three examples are given in this chapter to demonstrate the
approach to environmental evaluation and design:

(1)   an arid sub-tropical desert region;
(2)   a wet tropical rain forest region;
(3)   a semi-arid savannah region.

Only the first is illustrated graphically.

The area shown in Figure 7.2 is representative of sub-tropical desert
areas with hot, dry climates. It is a landscape of gravels, sands and salt

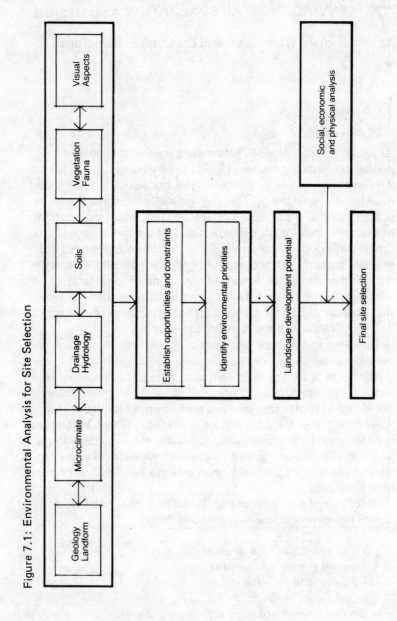

Figure 7.1: Environmental Analysis for Site Selection

Figure 7.2: Study Area; General Characteristics

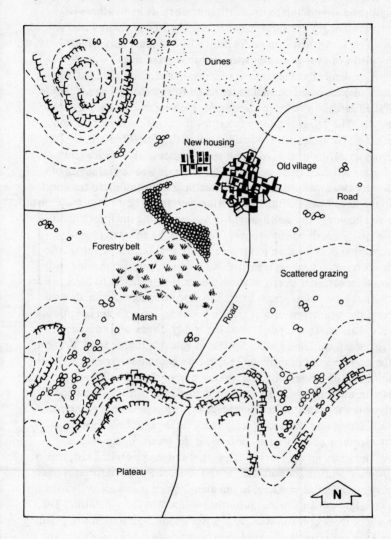

flats with only scattered pockets of vegetation. A rocky scarp to the south and an outcrop to the north provide relief in an otherwise overwhelmingly flat and windy terrain. The lack of rainfall has resulted in an economy based on pastoralism with the usual associated problems of over-grazing of sparse scrub vegetation.

A settlement at the crossing of a major and minor road has long been an oasis based on well water taken from a shallow aquifer below. Walled gardens provide protection for growing dates, vegetables and fodder. The village is also a market for the camels and goats of the nomadic herdsmen who live and travel in the desert hinterland. The compact nature of the old buildings contrasts starkly with a new housing scheme. These bear evidence to the increasing influence of development investment from oil wealth and the improved transport to the large town 20 miles away. However, the policy of the government is to encourage the development of self-sustaining small communities. To satisfy development pressure, a site must be selected for the expansion of the village or for an entirely new settlement. Here, the environmental analysis is carried out independent of economic and social aspects, but clearly the analysis must be sensitive to these factors.

The wet tropical area is located in sharply rolling terrain, derived from the weathering of soft granite bedrock. The soils are lateritic and very shallow. The tropical forest is a highly diverse and complex ecosystem, containing many species of valuable timber trees. However, the large number of different species, the enormous size of trees and difficulty of accessibility make extraction of timber a difficult process. Hence, although there is a growing demand for tropical hardwoods, there is a tendency either to manage the forest in a more economically exploitable way (for example by reducing the number of species and by shortening the rotation) or to clear the forest for agriculture.

The study area is sparsely populated and under-utilised but, with a growing demand for both timber and food, the tropical forest is under very considerable pressure. In our area, logging teams are systematically extracting valuable timber prior to development for agriculture. The scale of these operations requires government organisation and planning and the social implications of switching from a subsistence economy to a cash-crop economy (and one which is very dependent on world markets) are far-reaching.

The environmental goals are, in principle, the same as for the arid example, but the problems in achieving these goals are, of course, quite different. Environmentally the hazards of development of the tropical forest are serious. The soils are very shallow and the heavy rainfall leaches out most of the plant nutrients. The forest vegetation counteracts this problem by keeping most of the nutrients 'locked up' in plant tissue rather than in the soil. When the forest is cleared and the slash is burned, these nutrients are mostly returned to the soil but are vulnerable to leaching by rainfall. During the actual clearance process even a moderately heavy storm will result in run-off and erosion which will lead to the loss of topsoil and nutrients and the sedimentation and eutrophication of receiving waters (rivers and lakes).

Besides exposing soils to erosion and leaching, the development of farming in the tropics will frequently result in exposure of lateritic soils to sun and rain, and the process of laterisation can turn these soils into a pavement of hard rock within a few years. Perhaps to avoid this problem, traditional forms of agriculture in wet tropical areas are usually shifting types which tend to mimic the natural forest by keeping as dense a vegetation cover as possible, and encouraging regeneration of the jungle as fast as possible.

Although even rubber plantations and oil palms achieve some of the soil-protective characteristics of the natural forest, the scale of these developments causes concern for the stability of the ecosystem. In ecological terms, these developments involve replacing one of the most complex and diverse ecosystems on earth with what virtually amounts to a monoculture, or at the best an ecosystem of great simplicity, covering vast areas, and consequently vulnerable to disease and pest epidemics.

The location and form of urban areas will, to a very large extent, be determined by the land use of the hinterland. Negative locational factors such as avoiding highly productive agricultural soils, areas susceptible to flooding, erosion-prone steep areas, etc. should be taken into account at the earliest stages of planning.

In semi-arid savannah areas, the environmental problems associated with development are different from those in wetter tropical regions or in arid areas. The soils are very fragile, often laterites, but are protected by grassland, which can withstand prolonged dry periods. However, over-grazing or over-cropping may expose soil to both erosion and laterisation. Most areas of savannah would be vegetated with sparse woodland were it not for the practice of burning to convert it to range land. The management of good range land to prevent damage from over-grazing is a highly skilled task. Unfortunately efforts to farm these areas more intensively for tillage crops have often met with disaster.

The availability of water is frequently the limiting factor for the intensification of agriculture in these areas, but even if supplies are plentiful there are hazards involved. The dangers of laterisation and erosion remain, but irrigation may also result in a rapid increase in the concentration of salt in the soil. Irrigation water will contain some dissolved salts and if the concentration is high and the evaporation rapid, the build-up of salt in the soil may soon reach a point where it becomes toxic.

It is important to stress that an environmental analysis is a crucial step in development planning. A thorough understanding and response to environmental hazards can avoid natural disasters and adverse impacts and can enhance land values. Both wet and arid tropical environments demonstrate some of the worst extremes of climate which, if ignored, can cause considerable and unnecessary expense (e.g. cooling of buildings, loss of soil, lack of water, etc.). In order to develop an ecologically stable settlement a respect for the complexity of the natural environment is fundamental. The environmental goals to be achieved in the site selection process can therefore be stated as follows:

(1) to minimise the impact of a proposed development on the natural systems of the environment;

(2) to highlight the areas of environmental significance, areas of high ecological sensitivity, and areas containing unique natural features;

(3) to conserve the natural resources and to protect the regenerative capabilities of the natural processes of the area;

(4) to recognise the opportunities offered by the landscape character and natural processes of the area in the design process;

(5) to provide safe, rational and ecologically sound guidelines for directing the location and form of development in the designated area.

7.1.2 Landscape Elements

Landscape is best understood by describing the processes which have created it. An understanding of the observable natural environment and the ecological systems which shape it are necessary in order to plan for and prescribe land uses.

The complexity of a natural landscape can be simplified and summarised in describing systematically its geology, land form, climate, hydrology, soils, fauna and vegetation. Although each can be described in terms of several natural processes, the key factors relevant to the

overall objective of assessing the developmental potential of the area
are best summarised on a series of maps. For the example used here,
descriptive information is kept to a minimum since it only serves, first,
to demonstrate the type of data which is required and second, to
indicate factors which should be identified, summarised and recorded.

7.1.3 Geology and Land Form

Geological surveys are generally available at a regional scale. Mineral
and water resources which are economic to extract will often have led
to more detailed local surveys. However, frequently there are
insufficient detailed local data covering such topics as ground-water
availability, fault zones or breaking capacity, any of which could be
important locational factors. In some areas, the presence of a valuable
mineral, oil for instance, may have resulted in an unusual amount of
available data. However, this may provide invaluable information on
the local aquifers, their productivity and their sources of recharge (see
under Drainage and Hydrology). The geological bedrock may also
provide a resource for building materials which is worth recording. In
addition, such information will provide the planner with a better
understanding of the topography and surface features of the area.

Contour maps are usually available in sufficient detail to allow at
least a superficial assessment of land form as a limiting factor in
development. However, as the mapping of a number of important
development constraints (e.g. slopes, degree of slope, flood plains,
surface drainage) requires interpretation of reliable contour information,
a more detailed topographic survey will usually have to be
commissioned before more detailed design work can begin.

In the sub-tropical desert example, the lack of vegetation emphasises
land form. In this case, interbedded limestones and sandstones of
varying hardness are fundamental to the division of the area into a
lowland plain and desert plateau (hammada). The dramatic relief of
the scarp-face, the dry river beds (or wadis) and the rocky out-crops
(jebals) bear evidence to the strength of water erosion in what appears
to be a totally dry landscape. The forms of dunes and alluvial fans are
less dramatic but still indicate their wind- or water-borne origin. Both
provide evidence of the climatic forces and directions of drainage in the
landscape. The salt flats (sabkhas), easily definable by their white crusts
of salt, indicate drainage directions which may otherwise be
indistinguishable in an imperceptibly sloping plain or plateau. The
steepness of slope is frequently one of the most important limitations
for both urban and rural development. The degree of slope will be

Figure 7.3: Study Area; Land Form

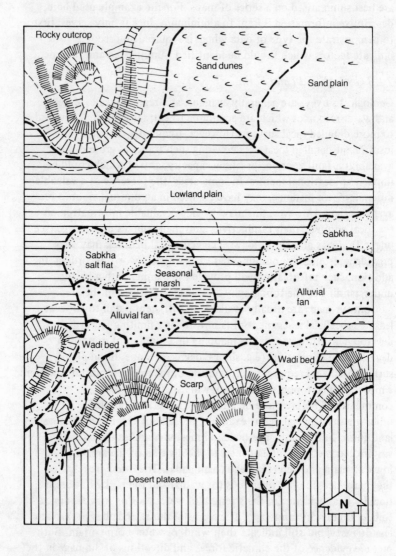

   Cliffs/rock outcrops

   Slope gradient > 10%

important in the location of buildings, services (particularly sewers and roads) and is also an important factor in designing measures to minimise erosion and run-off during and after development.

Four or five divisions of different slope gradients can be expressed as percentages. In the arid sub-tropics example only slopes of more than 10 per cent are emphasised as being too steep or unstable for building development purposes. Although not relevant in the dry arid context where insolation is more or less evenly distributed, slope 'aspect' (i.e. direction to which it faces relative to the sun) is a further interpretation of land form, which is an important locational factor.

In contrast to the arid sub-tropical example, the dense vegetation of the tropical jungle obscures land form so efficiently that topographic surveys carried out by aerial methods are subject to considerable error. Unfortunately, the difficulty of carrying out ground surveys is extreme and involves the laborious work of cutting transects. Consequently, the jungle is frequently cleared prior to detailed contour map preparation and hence the planner must strive to be as flexible as possible in preparing conceptual plans. Wet tropical regions contain a wide range of geologic and topographic conditions. However, a strongly rolling topography with a granite bedrock is representative of areas widely distributed throughout the tropics and has been chosen for the wet tropical example. The soils derived from the weathering of this material are laterites, but in the study area there are only two isolated areas where the laterite is of sufficient quality to make it worth while exploiting for road construction on site. There are no clays on site which can be utilised for the large-scale manufacture of building components, although small scattered deposits do occur. There are no other minerals on the site which can be exploited economically.

The topography is rolling, resulting from the weathering of the soft granite. Although slopes in excess of 10 per cent are quite limited in extent, generally following the valley sides, steep slopes are undoubtedly a major constraint to development as they are the principal factor affecting soil erodibility, workability in farming and general accessibility, and will of course result in higher engineering costs in building construction.

Capability for agricultural development is determined mainly by slope characteristics and soil type. Soil types usually reflect the land form closely (thinner eroded soils on the valley sides, deeper soils on flatter plateaus, and alluvial deposits in the valley bottoms). Slopes, in themselves, may not be a limitation to agriculture, but the susceptibility of slopes to erosion, particularly during the monsoon, excludes the

steeper slopes from agricultural practices, and may require modified
agricultural practices on lesser slopes (e.g. terracing or contour
cultivation and planting).

Land form is also a major limitation for urban development and will
be an important constraint, particularly in the planning of sewers and
roads. Minimising the cost of sewer construction usually requires a
gravity system, which will often be planned to follow the stream valleys.
Ridge (or watershed) routes for roads will minimise stream crossings
and flooding problems and will also serve the prime development land
plateaus). In very flat areas, the problem of impeded storm drainage
may result in stagnation and a consequent health hazard. There is also
the problem of obtaining sufficient fall in gravity sewers in flat areas.

The example for semi-arid tropical areas is set on a broad upland
plateau (elevation 1,750m). The land forms are very gently rolling
with stream valleys sharply defined, and cut deeply into the feralitic
subsoil. The soils which are lateritic are derived from weathered granite.

7.1.4 Climate

Some climatic statistics are usually available, often from the nearest
airport. Depending on their detail, they will require a varying amount
of interpretation.

In the sub-tropical desert area rainfall is limited to 100-500mm per
year, and may be erratic in its distribution through the year. A
pronounced 'wet' season, however, occurs in winter. Precipitation falls
in small but intense amounts. Temperatures are high (40°-48°C
maximum in summer) year round, but diurnal variations at ground level
are extreme. Winds blow in prevailing directions more continuously and
at more constant speed than in temperate climates.

In the example (see Figure 7.4) local variations will result in a
'microclimate' within the broad description outlined above. For
instance, the increased elevation of the scarp produces a slight increase
in rainfall. The wind from the north-west blows cool or cold in winter
but dry and dusty in the summer and prevails for two-thirds of the
year. It is associated with intense dust and sand storms in summer. The
wind from the south-east, on the other hand, blows for less time and is
also a warm wind but provides, during midsummer, a very refreshing
breeze in an otherwise hot and humid season. Areas of shelter or
exposure to these winds have great significance and should be recorded
(see Figure 7.4). Dust storms occur on as many as 30 per cent of total
days in the spring months. Damage to plants and machines can be
considerable. Blowing dust and sand cannot be totally avoided but areas

Figure 7.4: Study Area; Microclimate

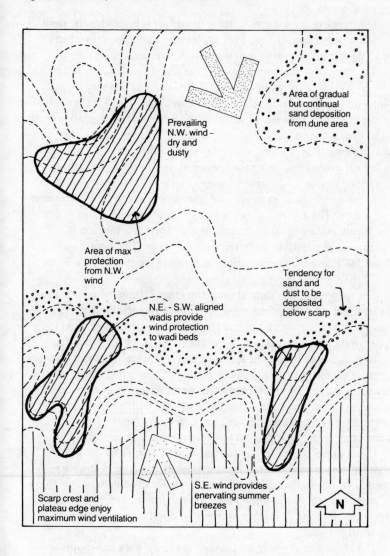

of extreme nuisance can be identified and frequently the problem can be ameliorated.

In summary, the extreme climate in arid areas highlights the need for wind protection, the need for exploiting cooling breezes whenever possible and the importance of water conservation.

The climate of the humid areas of the tropics is characterised by very high rainfall (often in excess of 2,000 mm/yr) and very high temperatures. There is usually a marked wet season, and a drier period of the year. Any seasonal variation in the behaviour of vegetation tends to be due to the wet/dry fluctuations rather than hot/cold. (Seasonal changes are subtle; for instance, most trees in the rain forest are broadleaf evergreens, losing their leaves throughout the year, though in varying amounts.) Diurnal temperature variation tends to be small.

In the wet tropical example, the monsoon season is from November to January. The annual rainfall is about 2,500mm with about 500mm per month occurring during the monsoon. There is a very small fluctuation in annual or daily temperature range. The annual mean is about 80°F and the normal daily temperature range is 75°-85°F. (24°C-30°C).[1]

The extremely high rainfall (in many areas 250mm of rainfall in a 24-hour period occurs occasionally) and high temperatures are two climatic characteristics which are the chief determinants of vegetation types, soil characteristics and the whole structure of the ecosystem.

In planning development activities in wet tropical areas it is essential to avoid excessive earth-moving or ground cultivation activities shortly before or during the monsoon season. Areas disturbed prior to the monsoon should, where possible, be protected with a vegetative cover crop, but if this cannot be established before the onset of the monsoon, some other form of protection to prevent erosion is essential.

High rainfall causes severe leaching of nutrients from the soil. But high temperatures also result in an extremely rapid breakdown of organic matter in the surface of the soil. Hence the ameliorative effects of humus matter in the topsoil are minimal, in terms of improving soil structure, drainage or making nutrients and soil moisture more available for plant growth.

The climate of the semi-arid savannah example is a sub-montane type, typical of the highland areas of central Africa. There is a rainy season from mid-October until the beginning of April, but there is rarely a deficiency of soil moisture for plant growth until the beginning of May. During May and June, however, there is a strong persistent wind which blows during daylight hours which increases transpiration and aggravates the soil moisture deficiency problem. The mean annual rainfall is about 1,300mm. Unlike the Mediterranean climate, the cold season does not coincide with the wet season. The coldest months of the year are May, June and July, when on cold nights frosts may occasionally occur. Mean annual temperature is about 20°C. Climatic factors are not, in this area, important locational constraints, but protecting housing from the persistent winds in May and June, protecting the soil, particularly in steep areas, from heavy rainfall and providing shade in urban development are design factors imposed by the climatic conditions. Some coastal areas in the tropics and sub-tropics are highly susceptible to damage from cyclonic storms. High winds and intense precipitation may cause damage and there is also a possibility of tidal waves.

7.1.5 Hydrology and Drainage

Reference has already been made to the lack of precipitation in arid or semi-arid landscapes. Of the rain which actually reaches the ground, only about 10 per cent permeates beyond the first few centimetres of soil, 20 per cent wets the ground, 20 per cent is immediately evaporated by intense solar radiation, and 50 per cent runs off. Collecting finally in salt pans, the run-off infiltrates to the water table or is evaporated. Wadis, or desert drainage channels, vary in size but all are subject to rapid run-off after intense rains. Every 10-20 years very destructive flash floods are recorded as a major hazard. These eventually dissipate in the saline sabkhas and seasonal marshes.

In many desert areas, subsurface water is available in aquifers. This may be either fresh or brackish (alkaline or saline) or both at varying depths. Large underground reservoirs are regional resources and are often recharged by ground water which occurs many miles away. Usually very little local information is available on the quantity and quality of ground water. It is quite likely that some regional aquifers contain 'fossil' water collected at a time when the climate was more equable and which are not now being recharged. Recent encrustations of surface soil in desert areas may have restricted recharge capabilities, thus making the water in that aquifer an irreplaceable resource. However, some recharge of aquifers will normally occur, and this rate determines the safe yield of the formation.

In the study area (see Figure 7.5) it is assumed that a shallow fresh-water aquifer lies below the lowland plain and is tapped locally by shallow wells at the oasis village. The seasonal marsh bears evidence of the closeness of the water table to the surface. Below this another

Figure 7.5: Study Area; Drainage/Hydrology

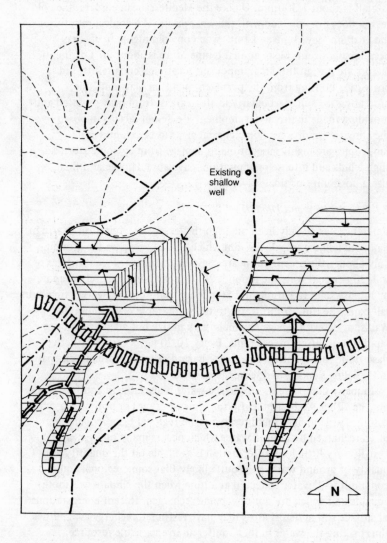

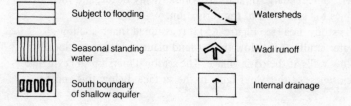

Subject to flooding		Watersheds	
Seasonal standing water		Wadi runoff	
South boundary of shallow aquifer		Internal drainage	

aquifer, containing brackish water, is sealed off by an impermeable strata.

The recharge areas for these ground-water resources are unknown, although the local wadis and sabkhas undoubtedly contribute some water after storms. There is a precarious balance separating the fresh ground water and the saline water of the marsh and sabkhas which results from a continual process of capillary action and evaporation. The watershed of the marsh extends over both the lowland plain and plateau. Management of the marsh watershed as a unit will be necessary to avoid irreparable damage to the wetland ecosystem.

In nearly all arid and semi-arid areas there is a need for more information on the quality and quantity of ground water, the rate of recharge and the potential safe yield. Although hydrologic data are often very limited, the planner must use the available information as best he can to judge the implications for development. Constraints may include areas susceptible to flooding and aquifer recharge areas. The planner should be aware of the catchment areas of streams and rivers in the area, and where appropriate, use of the watershed unit as a factor in design. Hydrologic data will be important in the design of sewer systems, the disposal of waste water, in assessing water-supply alternatives and the management of storm run-off.

In many areas of the tropics rainfall of over 2000 mm/annum is common. The lush vegetation of the tropical rainforest is a reflection of this heavy rainfall — 250 mm of rain may fall in a 24-hour period during the monsoon. The highly leached nature of tropical soils is a reflection of this drenching rain. However, under natural jungle cover only the heaviest storms generate sufficient run-off to cause serious erosion. Eroded soil is carried into streams and rivers as sediment, which itself may cause problems, clogging the channels and reservoirs, reducing fish and other aquatic life, and enriching the water with soil nutrients. In the wet tropical example heavy sediment loads in rivers caused both by logging and agricultural development have resulted in a serious reduction in the fish catch in major rivers.

The removal of tropical forest will produce an extraordinary change in the hydrologic behaviour of streams and rivers. An increase in the proportion of rainfall which runs off due to forest clearance results in a decrease in infiltration, hence a reduction in the amount of water available to vegetation. Decrease in infiltration also results in less water recharging underground water which keep springs flowing and seepage areas damp during dry weather. In areas which rely on underground water for supply, this reduction in recharge may threaten sustained yield from aquifers. In areas which rely on surface water for supply, the more erratic nature of stream flow is likely to make direct extraction from streams and rivers unreliable. Consequently, reservoirs are frequently constructed to impound water for dry periods. Unfortunately these reservoirs trap sediment caused by upstream development and may fill up with mud within a few years.

It is probable that little detailed hydrologic data will be available for most areas undergoing development. If possible, both water quality and stream flow should be monitored in order to assess the effectiveness of measures to minimise run-off pollution by sediments, fertilisers and agricultural wastes and also of measures to reduce the volume of run-off generated in the development area.

The effective treatment of sewage is essential to ensure the safety and usefulness of surface water. High capital outlay on sophisticated hardware for sewage treatment facilities is clearly inappropriate for all but large urban centres. Fortunately systems utilising a series of digestion ponds, of effluent, give a level of treatment as effective in most respects to more sophisticated tertiary treatment systems.

In semi-arid areas, water availability is likely to be the limiting factor for most plant growth and water conservation will be of the highest priority. Water which runs off into the drainage system will effectively be lost to the area, so efforts to reduce the run-off and to maximise the amount of infiltration into the soil during periods of rainfall are important. The rate of evaporation from ponds or reservoirs will also be very high in semi-arid areas and therefore underground storage in aquifers will generally be more effective than surface reservoirs. It may be necessary to drill a number of exploratory boreholes to assess the ground-water potential. Depending on the geology, it may be possible to recharge underground strata artificially using wells or seepage areas.

In semi-arid areas the re-use of urban waste water is generally feasible and it is often possible to utilise a low-cost 'biological' method of treatment to accomplish this.[2]

Flooding may be a problem which is aggravated by development, both urban and rural. During a storm, run-off builds up, the flooding in the river reaches a peak and then recedes. After an area has been developed, not only the volume of run-off increases but also it runs off more rapidly. The 'time of concentration' of a flood is vitally important as the peak will be highest and most destructive when the storm continues for long enough for run-off from all areas in the drainage basin to be contributing to flooding in the river. In planning the development of an area, therefore, attention should be given to measures to delay run-off and to reduce volume to a minimum and, in so doing, increase infiltration; but it should also be recognised that floods are a natural phenomenon and will continue to occur. Therefore generally any development of the flood plain should be avoided except for open-space uses.

In the wet tropical example the flood plains are fairly confined but monsoon rain may cause periodic inundation of valley bottoms due to the limited capacity of the channel downstream. Streams carry heavy sediment loads during heavy rainstorms, and this sediment tends to be deposited in extensive alluvial flats dispersed throughout the rolling topography. Flood-prone areas are identified partly by survey and contour interpretation using known flood levels, partly by vegetation indicators and partly by calculation. These areas are then designated for uses which will not restrict their ability to pass floods without damage. These include limited agriculture, recreation, some roads and parking and open space.

In semi-arid areas water for irrigation is likely to be in high demand. But before embarking on a programme of irrigation in a climate with a high rate of evaporation, the problem of salinity must be considered. 'Fresh' water will contain a varying amount of dissolved salts depending on the land across which it has flowed. When used for irrigation, a considerable proportion of water will be lost by evaporation, leaving all the salt behind. This tends to build up gradually in the soil and may reach a point when it is toxic to plant growth. Important factors are the salinity of irrigation water, the rate of evaporation and the availability of water. If enough water can be applied without causing drainage problems, excess salt can often be 'flushed' out. It is also important to try to avoid applying irrigation water by overhead sprinkler systems or drip systems where the rate of evaporation is considerably higher than by overland flow.

In the semi-arid scenario, stream channels are extremely unstable and will inevitably become more so when development results in an increase in both the magnitude and frequency of flooding. The instability of the stream channels has been aggravated by the removal of all riparian vegetation and the re-establishment of riparian trees would go far in stabilising stream channels and improving water quality.

7.1.6 Soils

There are very few areas of 'true' soil in arid areas. The high intensity of precipitation, the lack of vegetation (and consequently humus), the high winds and run-off rates (which tend to remove weathered material) all prevent the formation of soil as would be found in less arid climates. Rapid evaporation of surface water results in a high salinity in many soils. Rising saline ground water or mismanaged irrigation can further increase this problem. Desert soils are consequently poorly developed, thin, and usually contain a high percentage of sand, gravel and pebbles and areas of exposed rock. Where there is sufficient soil moisture to support plant growth a desert loam will gradually develop, often occurring in oases or in wadis.

The arid, sub-tropical area contains a range of different soil conditions. In the dune area there are moving sands while the plateau has a natural surface hard pan. A cementing of the gravel has produced a lithosol polished smooth by wind abrasion. Although all the soils have a degree of salinity, the extreme is demonstrated by the sabkhas (salt pans). Evaporation has created a white crust below which lie very unstable quick sands. The remaining soils of the lowland plain, wadis and alluvial fans are poorly developed in comparison to soils found in more humid climates, but with careful irrigation are productive in the desert environment.

If a detailed soil survey of physical and chemical characteristics of the soil has been carried out, the planner needs to interpret this data to assess the suitability of the soil for agriculture (irrigated and dry) for forestry and for urban development. Here the suitability of the soil for intensive irrigated agriculture and forestry is based on the degree of salinity, the absence of a hard pan, availability of moisture, the depth of soil and subsurface drainage.

The soil map (Figure 7.6) shows soil characteristics. Areas of soil best suited to irrigated cultivation should be conserved, since they are limited in extent (in arid situations). Unstable soils should not be built on, and advantage should be taken of soil where forestry shelter belts can be grown to protect urban development from wind. Tree and shrub vegetation also act as filters minimising the nuisance of wind-blown sand and dust. Every effort should be made to protect vegetated areas and to manage these to conserve and build up the soil.

In more humid tropical areas soil conservation is also of vital importance, especially in areas undergoing agricultural development. Many of the problems arise from 'laterisation'. Lateritic soils occur very widely in the tropics between about $30°N-30°S$.[3] They are mineral-rich earths, acidic and commonly derived from granite. Heavy rainfalll leaches most plant nutrients from these soils and they are almost devoid of organic matter. When these soils are exposed to air, the iron and aluminium are oxidised, and the soil becomes hard and intractable. As

Figure 7.6: Study Area; Soils

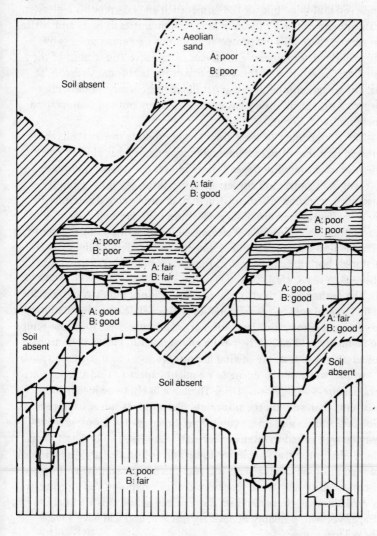

such, it has been used since ancient times for the construction of roads and even buildings, but for the farmer such an occurrence is a disaster. Laterites are a source of iron in many communities in India and Africa. In nature, these soils are protected from this hardening process by tropical jungle or by grassland 'savannah' in more arid regions of the tropics. The removal of this vegetative protection for any reason, as part of an agricultural or urban development scheme, should only proceed after a soil survey has been carried out and soil conservation measures worked out.

The vulnerability of these thin, highly erodible tropical soils to erosion resulting from extremely intensive rainfall has already been mentioned. Erodibility depends not only on the steepness but also on the length of slope. Soil conservation measures, say during jungle clearance or during urban construction, must be related carefully to factors affecting soil erodibility. Measures include temporary ground-cover of crops, 'windrowing' cleared slash and debris along the contours, construction of contoured diversion channels and mulching with various materials both natural (e.g. shed foliage and branches) or artificial (fibre-glass mats, etc.).

The 'lushness' of the tropical rain forest is *not* indicative of a rich soil. Tropical soils are characteristically severely leached by the heavy rainfall and contain low levels of most plant nutrients. They also tend to be highly acidic. Clearly, before any agricultural developments are undertaken soil tests are of vital importance.

In the 'wet tropical' example we might expect to find alluvial soils in small areas along flood plains. These are likely to be higher in nutrients than soils on the slopes and plateaus, yet suffer from periodic flooding and poor drainage conditions. Some garden crops, however, may be well suited to intensive cultivation on these soils. The soil on the slopes of the tract are likely to be thin and eroded and the removal of vegetation on sloping areas will result in an aggravation of this situation. Generally these soils should not be exposed and a protective cover kept at all times. Soils on flatter areas on hilltops are likely to be deeper yet, will probably be severely leached, and will have a weak physical structure.

The soils of the semi-arid savannah example are red or yellow ferralitic soils with lateritic material near the surface. The pH is between 5.5 and 6.0. The soils are extremely low in organic matter. (The practice of burning makes this problem worse.) Soils are frequently deficient in nitrogen and phosphorous. Unlike forest areas where the vegetation contains considerable plant nutrients, the herbaceous cover in the savannah contains little nutrient and that in the soil is found predominantly in the first few millimetres of the soil horizon. It is very important to retain vegetative protection of these fragile soils. Development or construction activities can of course expose them to erosion but so too can poor management, over-grazing particularly.

Thus a development scheme should contain a thorough analysis of soil types and their capabilities. The hazards of developing each soil type should be understood and conservation measures planned beforehand. It is essential to pay attention to annual patterns of rainfall when planning any activity involving earth-moving or removal of vegetation.

7.1.7 Vegetation

Vegetation cover in arid and semi-arid landscapes is very limited. However, introduced vegetation can play an important role in ameliorating adverse climatic conditions, providing shelter from the wind and shade from the sun.

Since desert vegetation is already stressed to its limits of tolerance by climatic extremes, it is particularly vulnerable to change or disturbance. Desert plants show remarkable adaptations to the lack of soil moisture. Maximum use is made of precipitation and dew; root systems are very extensive in order to benefit from whatever soil moisture is available, often at a considerable depth. Plant forms above the ground are adapted to minimise the loss of water, some changing the colour and shape of leaves to increase heat reflection, others having various storage mechanisms. Periods of growth and dormancy are related to the seasonal availability of soil moisture.

In the arid area (see Figure 7.7) the vegetation patterns generally match the distribution of soil types and land form. Some of the densest and most diverse cover grows in the wadis where considerable moisture and soil depth is available. In the marsh also there is a relative abundance of water, soil and vegetation forming a dense halophytic (salt-tolerant) community. A drastic lowering of the water table or artificial drainage would quickly eliminate this rich assemblage of plants and its associate wildlife. The marsh and its watershed is a rare habitat in this landscape and requires careful management and protection. The success of the existing forestry plantation (consisting of drought and salt-tolerant trees with their roots extending to a shallow water table) gives an indication of the potential tree species which can be established on the lowland plain area. The irrigation practised in the existing oasis

Figure 7.7: Study Area; Vegetation

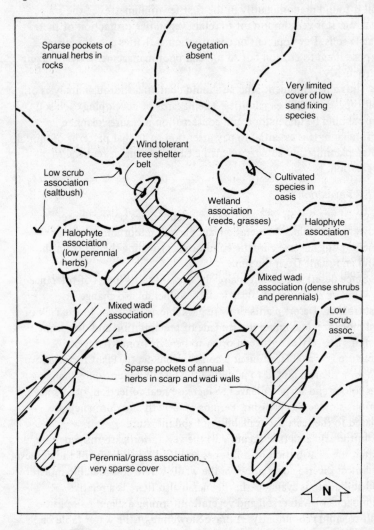

    Concentrations of Wildlife

gardens is of a small scale only, and does not necessarily prove the suitability of large-scale irrigation on the lowland plains. The scrub and perennial vegetation in the plain and on the plateau have suffered from serious over-grazing.

If no detailed vegetation survey is available much data concerning the plant community types can be derived from the soil maps and field surveys. At this stage the details of species are not important, but the type of plant community and the way in which it utilises soil and water in order to survive in this adverse environment should be studied.

The tropical forest is one of the most productive natural systems on earth. 'Productive', that is, in terms of the mass of vegetation which it produces, the biomass. It is also one of the most diverse natural systems of earth, containing a very large number of different species of plants and animals.

However, this 'biological productivity' does not mean that the tropical rain forest is very highly productive economically. Although the hardwood timber is of high value and is in heavy demand, the enormous trees are difficult to extract, and the large number of different species does not give the uniformity required by modern marketing methods. The wastage and inefficiencies involved in tropical hardwoods reaching their markets are serious problems. The actual logging procedure, too, often has serious environmental consequences. Accessibility for the heavy machinery required to handle logs means that a considerable network of temporary logging roads must be constructed. These roads are highly vulnerable to erosion.

Because of the difficulties and inefficiencies of exploiting tropical forests, efforts are being made to make them more productive economically. This may involve reducing the number of species or shortening the rotation. It may involve the clearance of the forest, and replacement by a tree crop, often rubber or oil palm; or it may involve clearance for agriculture, for grazing or tillage. It is interesting to note that in terms of 'biological production' (weight of vegetation produced) none of these systems comes close to the natural forest.

Inappropriate exploitation or development of the tropical forest has, in some instances, resulted in environmental consequences which have threatened or destroyed the economy of many areas. It is important to understand the relationship between forest, climate and soil before initiating any changes in the natural vegetation. Very heavy rain tends to leach out most of the plant nutrients from the soil. The vegetation therefore tends to store these nutrients up in the foliage wherever possible. However, the trunk and older wood of a tree does not contain much of this nutrient and therefore the removal of logs during logging does not represent a serious loss of nutrient from the system. However, if the small branches and slash are removed, or if they are burned and the nutrients which are released are not tied up rapidly by new vegetation, the system will suffer a loss. The removal of vegetation also results in increase in erosion hazard while the soils lie unprotected.

The distribution of vegetation in the semi-arid savannah landscape reflects topographic and soil changes much more obviously than does tropical forest vegetation. The availability of water is the critical factor in the distribution of vegetation in semi-arid areas. The savannah vegetation is burned frequently, and the open woodland (Brachystegia type) and savannah grassland are indicative of this practice, which is usually carried out in May and June. Nearly all the tree and shrub species of the savannah are fire-resistant to some extent. However, few of these species have any commercial value and most are of limited value for landscape use, although they are adapted to local conditions because of their extremely slow rate of growth. Introduced exotic species are rarely fire-resistant and consequently burning has to be carried out with extreme care. The savannah has been managed at a very low intensity for grazing and the principal management tool is burning. There are scattered cultivated plots, mainly in small alluvial areas in valley bottoms, but virtually no cash crops are grown.

In semi-arid areas vegetation may play an important role in ameliorating the effect of the wind. Ground-cover vegetation may prevent soil erosion by binding the soil; windbreaks or shelter belts of trees may also decrease wind velocity.

Timber is also vitally important as a fuel both for cooking and heating. In arid and semi-arid areas there may be serious shortages of wood and consideration should be given to establishing woodlots for this purpose. It is important that the landscape planner consider carefully the traditional methods of cooking and heating. Frequently wood is gathered wherever available and new plantations may be destroyed. However, if the need exists, it must be recognised and provision made.

7.1.8 Visual Character

The 'appropriateness' of development to the area, its terrain, climate and vegetation is far more important than a conscious effort to design for visual character. However, understanding and appreciating how the visual character of any landscape owes its origins to topography, climate and vegetation is valuable in understanding the appropriate use of land.

The dominant visual elements in a landscape may be topographic features, vegetation or man-made objects. The amount of visual enclosure created by these elements will vary greatly, and this factor will affect the way people respond to and behave in a landscape. An enclosed landscape may result in a feeling of security, an unenclosed landscape in a feeling of exhilaration.

The desert area in the example used here is strongly dominated by the scarp 'edge' of the plateau and the long views obtained from it. The outcrop in the north west is also a dominant but isolated visual feature. The lowland plain is visually open and undulates with only slight differences of relief. The wadis cutting back into the scarp are well defined areas of 'containment'.

The contrast between the visual characteristics of the tropical rain forest and the semi-arid savannah is extreme. It is hardly necessary for a conscious evaluation of visual character in designing a development for these areas *provided* that the designer gives careful attention to siting, materials, construction and techniques, the distribution of land uses and so on. However, the comparison of the visual character of traditional settlements in many tropical areas with the visual character of recent developments often emphasises the importance of recognising the potential of existing landscape elements.

Although often difficult to assess its practical application, a survey of visual characteristics is none the less an important part of the total description of the observable landscape for human use.

7.1.9 Interpretation of the Landscape

Development constraints will clearly vary considerably from area to area. The identification of major and minor constraints to development is an important task for the land-use planner early in the project. Constraints may be divided into positive and negative. For instance, for agriculture, level or gently sloping land with deep well-drained soils is an example of positive factors affecting the selection of land suitable for agriculture. Avoiding land susceptible to flooding, aquifer recharge areas or unstable areas are negative factors in the selection of urban sites.

In practice the schematic methodology of environmental analysis for site selection (Figure 7.1) involves the identification of major constraints affecting the distribution of land uses, followed by minor constraints which may result in minor adjustments and alterations in land-use allocations.

Here the desert example has been developed in some detail. On completion of the inventory of landscape elements the data are analysed to identify those factors which are liable to be influential in guiding the location and form of the proposed urban development.

Based on the descriptions of the arid example, the list of factors below may be typical but not necessarily comprehensive for all arid or semi arid areas:

slope gradients of more than 10 per cent;
cliffs or rock outcrops;
areas of moving sand dunes;
areas subject to excessive sand deposition;
scarp edges exposed to maximum ventilation for north-west and south-west winds;
areas of wind shadow, protected from north-west winds;
wadis and fans subject to flash floods;
sensitive watersheds;
extent of shallow fresh-water aquifers;
soils with inherent instability or difficult to drain;
local aquifer recharge areas;
soils unsuitable for urban effluent disposal;
soils suitable for irrigated cultivation;
areas containing extensive surface cover or density of vegetation;
unique areas or scientific values worthy of conservation;
high relief with extensive views;
features or areas of high visual impact locally;
opportunity for visual containment provided by topography or vegetation.

Using the overall objective for the area (in this case to select a site or area for a self-sustaining community development), the factors can be re-interpreted as 'constraints' or 'opportunities'. Each of these is represented graphically in Figures 7.8 and 7.9.

Due to the complexity of most landscapes and the natural processes creating them, more than one opportunity or constraint is liable to occur on the same area. For example, wadis have the best soil for cultivation, are sheltered from the wind, are subject to flash floods, have opportunity for visual enclosure and contain a relatively dense vegetation cover. To summarise and simplify the analysis, the designated area can therefore be divided up into a series of landscape zones or units (see Figure 7.10). The divisions are usually based on land

Figure 7.8: Study Area; Constraints

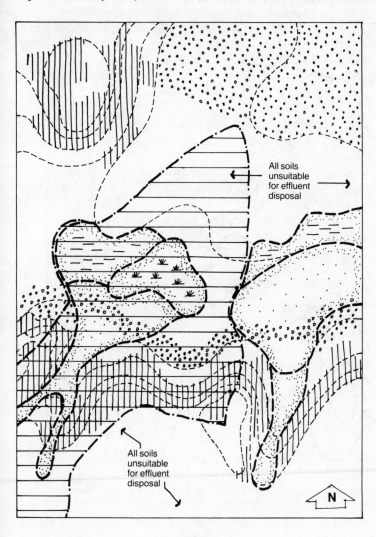

All soils
unsuitable
for effluent
disposal

All soils
unsuitable
for effluent
disposal

N

 Slopes <10%

 Conservation value

 Area subject to flooding

 Marsh watershed

 Soils difficult to drain

 Excessive sand deposition

Figure 7.9: Study Area; Opportunities

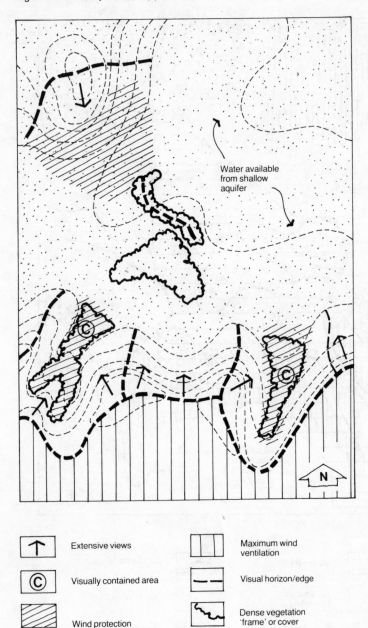

Water available
from shallow
aquifer

↑	Extensive views	⦀	Maximum wind ventilation
Ⓒ	Visually contained area	– – –	Visual horizon/edge
▨	Wind protection	⌇	Dense vegetation 'frame' or cover

Figure 7.10: Study Area; Landscape Units

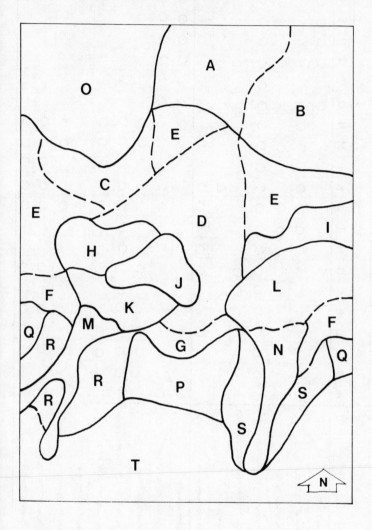

Clearly defined survey zone

Indistinct boundary to survey zone

Figure 7.11: Study Area; Landscape Analysis Matrix

		Landscape Units																			
		A	B	C	D	E	F	G	H	I	J	K	L	M	N	O	P	Q	R	S	T
Constraints	Slopes < 10%	O															O	O	O	O	O	O
	Area subject to flooding								O	O	O	O	O	O	O						
	Soils difficult to drain								O	O	O			O							
	Soil unsuitable for effluent disposal		O	O	O	O	O	O	O	O	O	O	O	O	O	O	O	O	O	O	O
	Subject to excessive sand deposition		O				O	O													
	Scientific value											O									
	Sensitive watershed				O			O	O		O	O		O				O		O		
Opportunities	Extensive views															O	O	O	O	O	O
	High visual impact locally	O														O	O	O	O	O	O
	Visual containment			O	O			O			O			O	O						
	Water available from shallow aquifer	O	O	O	O	O	O	O	O	O	O	O	O	O	O						
	Protection from N.W. wind			O										O	O						
	Maximum wind ventilation															O					
	Existing vegetation frame or cover			O							O			O	O						O
	Soils suitable for irrigated cultivation			O	O	O	O	O			O	O	O	O	O						
	Soils suitable for forestry			O	O	O	O	O			O	O	O	O	O						O

form (see Figure 7.2), but can be subdivided further to take into account minor topographic differences and visual characteristics revealed in field surveys. Each unit should have a general homogeneity which is the base on which a greater complexity of opportunities and constraints can be evaluated.

The opportunities and constraints of each landscape unit can be analysed individually or collectively in the form of a matrix (see Figure 7.11). The matrix thus provides the means of evaluating generally the possible negative or positive environmental impacts of the proposed development on any of the landscape zones. For example, landscape zone C is described in the inventory as a relatively flat part of the lowland plain with shallow, somewhat sandy-loamy soils covered sparsely with low scrub vegetation, and underlain by a shallow fresh-water aquifer. The latter provides easily accessible drinking and irrigation water. The matrix analysis shows that though featureless in itself, the zone is given visual definition by the steep rise of an adjacent rock outcrop which also provides considerable shelter from the north-west winds. Both of these factors are useful advantages for a new settlement in this area. Although the suitability of the soil is only rated as 'fair' for irrigated cultivation, this is interpreted as an opportunity in the analysis. Any potential for cultivation is an advantage where such soils are limited, and where self-sustenance is part of the settlement objective. However, excessive irrigation on the shallow soil could exacerbate present high salinity levels.

Suitability for forestry rates as 'good' and offers the advantages of future unirrigated shelter belts using the ground water. The prevention of the ground water from pollution by sewage effluent is a critical issue. The sandy soils allow fast infiltration and there is no significant improvement in effluent quality by passing through these soils. Protection of potable ground water from pollution and the protection of the natural process of local recharge to an aquifer of an as yet unknown size are major constraints for urban development in this area.

A similar assessment can be made quickly for any of the landscape zones on the matrix. The next stage is to establish criteria for judging the importance of the different opportunities and constraints.

7.1.10 Environmental Priorities

Priorities need to be defined to establish an order of importance for the opportunities and constraints of the analysis. It is clear from the summary matrix that there is, for different areas, a concurrence of opportunities and constraints.

The description of the landscape and natural processes of the study area has shown that certain constraints have critical ecological implications while others merely increase development costs. Thus constraints must be ranked according to their importance. To illustrate how this can be achieved, and to give some idea of the type of criteria used in establishing priorities, the desert area is again used as an example below. However, the criteria used should be generally applicable and acceptable, and the degree of response to each level of priority will vary according to the tolerances of a particular environment and the project objectives.

Priority 1: constraints identified as critical to the health, safety and welfare of the existing and future population of the area.
Priority 2: constraints identified as critical to the continued functioning and maintenance of the natural systems of the area.
Priority 3: constraints identified as resulting in additional development costs if minimal impact to the natural systems is to be achieved.
Priority 4: minor constraints which require little or no ameliorative action to avoid ecological impact.

Priority 1 constraints in Figure 7.12 are those areas subject to flash floods. The latter is the major environmental hazard in the study area and even though occurring once every 10-20 years, the floods may cause loss of life in wadi areas. Protection of the unique marsh ecosystem and its watershed is defined as second priority. These areas are particularly vulnerable to any disturbance of the rapid surface run-off on which they depend. Susceptibility to pollution from urban effluents is considerable and possible further lowering of the water table (by wells) would cause irreparable changes. Priority 2 constraints also include the protection of the aquifer recharge capabilities of the wadis and sabkhas which would be minimised by urban cover. In areas affected by constraints which fall into the first two priorities development for urban uses is prohibited. However, agriculture or forestry may be permissible. Clearly, if an area is affected by several constraints, those with a high priority take precedence over those with a lower priority.

Development constraints on areas above the shallow aquifer are considered as the third priority. This condition would require that the area be carefully planned to avoid reduction of its recharge capabilities, excessive withdrawal of water, and potential pollution hazards to the

Figure 7.12: Study Area; Environmental Priorities

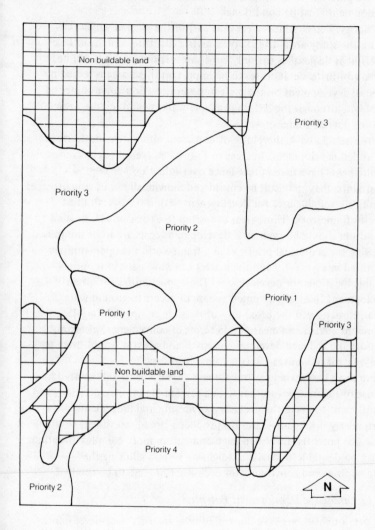

ground water. Thus development of settlements can occur but such development must be conditional.

Priority 4 constraints affect that part of the plateau which falls within the study area. The analysis matrix identifies soil unsuitable for effluent disposal as the only constraint. If this problem can be solved (for instance, it ceases to be important if the area is served by sewers), development on the plateau poses no serious environmental problems, although the lack of available water would require deep wells or outside sources.

Priorities 3 and 4, therefore, offer various alternative locations for controlled development. In areas of Priority 3, even though ecological requirements have taken precedence over other 'non-ecological' constraints, they may still be considered individually or as concurrences to indicate suitable area for development within the overall third priority framework. Thus, areas subjected to excessive dust or sand deposition should be avoided if development costs are to be minimised.

Using the ecological priorities as a framework, the opportunities identified in Figure 7.9 and the matrix can now assist in refining suitable locations for development. The opportunities for urban development (basically grouped as ease of access to ground water, visual, climatic and the proximity of possible complementary land uses) all present advantages measured in terms of convenience, pleasure, comfort and reduced development costs, and assist in establishing the development of various tracts within a landscape.

For most cases where a study area is as small as that illustrated here, the use of the matrix together with a few simple priority decisions will be sufficient to make the necessary environmental judgements (particularly if data are scarce) to produce a broad assessment of landscape potential for urban development. In more complex situations, it may be desirable to devise a weighting system allowing the opportunities and constraints for each tract or zone to be totalled.

7.1.11 Landscape Development Potential

The previous sections have illustrated how an analysis of development constraints and opportunities gives us a basis for assessing the suitability or development potential of the landscape for various uses. In the desert study area (Figure 7.13), the plateau, with no major environmental constraints, and with the advantage of extensive views and maximum wind ventilation, is the most suitable area for any scale of urban development. However, the cost of utilising the ground water available in the deep aquifer will be high and extensive treatment of soil

Figure 7.13: Study Area; Landscape Development Potential

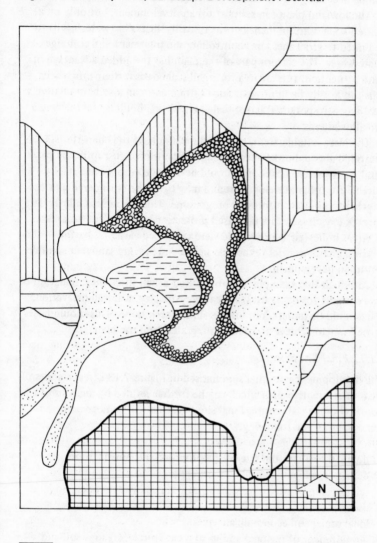

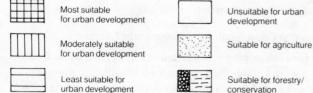

Most suitable for urban development		Unsuitable for urban development
Moderately suitable for urban development		Suitable for agriculture
Least suitable for urban development		Suitable for forestry/ conservation

will be necessary for any urban planting or shelter belts.

The lowland plain can support urban development, but only on a limited scale. Careful management of easily accessible water needs to be linked to strict measures controlling the treatment and recharge of waste water. The eastern part of the plain has the added advantage of wind protection. It is an area for small-scale oasis settlements where soils can locally be improved. Such settlements can also have relatively easy access to potential larger-scale agricultural holdings on the wadis and alluvial fans.

The least suitable areas, also on the plain, have the characteristics as described above, but have the added discomfort of susceptibility to windblown sand. These areas should be considered only marginally suitable for urban development and may better be considered as areas on which to initiate a forestry programme. This use may at a later date upgrade (by virtue of its increased protection) the area for urban uses.

Areas indicated as unsuitable were identified earlier as having physical characteristics (excessive slopes and moving sands) unsuitable for urban development.

Although this example has emphasised urban suitability, selection of land suitable for other uses, agriculture, forestry, water conservation, etc., should be undertaken using a similar technique. This should be carried out to achieve a rational, integrated land-use plan.

7.1.12 Final Site Selection

The development potential summarised in Figure 7.13 offers a series of areas or alternative sites which can be further refined by analysis of a non-environmental nature. Final site selection will be dependent on some or all of the following:

> detailed brief for the size of the proposed settlement, water demands, expected employment, etc.;
> relationship of site to existing village, transport networks and land uses;
> local social and economic analyses;
> development of regional and local agricultural, forestry, soil and water conservation programmes.

7.2 Environmental Considerations in Community Design

The method for environmental evaluation which has been described results in the identification of areas which are broadly suitable for development and areas which are suitable for development subject to certain conditions. Following final site selection the environmental planner should accomplish the following tasks:

(1) specify density restrictions and/or performance controls appropriate to the constraints in areas which have been identified as suitable for conditional development;

(2) recommend how the detailed design of the settlement can make the most of the climatic characteristics, the topography, vegetation and other natural features and processes and also minimise adverse environmental impacts for the well-being of future residents;

(3) identify an open-space system, where appropriate, within the proposed urban area;

(4) consider the environmental implications of alternatives for the provision of utilities and services;

(5) specify precautions necessary during the development process and identify urgent tasks for immediate implementation (e.g. setting up a plant nursery, initiating monitoring programmes, etc.)

7.2.1 Performance Controls and Density Restrictions

Some areas selected for urban development will have some constraints (mostly Priority 3 or 4) which make density restrictions or performance controls necessary. It is very important that these planning controls are clearly related to the areas where the constraint applies and that the controls are appropriate to the nature and magnitude of the constraint.

To enable performance controls and density restrictions to be formulated, the planner must be able to describe each land use in terms of the characteristics which are relevant to the constraint in question. Thus, where there is a need to maintain aquifer recharge, the extent of impermeable coverage (paving, roofs, sidewalks, etc.) which will prevent water infiltrating the ground must be known for each land use. In this case, the planner may then restrict development in the area to a density in which the extent of impermeable cover does not reduce recharge excessively. Or in some cases a performance control may be more appropriate. In this example, the developer may be required to take measures to maintain infiltration at the pre-development level, by, for example, constructing soakaway pits, recharge basins, using permeable paving or perhaps injection wells.

It is emphasised that for such planning controls to be enforced effectively they must be reasonable; the rationale on which they are based must be absolutely clear and the values which they embody must be generally held.

7.2.2 Design Considerations Arising from Natural Processes and Features

In desert communities adaptations to climatic extremes and the conservation of water are the most critical considerations in building layout and design. In most areas, a study of traditional settlements and dwellings often reveals remarkable attention to environmental factors. In arid sub-tropical regions, the compact nature of traditional settlements offers distinct advantages in this adverse climate. The low buildings are densely grouped together so that they shade each other and the open spaces around them. Small-scale spaces, yards and gardens next to houses are protected by walls from low-lying dust swirls within settlements. The streets are narrow and winding (but still with an ordered hierarchy) and orientated to reduce the wind-tunnel effect which is often created when streets are aligned in the direction of the prevailing wind. Houses are built around courtyards which are protected from blown sand and dust by perimeter walls or shelter belts.

Such patterns are rarely evident in modern desert settlements where grid iron layouts more suitable to temperate climates are commonly found. This is unfortunate, since in traditional towns, both in overall layout and in individual houses, there has been careful adaptation to climate extremes and water conservation. To create environmentally and culturally successful settlements, similar care must be taken in the layout and design of new development. Generally, broad streets should be avoided, and streets which lie in the direction of the prevailing wind should, where possible, be staggered, using small 'blocks'.

Wind tunnelling is almost inevitable if a grid street layout is used. A hierarchy of small streets and pedestrian footways should link residential areas to the commercial centre. In hot climates, especially where vehicular ownership is low, the size of development and the distribution of uses within it should be carefully related to walking distance. In the detailed design of circulation systems consideration must be given to the provision of shade and wind protection for the pedestrian. Walkways can be narrow, taking advantage of shade from adjacent buildings and minimising run-off from paved surfaces.

'Courtyard' housing offers great advantages in an arid hot climate, providing mutual shade and a cool, private internal space within the dwelling unit. This is in direct contrast to traditional housing in temperate climates which is usually surrounded by open space. High densities can be achieved using courtyard housing. Individual housing groups should be organised around courtyards. This is the opposite to the temperate pattern where central houses are surrounded by open space. As well as providing climatic protection to small-scale internal pleasure space, courtyard housing in groups can offer greater opportunities for higher densities. Although cultural patterns for families will vary from country to country, the traditional extended Arab family, for example, is well suited to the courtyard which acts physically as a family focus, yet provides complete privacy. The protection of buildings creates a microclimate favouring plant growth in internal gardens. A concentration of vegetation creates cooler night temperatures and offers a psychological relief to the static monotones of building and ground surfaces.

The courtyard principle can also be applied at the neighbourhood level; groups of houses enclosing a small semi-public open space. The space might be used for growing communal crops, i.e. an urban oasis garden.

In the town centre of communities in arid regions the dense fabric should not be interrupted by excessively large spaces for administrative or religious uses. Where larger spaces do create exposure to wind, protection from small berms and shelter trees should be used to subdivide them. Where water supply is limited, the planner should make the maximum possible use of the buildings themselves, both in their layout and in their detailed design to provide shade and wind protection in public spaces. If sufficient water is available only for a limited amount of vegetation, this should be concentrated in courtyards and small neighbourhood spaces. At the fringes of the settlement, extensive landscaping for wind shelter must have a high priority for water use.

On the fringes of desert towns, regardless of internal layout, protection is needed against the sand- and dust-laden winds. Berms or mounds can be constructed which will reduce wind speeds for as much as twenty times their height. Similarly, shelter belts of trees can be planted which will not only reduce wind speed but will also act as filters for blown dust and sand. Tree species should be wind- and drought-tolerant, requiring a minimum of irrigation water. Traditionally, high walls have been used as windbreaks; these offer local protection but sometimes create turbulence. For optimum shelter a combination of berms and vegetation is best. The windward side of the berm should have a shallow slope which has been stabilised by indigenous ground-cover species tolerant of dry conditions. Planting may take some time to establish and 'rip-rap' rock veneers can be used to stabilise the slope temporarily. Asphalt sprays have also been used, but these prevent the possible use of plant material. The berm must be planted below the crest while wind-resistant and wide-spreading trees should be planted near the crest. Both sides of the berm should be carefully fenced against grazing animals, at least until plant material is established. Once the wind has been raised it must be maintained above the roof line height. The wind will tend to return to ground level if internal open spaces are greater than five times the height of the building or berm. Spaces between the berm and the first houses, road rights of way, courts and neighbourhood spaces should all therefore be less than three times the height of the buildings (see Figure 7.14(A)). This emphasises the need for compact town layouts.

In wet, tropical areas, climatic factors do not dictate the close grouping of dwelling units in traditional villages. Indeed most families will cultivate a garden and many will also enclose a small area for livestock. In some cases the garden itself is enclosed to keep out livestock which are permitted to forage throughout the village for food. Fruit trees, particularly papayas, loquats, bananas and coconuts, are common within the curtilage of the village, often performing a dual function as shade trees. The mutual protection afforded by clustering dwelling units closely together in arid areas is unnecessary in wetter areas of the tropics and the villages are much more dispersed. The provision of shade, good ventilation and the required space to grow what is needed are important factors in the layout of urban development.

In arid climates the amount of vegetation used in private and public spaces within the settlement should depend on the amount of water available. The use of planting must be 'functional'. Species should be carefully chosen to optimise their uses and thus avoid waste of water.

The landscape designer must be aware of the patterns and routines of use of outdoor areas, in order to be able to assess the need for shade, and at what periods of the day. When sufficient water is available shade will generally be provided by trees or vines growing over arbours, yet artificial shading devices may also be feasible. Plants can be used to provide shade, wind shelter, filtering of dust, to give direction to breezes, evaporate cooling, and psychological refreshment. For each location there are a variety of species which will be tolerant to the local conditions. Their different characteristics of foliage, shape, height, tolerances and water demand should be carefully evaluated.

In arid areas residential courtyards and neighbourhood spaces should be an integral part of the buildings (see Figure 7.14). Small in scale to

Figure 7.14 (A): Wind Protection

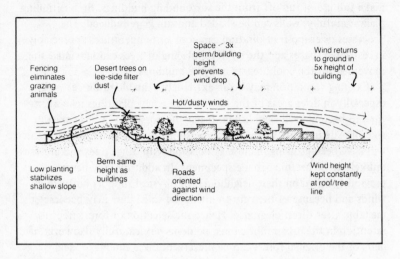

Space ~ 3x berm/building height prevents wind drop

Wind returns to ground in 5x height of building

Fencing eliminates grazing animals

Desert trees on lee-side filter dust

Hot/dusty winds

Low planting stabilizes shallow slope

Berm same height as buildings

Roads oriented against wind direction

Wind height kept constantly at roof/tree line

Figure 7.14 (B): Landscaping for Housing

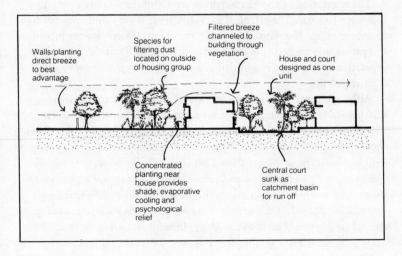

Walls/planting direct breeze to best advantage

Species for filtering dust located on outside of housing group

Filtered breeze channeled to building through vegetation

House and court designed as one unit

Concentrated planting near house provides shade, evaporative cooling and psychological relief

Central court sunk as catchment basin for run off

prevent wind drop, the spaces should be sunk by a few centimetres to make full use of run-off from the surrounding buildings. By positioning plants carefully, walls can be shaded and sun glare reduced. The processes of evapo-transpiration can cool air temperatures appreciably in restricted spaces and the strategic placing of trees can maximise the movement of the cool breezes into the buildings.

Existing vegetation may be an extremely valuable resource, especially in drier areas of the tropics where new plantings take a long time to become well established. It may be possible to utilise existing trees on site in urban areas. In previously forested areas, however, trees will have been growing in close association with other trees and are unlikely to be useful as shade specimens. In addition they have previously relied on their neighbours for physical support during high winds and because of the very thin tropical soils, they may become unstable after forest clearance. Hence the selection of forest trees for retention in the urban fabric must be done very carefully. However, if belts of the original forest can be preserved, these can make ideal corridors for shaded paths, cycle tracks and roads. Playgrounds, playing fields and institutional uses can be located along these corridors to maximise their value as open space. Shading of asphalt roads in tropical climates will significantly increase the life of the paved surface by keeping it cooler (see Figure 7.15).

The vegetation of the 'savannah' in semi-arid regions has a very low tolerance to wear. The effect of excessive wear is very similar in nature to over-grazing. The natural ground-cover vegetation no longer provides soil protection and erosion and laterisation set in. Thus the natural vegetation will require modification or even paving where heavy wear is anticipated.

Although few of the native trees and shrubs of the savannah are suitable for landscape uses, there are many species which have been introduced which are well adapted to the growing conditions. However, some species will require supplementary irrigation during the dry season and the landscape architect should see that this can be accomplished using simple flooding techniques rather than elaborate sprinkler systems. Vegetation requiring irrigation should be planted in slight depressions or swales to permit this. Because of its need for irrigation, grass as ground cover should be used sparingly. In semi-arid areas there is a fire hazard during the dry season. It is important that the landscape architect takes steps to minimise this hazard.

Figure 7.15: Trees for Shade

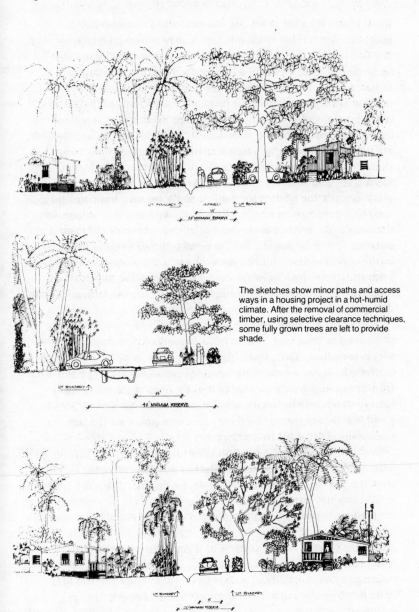

The sketches show minor paths and access ways in a housing project in a hot-humid climate. After the removal of commercial timber, using selective clearance techniques, some fully grown trees are left to provide shade.

7.2.3 Open Space Systems within the Urban Area

When planning an urban area, it is important to recognise the multi-functional roles which open space may perform. Open space may satisfy a specific demand, say, for recreation or it may, by its undeveloped nature, protect a localised unique or fragile natural resource. In most areas the environmental analysis will probably have resulted in the identification of certain areas where development would result in severe adverse environmental impacts. In some cases these anticipated impacts can be made acceptable by taking precautions and installing protective measures. But in other cases, hazardous areas should not be developed for intensive uses. However, this does not mean that these areas are not useful. Having identified them systematically the planner should first study the distribution of these areas in order to assess whether they serve any important linkages in the circulation, services or open-space infrastructures of the town. For instance, it may be possible for the flood plains of stream valleys to incorporate a pedestrian/cycle network and gravity sewer system without serious environmental impact or reducing the principal function of the flood plain (to allow passage of a flood without causing damage).

Having made this assessment the planner should examine the role of these areas as open space, for any of a number of open-space uses within the urban fabric; where they are adjacent to public housing or commercial areas, they may be valuable for parks or playing fields. Institutions may have a number of uses for open space, particularly schools which may utilise them for playing fields. It may also be possible to locate gardens on these areas, to supplement the lack in neighbouring dense urban development.

It should be emphasised that the identification of these 'hazard' areas cannot follow a rigid set of rules but will depend on the local conditions. In the wet tropical example, for instance, areas susceptible to flooding and slopes in excess of 10 per cent should be protected from intensive development (both urban and agricultural). It is also recommended that an absolute minimum of 150′ (46m) from the centre line on each side of streams be maintained as a buffer during development of the area. These will have a considerable effect in maintaining water quality as well as serving as a refuge for wild life. After development is complete they may receive some landscape treatment.

7.2.4 Some Environmental Implications of Alternatives for the Provision of Services and Utilities

In arid and semi-arid climates, there is a constant need to conserve water. Even in more humid areas of the tropics periods of considerable excess during the monsoon may be followed by periods when water is unavailable or is of a quality unsuitable for domestic use. In arid and semi-arid regions few rivers are perennial and evaporation loss from stored surface water is very high. Most water utilised is from ground-water sources and in such cases it is clearly important that ground water is pumped at a rate which does not exceed the sustained yield of the resource, which depends on the rate of recharge. Thus the planner must have knowledge of the sustained yield of the aquifer, and the location and extent of the recharge area. This may require a detailed hydro-geologic study and a number of exploratory boreholes. The demand for water can, to a limited extent, be minimised by keeping irrigation requirements of landscaped areas and agriculture to a minimum and by encouraging conservation, but it is important that the total demand of the projected population does not exceed the safe yield of the surface and ground water.

Serious consideration should be given to making the best use of sewage effluent. After primary and secondary treatment (stabilisation ponds are suitable for use in most tropical and sub-tropical climates), effluent can be used to irrigate agricultural crops which will remove a large percentage of the dissolved nutrients. Effluent may also be used to recharge ground water, to irrigate open space, for industrial use, for agriculture projects, etc.

The management of storm water is also a vitally important design consideration, particularly in arid and semi-arid climates. The incorporation of elaborate cisterns and catchment systems has, of course, always been a feature of most urban settlements in dry areas. First, care should be taken to avoid run-off pollution and, second, as much water as possible should be collected and stored. Usually the cheapest storage is in aquifers, but before using storm water to recharge an aquifer, a geologist should be consulted to make sure it is retrievable. Generally costly 'engineered' storm drainage systems can be minimised by using recharge and soak-away devices whenever possible. Consideration should be given to flooding areas during storms; playing fields, for instance, can often be flooded to a depth of several inches, providing care is taken during construction to ensure good surface fields, for instance, can often be flooded to a depth of several inches pro-viding care is taken during construction to ensure good surface drainage.

In the wetter regions of the tropics traditional villages have very few paved surfaces. During storms, water shed from roofs usually either infiltrates the ground or is allowed to run off slowly in natural water courses. Houses are frequently on stilts which give them tolerance of temporary standing water. Some new developments, however, have considerably increased paved areas (to accommodate the motor vehicle) and consequently the run-off during storms may present a problem, particularly on sloping sites. Hence it is found that, while traditional villages rely on seepage and natural water courses to handle storm water, newer developments, which may be only slightly more dense, must be equipped with a more elaborate system of storm-water drainage.

In many cities, authorities have incurred great expense by constructing separate storm and septic sewer systems. Because of the seriously polluted nature of run-off from some urban uses, it may be considerably cheaper to discharge polluted run-off into the septic system and attempt to handle clean run-off by various soak-away devices and natural drainage courses. However, it must be recognised that the increase in roofs and paved areas which will result from urban development will greatly increase the volume of run-off. Consequently the capacity of natural water-courses to handle new peak flows without eroding their banks or otherwise modifying their channels must be calculated.

In humid areas with very flat terrain there may be serious problems caused by impeded storm drainage, which results in stagnation and a consequent health hazard. The environmental evaluation process may have excluded areas with insufficient slope to ensure adequate surface drainage, but if not, the designer must give very careful consideration to storm drainage requirements.

Also, in areas of flat terrain it may be difficult to obtain sufficient fall for the use of gravity sewer systems. Sewerage is often the largest item of expenditure in development and redevelopment projects and consideration of the factors determining the cost-effective layout of sewer systems can result in very substantial savings. The cost of both roads and sewers can be reduced by careful allocation of suitable development land. For instance, if roads are routed for a large part of their length along watersheds, culverts and other expensive drainage structures can be minimised. In the case of sewers, if the areas to be served can be drained by a gravity system the cost will be considerably less than if force mains are required.

7.2.5 Environmental Precautions during Development

It is very important that the environmental planner consider carefully
the impact of the development phase on the environment. It is well to
make up a detailed flow chart of all activities and then various seasonal
constraints such as the monsoon or the dry season can be plotted on a
time scale.

During the development process there will be a number of
environmental problems. For instance, erosion may cause heavy
sediment loads in run-off and it may be advisable to construct
temporary check dams in minor streams. These may be semi-permeable,
of brushwood or rock, and their function is to impound water for
enough time for the bulk of the sediment to settle out. Buffer strips
should ideally be left undisturbed around all 'sensitive' areas,
particularly streams and water-courses.

7.2.6 Plant Nurseries

It is also important to initiate the establishment of a plant nursery as
early in the development process as possible (unless of course there is
a source of plant material already accessible). The nursery should be
located on the best available soils and should be phased so that trees
and shrubs are available for shelter planting before construction begins.
The nursery would also be used to acclimatise imported materials to
the rigours of the local climate and encourage the selection of suitable
indigenous plants. In most countries there are established forestry
departments which usually run tree nurseries growing large numbers of
commercially valuable species, generally for planting at the seedling
stage. The policy varies from country to country, whether these are
available to agencies other than the forestry service; however, provided
sufficient notice of requirements is given, it is usually possible to make
satisfactory arrangements. Usually the environmental planner will find
that commercially grown species can be used for many of his needs,
with the knowledge that the strains are selected for rapid and healthy
growth. It is also important that nursery material, particularly fruit and
shade trees, and shrubs for hedges, screens, etc. should be available to
residents at low cost from a community plant nursery. This aspect of
self-help landscaping is an important function of the plant nursery and
also applies to other living spaces.

Notes

1. Freeman Fox and Associates, Akitek Bersekutu, Tahir Wong, Alan Turner and Associates and Roger Tym and Associates, *Summary Report: Six New Towns in Pagang Tenggara* (November 1976).
2. T. Tourbier and R.W. Pierson (eds.), *Biological Control of Water Pollution* (University of Pennsylvania Press, Philadelphia, Pennsylvania, 1976).
3. M. McNeil, 'Lateritic Soils', *Scientific American* (November 1964).

Annotated Bibliography

1. Cloudsley-Thompson, J.L. *Man and the Biology of Arid Zones* (Arnold, London, 1977). An account of the physiology and ecology of desert flora and fauna; present exploitation of the desert environment is discussed together with its potential for future development in accordance with modern ideas of regional conservation.
2. Clouston, B. (ed.) *Landscape Design with Plants* (Heinemann, London, 1977). A comprehensive work which covers planting, design techniques and management. Chapters 15 ('Planting in Tropical Lowland Areas' – W. Bowen, B.T. Siedlecki and Dr T.G. Walter) and 16 ('Planting in Hot Arid Climates' – Ann Willens) are particularly useful in the context of community development. The latter chapter discusses detailed aspects of soil analysis and water quality, needs and application (irrigation) for planting in arid areas. Planting problems are discussed and an expansive plant list is included.
3. Costello, V.F. *Urbanisation in the Middle East* (Cambridge University Press, Cambridge, 1977). An urban geography text, this book studies the social demographic, political and economic processes involved in the growth of cities in the Middle East. It examines the causes and consequences of the change in the character of the Middle East city from a traditional to a modern pattern.
4. Erskine, R. *Influence of Climate on Architecture and Planning* (unpublished paper, 1977). As a result of his extensive research into the architecture most suited to peoples of cold (arctic) climates, Ralph Erskine outlines some principles which have parallels in hot arid areas. Responding mostly to climatic constraints and opportunities, he outlines ideas for the laying out of a new coastal town (with a population of about 400,000 people).
5. FAO/UNESCO *Irrigation, Drainage and Salinity: an International Source Book* (UNESCO, Paris, and Hutchinson, London, 1977). This book is a detailed compendium of pre-1973 work carried out on irrigation and soil salinisation. It is a source book which is intended to provide a synthesis of up-to-date knowledge, a guide to practical experience obtained by leading countries in the field of irrigation and drainage methods in relation to salinity and alkalinity of arid lands and generalisations useful in the solution of practical problems in the field.
6. Kaul, R.N. *Afforestation in Arid Zones* (Junk, The Hague, 1970). As a result of the over-use and abuse of the limited vegetation in arid and semi-arid zones efforts have been made by some countries to reafforest their environments. The knowledge derived from these efforts over the last two decades is made available to planners and managers in this book. Discussed by countries, the book gives latest information on species, site relationships, raising of nursery stock, etc., as well as a broad picture of the whole ecosystem which constitutes arid environments.
7. Kelly, K. and Schnadelback, R.T. *Landscaping the Saudi Arabian Desert* (Delancy Press, Philadelphia, Pennsylvania, 1976). From the point of view of the

landscape architect and an environmental planner, the natural processes of the Saudi Arabian desert are described and interpreted in terms of their implications for the design of 'outside' space. The book demonstrates landscape and architectural adaptations to wind, sun and water and provides guidelines to successful implementation of designed desert 'landscapes'.

8. Mousalli, M.S., Shaker, F.A. and Mandity, O.A. *An Introduction to Urban Patterns in Saudi Arabia: the Central Region* (Art and Archaeology Research Papers, London, 1977). This is a report on work in progress concerned with the identification of traditional architecture and urban patterns in the Kingdom of Saudi Arabia. It is part of a larger survey which is intended to record visually the traditional architecture of Saudi Arabia's different regions. It is hoped that it will provide an opportunity for foreign consultants working on major projects for the Saudi government to develop a better understanding and appreciation of _ indigenous architecture. The introduction in particular highlights living and environmental patterns which are widely applicable.

9. Saini, B.S. *Building Environment: an Illustrated Analysis of Problems in Hot Dry Lands* (Angus and Robertson, Sydney, 1973). Despite the title, this book covers a wide range of planning and design ideas for arid environments. In particular, Chapter 2 ('The Needs of Man in Hot Dry Environments') and Chapter 5 ('Planning and Design of External Space') are relevant to the evolution of 'compact' planning and design necessary in hot climates. The book also discusses the philosophies of resource development, building design, control of indoor climate, building materials and professional responsibility.

10. Shankland Cox Partnership, Salem Al Morzouk and Sabah Abi Hanna *The New City of Subiya, Draft Final Master Plan* (Report for National Housing Authority of Kuwait, 1977). This report describes the preparation of a Master Plan for a new city (satellite) in Kuwait (projected population 500,000). It also includes the development of a socio-economic framework and the selection of an area within a designated region.

11. Fiddler, A.G. and Associates, Lovejoy, D. and Partners, and Mander Raikes and Marshall *Settlements in Dry Countries: a Design Approach* (Limited Edition Report, 1977). The report is the result of a collaboration between three UK-based consultants who are actively involved in the planning and construction of new settlements in the Middle East. Using a hypothetical guideline settlement of 10,000 population, the report discusses the cultural and energy dilemmas, the form and structure of new settlements, basic services and the need for integrated architecture and designed landscapes (courtyards, etc.). (The report upholds fine ideals but sadly misses the key to the problem – how to increase local environmental awareness.)

12. Walter, H. *Ecology of Tropical and Subtropical Vegetation* (Oliver and Boyd, Edinburgh, 1971). This book (now fairly old) discusses in some ecological detail the vegetation of all the tropical and sub-tropical zones throughout the world. Since it controls ecology, the climate aspects are also described in detail. After studies of general vegetation types, wet and arid tropical and sub-tropical regions are described in detail.

13. Winston, J.T. and Blandford, C.J. *Open Space for Boca Raton, Florida* (Centre for Ecological Research in Planning and Design, Philadelphia, Pennsylvania, 1975). The natural systems of sub-tropical south Florida coast environment are used, in this report, as a basis for developing an ecological methodology for the analysis and allocation of open space in an overall land-use plan for a town of 30,000 people. Methods of achieving environmental conservation objectives are proposed and the report demonstrates the necessity for ecological planning and design to maintain vital natural resources.

PLANNING AND DEVELOPMENT STANDARDS
Alan Turner

8.1 Definition of Standards

According to the *Concise Oxford Dictionary*, a standard is a 'thing serving as basis of comparison' or a 'thing recognized as a model for imitation'. Clearly to have high standards in performing any activity does not necessarily mean that they are always attained. Standards are something to be aimed for: desirable models. Unfortunately, in the case of housing and infrastructure, legislated standards are not usually seen in this way, but are mandatory and inflexible, requiring an absolute level of service or specification before, say, a house or a sewer can be approved under the law. Minimum standards are required in new construction by housing authorities or building codes, but are not achieved in the vast mass of existing housing which in theory becomes 'substandard'. This applies in developed and developing countries alike; it is safe to say that most of the older houses in cities like London or New York do not fully comply with the building codes, but millions of people of all income groups live happy and healthy lives in them. (This, of course, excludes slums where environmental standards are by definition unacceptable.)

Clearly standards are relative and must vary greatly from place to place and from time to time. They cannot have general applicability and should not be thoughtlessly transferred from one environment to another where they may be economically and culturally irrelevant. (The most extreme example in my experience is in the building code of a tropical country where roofs are required to support snow loads, presumably to placate the gods of the European country from whence the regulation came.) In housing, particularly, the level of service in infrastructure, lot sizes and facilities has to be adjusted to the ability of the residents to pay. Unrealistic standards inevitably result in the eventual occupation of the housing by a higher-income group than the intended families, who are unable to afford the rents to pay for the level of service provided. In developing countries, especially, it is vital to base project design on estimated levels of affordability rather than on predetermined standards of infrastructure, construction or facility provision. In this respect, a World Bank paper recommends an 'ad hoc iterative approach', basing levels of service on existing norms, which would then be explored in terms of improving or reducing standards to produce a project within the cost ceiling imposed by the need to recover costs from the beneficiaries. 'The pattern of facilities to be provided can be roughly tested for realism by comparison with the pattern of household budgets in the income category concerned.'[1]

It is quite pointless to tear down 'substandard' housing and to replace it with housing which the occupiers cannot afford and which is, therefore, a burden on the nation as a whole through subsidies, or is occupied by people who do not need government assistance to satisfy their housing needs. However, these arguments do not imply that there should be no standards at all or that building and development should be anarchic. It is not possible to plan a new area, nor to upgrade an existing one, without a set of guidelines or criteria to follow. The problem for administrative control is how to prepare such guidelines so that they are neither over-restrictive nor so loose as to be ineffective. Which requirements will be mandatory minima or maxima and which will be discretionary? If a project fails to meet a certain norm is the whole project rejected or can the norm be lowered? In this respect, the World Bank's 'iterative approach' seems to make the most sense and lends itself to appropriate solutions.

8.1.1 Performance Standards

Most standards are expressed as specification standards which prescribe sizes (e.g. hectares of open space per thousand people or the thickness of a wall), dimensions or materials. This is fairly easy to administer as it leaves no flexibility; a wall is either thick enough or it is not. Performance standards are much more flexible and, therefore, much more desirable in practice, but unfortunately they require a degree of sophistication which may not exist in a particular country. For instance, a specification standard requiring a fire wall to be 200mm of concrete is easy to understand and to apply. A performance standard allowing any material to be used which will resist fire for two hours is more flexible and would allow, say, local materials to be used. It would, however, imply the existence of a testing laboratory which would certify such materials, and this may be out of the question in many developing countries. It is, however, quite possible to use performance standards for levels of service. For instance, to require that 'all dwellings should be accessible from footpaths which are usable without danger or discomfort at all times of the year' implies certain standards of construction or levels above flood water, without specifying particular materials or methods. In spite of the difficulties of monitoring, evaluation and control, performance standards are usually preferable to rigid specifications.

8.1.2 Mutually Exclusive Definitions

When compiling a comprehensive list of planning standards, great care must be exercised to avoid conflicts between one requirement and another. For instance, a facility may be required for so many thousand people; if at the same time another requirement specifies the maximum distance between these facilities, this has the unintended effect of defining housing density. At lower densities, either the facilities would be further apart or they would serve fewer people. This is fairly obvious, but there are a great many examples of such conflicts in legislation throughout the world.

8.1.3 Existing Standards

One of the most difficult problems in the planning and design of low-income areas is to adapt projects to the requirements of existing agencies. Many of these will be guidelines subject to negotiation; others may be rigid and inflexible and may require new legislation to enable affordable projects to be designed. To apply the average building code in a typical squatter area would imply complete demolition and this, in fact, is what many housing officials would like to see. Such areas are often viewed as being a discredit to the town and there is a feeling that they should be 'cleaned up' and that the people who live in them should be rehoused. Their importance as the houses of the *majority* of people is often completely misunderstood. However, if new legislation can be brought in, which in effect legitimises informal construction, while imposing certain achievable (probably incremental) standards, the view of the administrator may change. He is, after all, required by his government to impose the law, even though it may be manifestly absurd. His task should be made easier by practical legislation which both he and the community can see a way of achieving.

8.1.4 Variable Standards

There is no reason why standards should not vary within a town or even within a project; only a bureaucratic desire for orderliness would insist otherwise. At first sight this statement may appear discriminatory, but on reflection it will be seen that such a pragmatic approach is necessary if the living conditions of the very poor are to be raised and if the desires of the slightly better-off are not to be frustrated. In a high-density slum area, lot sizes may have to be very small to avoid extensive relocation, but it does not necessarily follow that in a new area the sizes should be the same.

While sites and services projects must be affordable, the tendency to concentrate only on the smallest lots and the lowest standards should be avoided for two reasons. In the first place, a better social mix (and possible cross-subsidies) may be achieved with variable standards and, in the second place, incomes and expectations may improve over time and space standards which were too low in the early stages may result in obsolescence during the later years of the project, long before the end of its economic life.

This, of course, applies specifically to housing for low-income groups, where, aside from small areas of community facilities, there is only a single land use. In the case of larger projects involving a number of urban functions, it is most important to consider not only the current levels of income and demand but to give due weight to the needs of the community in the future when it is probable that larger real incomes will increase the pressure on land. Under-provision at the beginning can be a serious constraint in later years and an attempt must be made to propose a reasonable and flexible land-use allocation. For instance, it is not uncommon for a planner to be asked by a government how much land should be acquired for a new development which may include housing, industry, social facilities and open space. The planner cannot react by saying that there are no standards on which he can base a judgement; in the initial stages he may have to turn to previous examples, study them and adapt them to local requirements to suggest a reasonable figure.

8.2 Main Categories of Land Use

A useful basis for establishing the major urban land uses is given by Robin Best, following the original data requirements for the British new towns, which distinguish four main categories:

(1) housing (net residential area);
(2) industry;
(3) open space;
(4) education.

In addition to these, Best refers to residual uses which are 'many and varied and some of them may cover larger areas in individual towns or even in the country as a whole than certain of the four main uses.'[2]

Table 8.1: Land Use in Selected New Towns
Amounts of land for main uses in selected examples of new towns in
the UK and developing countries, in hectares per 1,000 population

Town	Total urban area	Housing	Industry	Open space	Education	Residual
Milton Keynes, England	35.5	18.8	3.2	4.6	1.5	7.5
New towns near London, England	23.2	11.7	2.0	4.0	2.3	3.2
Cumbernauld, Scotland	14.9	4.7	2.7	4.7	1.0	1.8
Average	24.5	11.7	2.6	4.4	1.6	4.1
Average percentage	100	47.7	10.6	17.9	6.5	16.7
Huambo, Angola	13.4	8.0	1.92	1.0	1.0	1.5
Rural new towns, Malaysia	25.7[b]	10.75	2.6	2.9	2.7[a]	6.75
Ciudad Losada, Venezuela	16.7	5.5	3.4	4.6	0.4	2.8
Alta Gracia, Venezuela	17.1	8.3	1.2	3.0	0.6	4.0
Average	18.2	8.1	3.4	2.1	1.1	3.7
Average percentage	100	44.5	18.6	11.5	6.0	20.3

Notes:
a. A high figure required by the Malaysian authorities including reserves for
expansion.
b. This figure relates to the area designated for the uses in this table. An 'urban
fringe' comprising jungle reserve, service wayleaves, agriculture and reserves
for urban expansion is omitted. If included, this would bring the total land
use up to 83.5 ha. per 1,000 people, and would give a misleading comparison.

Residual uses include transport, commercial, public buildings,
government establishments and public utilities. In the British new
towns, housing takes up about 50 per cent of the total area, followed
by public open space with about 18 per cent; education and industry
account for 6-10 per cent each.

Based on this classification, Table 8.1 shows the land uses in a number
of examples of new towns in developing countries compared with

Table 8.2: Land Use Areas: Angola

Use	Area per person m^2
Housing lot	19.00
Open space	10.00
Schools	2.00
Commercial	0.50
Social, cultural, religious	0.80
Administration	0.50
Circulation	11.00

Source: T. de Sampaya[3].

several British new towns. Using this as a guide, it is fairly simple to estimate the amount of land required for these land uses as a first approximation. Further study will refine and alter the land requirements; for instance, the amount of industrial land is related to the type of industry, the density of workers per hectare common in that industry and the number of industrial workers predicted in a given population. The amount of land devoted to educational use or open space can vary greatly, depending on whether playing fields are included as 'education' or 'public open space'.

Other authorities express normative land-use areas quite differently; for example, areas were recommended for low-income housing in Angola, expressed in square metres per person. These figures relate specifically to gross residential area and exclude industry and residual use outside the immediate housing area.

An example from Jamaica recommended (for a sites-and-services project) 3.6-4.8 ha. per 1,000 lots (4,500 people) for open space and 4 ha. per 1,000 lots for schools and recreation. In this example an important point was raised which should be considered in all low-income areas; namely that schools should be adequate to cope with more children than would be found in the initial projected population, in order to allow for subletting.[4]

Although it is obviously necessary to make rough assessments of this kind in the early stages of a project, great care should be taken with measurement and definition and every figure which may be given regarding an existing situation should be double-checked. For instance, the city of Davao in the Philippines is one of the largest in the world in terms of area ($2440 km^2$) but has a population of only about half a million on a very small percentage of the land. Most of the area of the 'city' is composed of forests and mountains. Some 'municipal' statistics can, therefore, be very misleading and it is usually necessary to draw an arbitrary boundary round an urbanised area rather than use legal boundaries, even though this may produce problems of disaggregation of data.

A further point to consider at the town scale is the fact that different kinds of facility require certain minimum population levels and can only be designed into phases of development where the necessary support population has been reached. Again, there are no hard and fast rules and there are towns all over the world which have exceptional facilities which would normally only occur in much larger cities. However, Figure 8.1 shows a selection of facilities ranging from the neighbourhood to the city centre and the populations which would normally support them.

8.3 Concepts of 'Neighbourhood' and 'Community'

A great deal of work has been done during the past two or three decades on a number of ideas concerned with the size of a planned community and the way in which people use the available facilities and relate to other people within the community. In Britain after the Second World War emphasis was placed on a series of new towns which were to have populations of about 50,000 divided into 'neighbourhoods' of 10,000 people. It was thought that this would foster the growth of community spirit and neighbourliness.[5] However, later research has shown that these ideas have little significance for social relationships. Margaret Willis has shown that needs vary with age, sex and economic status; a small child's contacts are limited to the people next door; at school the child's interests widen and extend beyond the neighbourhood, but with marriage and children the young mother is again restricted to the neighbourhood.[6] In a survey in 1962 Peter Willmott concluded that for the majority of people, a neighbourhood of 10,000 people is 'not a meaningful concept' and that they tend to identify with a much smaller residential area. He also concluded that physical planning of large areas does not create 'communities' or 'neighbourliness'.[7]

Emphasis is now on much smaller residential groups and various sizes have been put forward — 60-100 families or 12-50 dwellings (Washington New Town, England) or 30-60 houses (Runcorn New Town, England) which allow a reasonable number of contacts to be made.

Figure 8.1: Population Required to Support Major Public Facilities

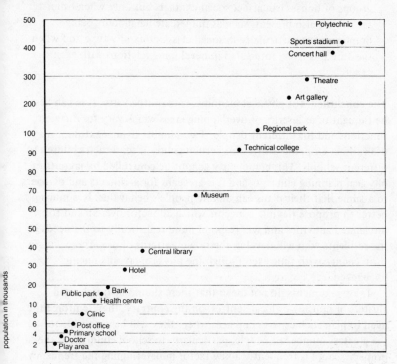

The figures given above are based on those used in the design of a new city in Britain.* They are not necessarily correct for other situations, but research in a particular country could suggest appropriate figures, based on local needs.

* Central Lancashire New Town, HMSO, London 1971.

On the whole, sociological research suggests that the layout of small groups of houses can affect social contacts but only when other factors are also present, such as immediate neighbours being homogeneous particularly in social class and family type and when they are positively interested in developing relations with each other.[8]

The conclusion, for physical planning, is that urban structure can best be thought of as a series of overlapping areas which vary for different functions and for different people. Two families living next door may use various shopping centres for certain goods or send their children to different schools. This complexity cannot be controlled by layouts or physical planning concepts and it is arrogant for architects and planners to assume that their plans can dictate people's behaviour. It is much better to propose flexible concepts which allow for overlap and for unplanned activities and will respond more realistically to the needs of the residents who will develop their own patterns of use. These will, in turn, change with time even though the physical layouts remain unchanged (see Figure 8.2).

These arguments do not mean that there should be no planned clusters of housing or local centres; on the contrary, they reinforce the need to plan such centres in places where they will be accessible to the greatest number of people, particularly to school children, as the primary school is frequently a key factor in determining the frequency of local centres. The usual assumption is that primary schools should be near to the centre of the area they serve, but the problem is that the extent of a school's catchment area will depend on dwelling density, the average number of children of primary school age per family and the annual intake and number of children in a school. This is shown in Figure 8.3, which relates densities, numbers of children per lot and school catchments. Schoolchildren have been related to the lot rather than the family as it is common in developing countries for more than one family (or an extended family) to share a lot.

The need for a flexible system for the educational policy-maker and for some freedom of choice of school for the family will lead to overlapping areas. A study of the location of primary schools in Britain showed that in a large area of new development, zones will tend to peak in the order in which they were constructed, but when birth rates put a strain on one school others can be used to relieve it, provided there is some overlap in the catchment areas. School buildings cannot be matched to such variables and in general can only be more or

Figure 8.2: Social Facilities; Catchment Areas

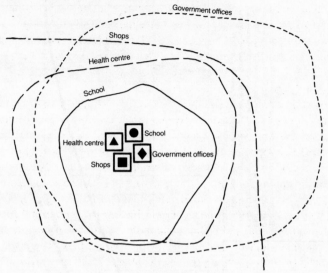

Social facilities may draw their users from widely different areas. Placing these facilities in a local centre does not ensure that they serve the same geographical "neighbourhood". However, combining them together enables residents to visit more than one facility with a single journey to the centre.

less evenly distributed over the area to be served. An ideal size for a new development might be enough housing to support 5 or 6 primary schools with each dwelling having two schools within about 800 metres that can be reached easily and safely. In this respect, the same study found that a school less than 650 metres away will be regarded as accessible to a five-year-old, but that one more than 1.5 km away will be regarded as inaccessible.[9]

8.4 Housing – Standards/Density/Lot Sizes

8.4.1 Density

While it is clear that there are no absolute standards of lot sizes or density, the places to which this book relates are usually areas of single- or two-storey houses built on individual lots. In squatter areas, there may be no defined lots; families may have built their own shacks on unused ground, often in an erratic and congested fashion. Their methods are simple and direct and the houses tend to be little larger

Figure 8.3: School Catchment Areas

Children of primary school age per lot	3	2	1
Number of lots per 600 place school	200	300	600
Hectares of catchment area per school			
Density 150 lots/ha	1.3	2	4
" 100 " "	2	3	6
" 50 " "	4	6	12
" 25 " "	8	12	24

The catchment area for a school depends on the housing density and the number of children of school age per lot. This example shows how the catchment area for a 600 place primary school could vary from 1.3 ha to 24 ha. As the majority of families will tend to remain in the area while the children grow up, the area served by a school will vary over time. This demonstrates the need for overlap when planning the location of schools in a community.

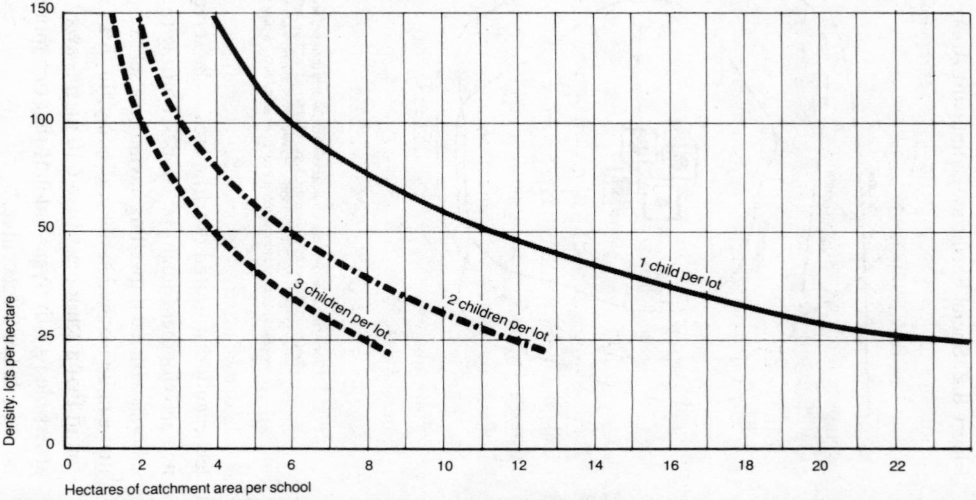

than basic shells for sleeping and sometimes eating (although in many countries the cooking is done out of doors). Consequently the pattern of houses tends to flow into available spaces and fill up voids until a saturation point is reached (given sufficient pressure). The density of a squatter settlement increases with its age and if the local circumstances are known its age can often be judged approximately from the closeness of the houses.

There are two primary considerations:

(1) lot size;
(2) area of lot which is built on.

There is no particular relationship between these, as at one end of the scale in an urban slum the house may be virtually as big as the lot, whereas in low-density areas it may be only a small portion of the lot. Lot size depends on a number of factors including

cultural and social needs — in a newly urbanising situation families newly arrived from country areas may need space to grow food for some years after they become city-dwellers;
affordability — where a family is paying rent (as distinct from squatting) the size of the lot is obviously limited by the ability of the family to pay and the level of subsidy, if any;
land availability — even though families could pay more, the lot size may be limited by the supply of suitable land;
economic service runs — in newly planned areas there is a close relationship between lot size (and shape) and reasonably efficient services layouts. At very low densities, service runs are too long and at very high densities services may become complex and pass through a cost threshold. There is usually a zone of 'reasonably efficient' density.

In the case of built area there is an equally large range of acceptable norms which makes it impossible to be specific. For instance, poor areas in Asia or Africa may have only $2\text{-}4\,\text{m}^2$ of built dwelling per person, whereas comparable areas in the UK are as high as $16\text{-}17\,\text{m}^2$ per person; $4\text{-}6\,\text{m}^2$ of built dwelling per person might be a reasonable standard to aim for in low-income areas in developing countries.

However, all these considerations are further complicated by the vagueness of the concept of density. It is now normal to use figures related to habitable rooms or bed-spaces per hectare in developed

Table 8.3: Some Recorded Examples of Existing Lot Sizes and Densities from a Number of Countries

Place	Source	Sizes m² House	Lot	Occupancy	Built area per person m²	Density dw. per ha.	Notes
1 Angola	Sampaya,[3] p. 180	50-60	279	5-11	4.6-7.4	30	
2 Luanda, Angola (musseques) (a)	aerial photos high	—	114	—		70	Urban, developing squatter areas, filling in gradually
(b)	medium	—	217	—		36.8	
(c)	low	—	444	—		18	
3 Jamaica	SCP Report[4] Tower Hill (Sites & Services Project)	92	167	2 persons per habitable room 8	11.5	23.4	Original figures — since then open space has been 'captured'
4 Cuevas, Lima, Peru	Caminos,[10] p. 138	87	128	6	14.5	30.5	Includes 30 m² for walls
5 El Ermintano Lima, Peru	Caminos,[10] p. 145	110	160	10	11.0	26.06	Includes 27 m² for walls
6 El Augustino Lima, Peru	Caminos,[10] p. 159	43	61.8	6	10.3	68.05	Includes 5 m² for walls
7 El Gallo Ciudad Guayana, Venezuela	Caminos,[10] p. 215	65	300	6	10.83	10.56	
8 Villa Socorro Colombia	Caminos,[10] p. 229	43	96	6	7.16	38.25	
9 Davao Philippines (Piapi)	Social survey of area	24	48	9	2.6	176.00	high-density urban slum — all houses on ground — no multi-storey

Table 8.4: Some Recorded Examples of Proposed New Housing from a Number of Countries

Place	Source	Sizes m² House	Sizes m² Lot	Occupancy	Built area per person m²	Density[a] per ha. net	Notes
10 Kaduna, Nigeria	Max Lock[11]	84.5	232	7-8	10.5-12	34.4	
11 Luanda, Angola (Ilha do Cabo)	OTAM[12]	60 84 88	95 145 150	4 6 8	15 14 11	)24	Semi-urban
12 Luanda, Angola Bairro do Cazenga	Observation	60	162	6	10	43	Urban
13 Huambo, Angola Bairro do Cacilhas	Observation	64	375	6	10.6	21	Rural
14 Alto Liro, Angola	Lobito[13]	36	144	6	6	55	Urban self-help project. Houses to be extended
15 Angola	Sampaya[3] p. 184	50-60	130	6	8-10	60	
16 Jamaica	Shankland Cox[4]	45.5 36.2	93.6 93.6	6 4	7.5 9.05	69 69	

Note: a. Where not specifically indicated, 20 per cent of the area has been deducted for roads and footpaths.
Footnotes are at the end of this chapter.

countries where 'habitable rooms' or bedrooms are easily defined. However, in many developing countries, rooms are used for eating. living and sleeping and all are 'habitable'. Given that houses are all single- or double-storeyed (we are excluding discussion of high-rise apartments) the most useful measure is lots per hectare. This does not necessarily relate directly to population density as there may be one, two or more households sharing a lot, but it gives a useful guide to achieving a certain 'base' standard which will vary from lot to lot with occupancy. In other words, we are saying: with one household this represents a reasonable standard of accommodation but if the household rents to another one (and tacks on an extra room) it is still not too bad.

8.4.2 Percentage of Land used for Lots: Saleable Area

An important measure in terms of maximising the return on investment in housing land is the proportion of the total area used for actual lots. Obviously a percentage must be used for roads, community facilities and open space, but in low-income areas, where subsidies should be low and where costs must be partially recovered from the beneficiaries, this should be kept to a reasonable minimum. Table 8.5 illustrates a number of projects and indicates a wide range. It is usually assumed that the percentage of private land (i.e. lots) decreases with density and that the requirements for public space, including roads and footpaths, increase with density.[14] While this is true in general, the projects in the table, which vary from very high to very low density, show that it is not necessarily always true in practice. This is because the developing authority does not always provide the appropriate amount of space for social facilities, or in some cases (such as Indonesia) the amount of space for circulation is very low. The projects in Table 8.5 are shown graphically in Figure 8.4 and it can be seen that they are not distributed in any clear pattern. A high percentage of land can be in private use at either high or low densities. However, a much clearer relationship exists between lot size and density as shown in Figure 8.5, which records the numbered projects in Tables 8.3, 8.4 and 8.5. Clearly there would be a simple arithmetical relationship if all the space were taken up with lots and this is shown at the top of the graph; it is in practice an unobtainable relationship, but it demonstrates the curve which tends to be followed by actual projects. The projects plotted show two distinct groups; the first lies at the higher part of the graph and comprises projects with few other uses and minimal circulation space. They have a high percentage of land in private use. Another group lies

Table 8.5: Percentages of Public and Private Use in Some Typical
Sites-and-Services Layouts

Project	Lot size m^2	Net density lots/ha.	Percentages of land use			Source
			Lots	Social facilities	Roads and footpaths	
17 Nicaragua	110	50	55	25	20	IBRD, Sites and Services Projects
18 Senegal	150	44	61	15	24	Annex A, p. 10
19 Indonesia	64[a]	95	61	21	18	''
20 Jamaica	77[a]	77	60	20	20	''
21 Botswana	330	20	66	14	20	''
22 Zambia	210	21	50	15	35	''
23 Tanzania	130[a]	38	50	34	16	''
24 Kenya	150[a]	40	60	20	20	''
25 Korea	105[a]	72	76	5	19	''
26 Philippines	68[a]	100	68	17	15	Alan Turner
27 Curacao	320	18	59	25	16	Alan Turner

Note: a. Average lot size in projects where a range of lot sizes is used to provide
greater choice.

at the lower part of the graph and has a high proportion of land used
for community facilities and circulation. This group has a low
percentage of land in private use. A third group lies approximately
along a line represented by a theoretical split — 60 per cent private
space, 20 per cent public space and 20 per cent circulation. It is
suggested that this is a reasonable guide in practice; the graph can be
used to show the density for a given lot size assuming this utilisation.
Thus, in this example projects with lots of 200m^2 vary in density from
20 lots/ha. to 35 lots/ha., but the optimum is shown to be 30 lots/ha.

However, it must be stressed that while this is a useful guide,
exceptions must be made depending on local conditions. For instance,
in a small project situated near to existing facilities the land devoted to
public use can be decreased, whereas in a very large project, school sites
and other major facilities may reduce the proportion available for
private use.

Figure 8.6 illustrates this diagramatically and also shows how the
percentage of land devoted to other uses may vary considerably with
density. The graph indicates a range of percentages which forms a

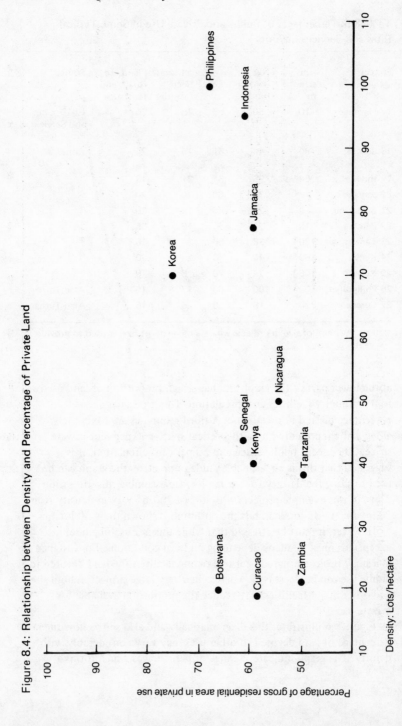

Figure 8.4: Relationship between Density and Percentage of Private Land

Figure 8.5: Relationship between Lot Size and Density

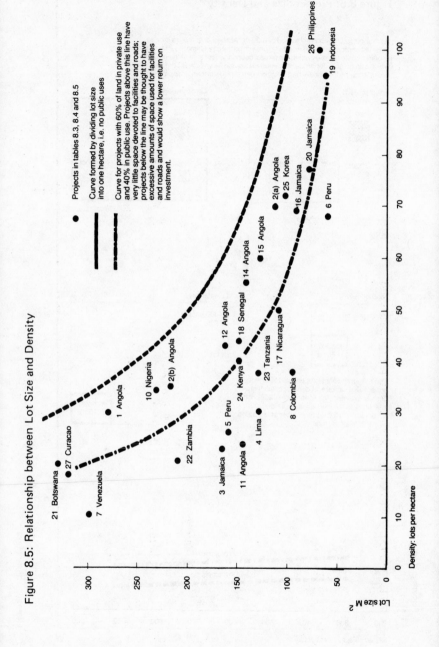

Density: lots per hectare

Lot size M²

Projects in tables 8.3, 8.4 and 8.5

Curve formed by dividing lot size into one hectare, i.e. no public uses

Curve for projects with 60% of land in private use and 40% in public use. Projects above this line have very little space devoted to facilities and roads; projects below the line may be thought to have excessive amounts of space used for facilities and roads and would show a lower return on investment.

Figure 8.6: Project Size and Density

A small project may be well served by existing facilities, or new ones located outside the project boundary. A large project, on the other hand may have to accommodate facilities within the project boundary. The area of the project which can be used for producing revenue (residential and small commercial lots) may be proportionally much higher in small projects than large projects.

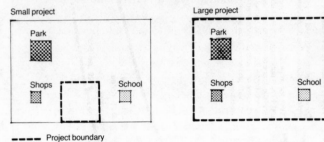

- - - - Project boundary

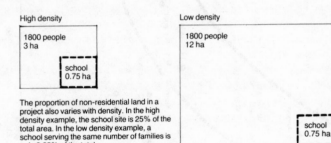

The proportion of non-residential land in a project also varies with density. In the high density example, the school site is 25% of the total area. In the low density example, a school serving the same number of families is only 6.25% of the total.

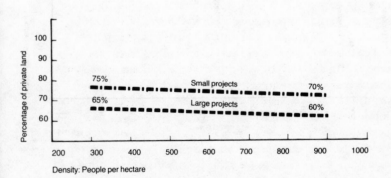

This graph gives a guide to the percentages of private land which may be achieved in projects of different sizes and densities

useful guide at the planning stage.

8.5 Social Facilities

There are normally two categories:

(1)   publicly provided: schools, clinics, hospitals, community centres, parks, etc.;

(2)   privately provided: churches, some schools and hospitals, clubs, shops, restaurants and many recreational facilities.

The first category can be directly controlled by planning; available resources, construction budgets and timetables will usually be known to existing agencies and the necessary land can be planned into the development programme, both in terms of space and time. That is, the necessary area based on local standards can be programmed to be available when needed, allowing time if necessary for compulsory acquisition or expropriation. However, the facilities in the second category cannot be 'provided' by planning and development agencies; they can only be encouraged to happen by sensitive plans and programmes which allow space for them and, more importantly, do not actively discourage development by means of inappropriate zoning or construction regulations.

It is not uncommon for such legislation to be nation-wide and based, perhaps, on examples borrowed from foreign countries. The regulations found in such cases are often counter-productive in a low-income community and will be either ignored or will cause hardship and stagnation.

In one country in Asia, there is a regulation (sensible in the crowded metropolis) that new housing should have back alleys to provide fire-breaks; this has the effect of placing a road on either side of a plot. According to the law, it applies in rural areas, but in this case 'the law is an ass' and to penalise low-income people with such a high level of expensive circulation is a policy that cannot be defended. In another developing country it is illegal to use part of an ordinary house for retail purposes although the vast majority of the population relies upon informal 'corner shops' (sari-sari stores in the Philippines or tokos in Indonesia — most countries have them). To attempt to enforce such laws in low-income settlements would be virtually impossible and if it were successful such enforcement would wreck the local economy.

The need, then, is for flexible policies; there is no compelling reason why zoning ordinances or building regulations should be exactly the same in different parts of the city. What may be appropriate in a middle-income subdivision may be entirely out of place in a sites-and-services project. Policies should allow and encourage the use of private residential lots for small-scale commercial activities, subject to minimum requirements for health and safety — for instance noxious fumes, excessive noise or fire hazards. The importance of small-scale enterprises is discussed in Chapter 5 and grants and loans for the development of small, labour-intensive businesses are now an important part of urban and rural programmes, so that it becomes increasingly important not to stifle initiative by over-rigid physical planning policies.

It is not possible to give more than a general guide to the provision of facilities, as standards vary so much from country to country. However, it should be borne in mind that for low-income communities standards may need to be lower than the legislated norms applied in more affluent parts of the city. This is a difficult philosophy to put forward and I am not suggesting that the poor should be treated unfairly. The point is that, if the rules require piped sewerage and all that can be afforded are pit privies, then these are better than nothing at all. Similarly, a school built to lower standards in the early stages of a new settlement is preferable to waiting for years to build one with 'approved' standards, by which time a lot of children will have missed their chance of a basic education.

The appropriate standards will be generated by:

available resources and level of subsidy or degree of cost recovery required;
land costs/development costs;
density and transportation;
in the case of schools, the numbers of pupils per classroom and whether there are single or double shifts;
the staff resources available to provide the particular service — for instance, the number of doctors, midwives and auxiliary health workers available will help to determine the physical facilities to be provided. A well equipped but unstaffed clinic is of little use to anyone.

It is clear that schools are one of the major land uses (see Table 8.1) and need special attention to avoid the waste of resources by over-provision. It is common for education authorities in developing countries to have exorbitantly high standards for land for schools; sometimes as much as 1 or 2 ha. per 1,000 people may be required (although often not obtained). The British examples in Table 8.1 average about 1.6 ha. per 1,000 people, but this includes very large areas for football fields and other outdoor sports. The planners in developing countries who have worked out the standards have often been educated in the West and may be over-influenced by Western models. As a guide, the Venezuelan example of 0.4 ha. per 1,000 may be nearer to the mark and should prove to provide enough space for the basic teaching requirements, divided roughly equally into primary, secondary and collegiate levels. Sports fields should, wherever possible, be combined with wider use by the whole community so as to maximise the return on the investment.

8.6 A Check-list of Standards for Low-income Housing

The following check-list sets out some standards which have been found to be appropriate in low-income communities in various projects in less developed countries. The list is neither definitive nor prescriptive and should be used as a guide for testing against local conditions, so that a specific set of standards can be devised based on local uses and levels of income.

8.6.1 Lot Size and Shape

Figure 8.7 indicates how lot size is influenced by single- or double-storey construction, the position of the house within the lot and the type of sanitary disposal system. Ideally lots should be rectangular with the short side adjacent to the street, path or piped services; this is more efficient in terms of the length of services per lot which is a major determinant of total cost. Clearly there is a minimum practical width (possibly affected by fire regulations) and the following are some recommended ratios:

Agency	Width (m)	Depth (m)	Ratio
USAID	7.5	14.0	1:2
UNWRA	5.0	16.7	1:3
OAS	5.0	8.0	1:1.5

Source: World Bank.

8.6.2 Access

Classification of Roads and paths (see Figure 8.8):

Figure 8.7: Lot Size and Built Area

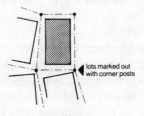

In some upgrading schemes, the houses may be so close together that they almost fill whatever lot can be defined. Where this is the case, there is little that can be done but accept the de facto lot sizes even though they may be smaller than a desirable minimum. This will leave no space for expansion (except by adding a second storey), or for pit latrines. Communal sanitary facilities will be required since piped sewerage is unlikely to be affordable at this level.

lots marked out with corner posts

40m² lots

If an arbitrary minimum lot of 40m² is assumed, the built area (single storey) will be about 22.75m² or 2.85m² per person, assuming an occupancy of 8 people (1.3 households with 6 people per household).

50m² lots

Where there is a little more space, minimum lots may be calculated, assuming a desirable minimum built area per person – in this example 4m² or 32m² for 8 people. The resultant minimum lot would be about 50m².

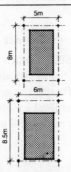

40m² lots
density 168 lots/ha

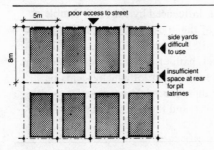

poor access to street

side yards difficult to use

insufficient space at rear for pit latrines

This and the following diagrams represent basic sites and services lots with minimum on-lot development. In some countries, two storey timber houses are common this makes it possible to provide more open space on the lots, while retaining a reasonable amount of built area. The densities quoted in these examples assume 67.5% of land use in private lots (saleable area).

40m² lots
density 168 lots/ha

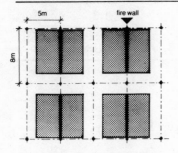

fire wall

If the houses can be paired, the side yards are more usable and access to the street is improved. However, fire resisting brick or block dividing walls must be built as part of the site development contract. This increases on-lot costs and affects affordability.

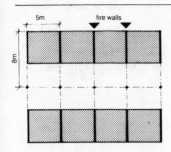

40m² lots
density 168 lots/ha

This example maintains the same house size (21.75m²) but shows that with row houses the shape of the yard space is improved. However access must be through the house which means that although there may be room in the yards for pit latrines, they are probably not acceptable. With lots of this size, communal facilities or piped sewerage will be required.

With the minimum suggested house of 32m², the lots will be about 51m² but the same arguments will apply.

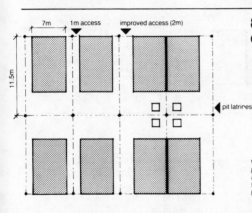

80m² lots
density 84 lots/ha

With 80m² lots and 40m² houses it becomes possible to accommodate pit latrines and to allow reasonable access from the street to the back yard, especially with paired houses.

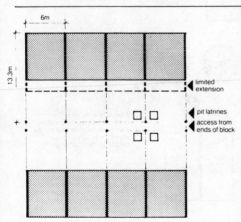

80m² lots
density 84 lots/ha

A house size of 40m² with a row house form gives better shaped yards, but requires access through the house, or, at this density, it may be possible to provide a narrow footpath between the yards.

Limited extension of the house may also be permitted and there may be room for small fruit trees (valuable as an addition to the family food supply).

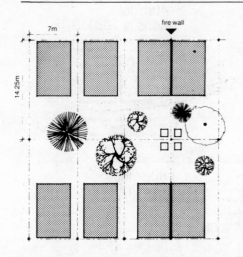

7m

14.25m

fire wall

100m² lots
density 67.5 lots/ha

When the lot size reaches 100m² the yards are relatively spacious. even with detached or paired houses. There should be space for pit latrines. limited house extension and small fruit trees.

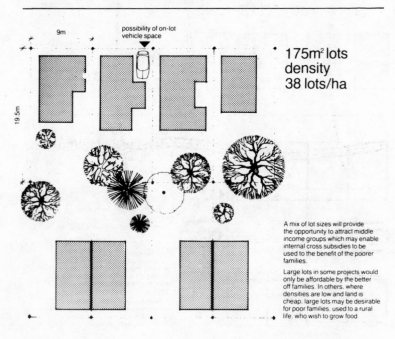

9m

19.5m

possibility of on-lot vehicle space

175m² lots
density
38 lots/ha

A mix of lot sizes will provide the opportunity to attract middle income groups which may enable internal cross subsidies to be used to the benefit of the poorer families.

Large lots in some projects would only be affordable by the better off families. In others. where densities are low and land is cheap. large lots may be desirable for poor families. used to a rural life. who wish to grow food.

Figure 8.8: Circulation Network

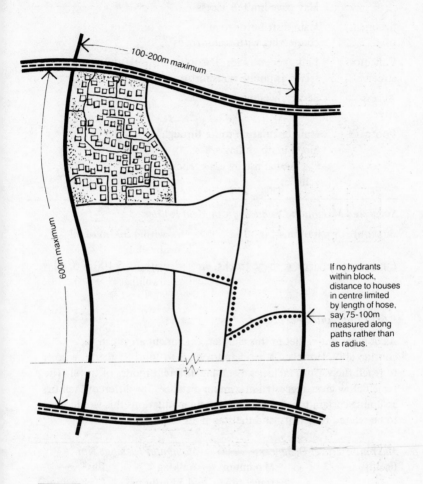

100-200m maximum

600m maximum

If no hydrants within block, distance to houses in centre limited by length of hose, say 75-100m measured along paths rather than as radius.

═══ 10m street

━━━ 6-10m street: depending on local conditions

──── 6m access streets

───── 2-4m footpaths serving groups of houses

------ bus or para transit route

Name	Function	Width (right of way)
Major road	Links parts of the city. May have limited access	30-45 m
Secondary road	Main distributor road connecting with major roads	25 m
Collector street	Links access roads. Possibly serves as public transport route	10 m
Access street	Serves dwellings	6 m
Footpath	Main circulation route through block in upgrading areas. Occasional use by emergency vehicles	2-4 m

Suggested Maximum Distances from Main Routes

Bus route or para-transit route	– within 300 m of all dwellings
Emergency services, garbage trucks, etc.	– within 75-100 m of all dwellings

8.6.3 Community Facilities

As pointed out earlier in this chapter, catchment areas can vary considerably. However, a good approach is to consider the time taken to reach the various facilities assuming different modes of travel. The table below gives suggested maximum distances for different facilities assuming certain travel times. In particular situations this would need to be related to density and the standards of provision.

Maximum Travel Distances		Maximum Distance Km	
Facility	Maximum travel time (minutes)	Walking (4.5 km/hour)	Bus[a] (25 km/hour)
Day-care centre	10	.75 km	–
Elementary school	20	1.5	2.0
High school or local shopping centre	30	2.25	6.25

Note: a. Assuming 5 minute walk to bus stop, 5 minute wait for bus and 5 minute walk to destination.

Area of Land for Schools. Assume

40 pupils per classroom and $50 m^2$ per classroom;
1/3 of built area maximum for circulation administration and
ancillary uses;
total site area of not more than 10 times the area of the buildings,
allowing limited space for outdoor games.

No. of classrooms	Classroom area m^2	Circulation and Admin. m^2	Built area m^2	Site area ha.
10	500	250	750	.75
20	1,000	500	1,500	1.5
30	1,500	750	2,250	2.25
40	2,000	1,000	3,000	3.0

The area of land per 1,000 population can be worked out once the
number of children of school age is known. If it is assumed that 25 per
cent of the population is below high-school age, then the number of
school spaces would be 250 per 1,000 people, or 6.25 classrooms. This
gives 0.46 ha. of land per 1,000, which is comparable to the Venezuelan
figures in Table 8.1. Higher figures are the result of large playing fields;
wherever possible recreational space of this kind should be a shared
community facility and not solely reserved for school use.

Community Centre. The size of facilities would obviously vary with the
size of the community to be served, but the following basic spaces
should be provided where possible. In some countries the spaces may
only be roofed over to provide shade, with a small lockable area for
storage.

		Suggested size
(1)	Multi-purpose meeting space	200-$300 m^2$
(2)	Day-care/nutrition facility	$50 m^2$ for each 45 children served
(3)	Health care centre or clinic	$75 m^2$-$350 m^2$ depending on population. Space for pre-natal and post-natal clinic, first aid, immunisation, treatment room, baby clinic, dental services and lecture space for health-care education

(4)   Work-room, for $100\,m^2$ minimum with allowance of $1\,m^2$
      employment and   per person for 25 per cent of women in
      training of women   area, e.g. about $200\,m^2$ for community
                              of 5,000 with family size of 6 and one
                              woman per family

Recreational Open Space

Category	Provision
Play lot	$0.5\,m^2$-$2\,m^2$ per lot depending on density and land cost. Minimum area per play lot of 20-$30\,m^2$
Playing field	$1\,m^2$ per person for general purposes, including use by schools
Small park	About 1-$2\,m^2$ per lot for 'vest-pocket' parks. Minimum size $100\,m^2$
Community park	About 1-$2\,m^2$ per lot with minimum size of $400\,m^2$
Large park	To serve community of at least 5,000, $1\,m^2$ per person

The suggestions given above equate to about 0.3 ha. per 1,000 persons. This is very much less than the average of 2.1 ha. per 1,000 for several developing countries given in Table 8.1. However, it excludes major facilities such as sports stadia, regional parks or large-scale conservation areas such as those along stream banks. The figures in Table 8.1 are at the *town* scale; the figures above are at the neighbourhood scale.

8.6.4 Infrastructure

Water Supply. Water for industrial use cannot be quantified without a knowledge of the specific industry. For residential uses the following figures are often used as a guide:

- 80 litres *per capita* per day with pit latrines;
- 100 litres *per capita* per day with water-borne sewerage;
- 40 litres per minute per tap for community stand-pipes;
- 400 litres per minute per fire hydrant.

Communal standpipes should be located within 75 m of all dwellings.

Where a service to each house is provided, the reticulation should extend to a point on the lot boundary; extension to the house should be the responsibility of the owner.

The location of fire hydrants depends on the maximum hose length used and will vary considerably.

Roads and Footpaths. Construction standards:

low standard: 150 mm to 200 mm of compacted rubble or gravel;
moderate standard: 200 mm of compacted gravel with asphalt seal;
high standard: 50 mm of compacted gravel with 150 mm of concrete.

Footpaths:

low standard: 75 mm compacted gravel;
high standard: 60 mm concrete.

Drainage. Storm water:

footpaths graded to parallel open drain;
open drains concrete lined where adjacent to paving or earth lined where adjacent to rubble or gravel;
concrete pipes where necessary.

Waste water:

open channels from house to stormwater channel or pipe.

The volume of waste water will depend on whether the houses have individual water connections. If this is the case, allow for 45 litres *per capita* per day.

Sanitation. The disposal of human waste is one of the most serious problems in all low-income communities except very low-density rural settlements. Wherever concentrations of people are found without an effective disposal system, there will be severe health hazards. The subject is too complex to deal with in a few pages and the reader is directed to two excellent appraisals of the available methods which are appropriate to low income communities. These are:

Overseas Building Notes No. 168, published by the Overseas Division, Building Research Station, Garston, Watford, England, June 1976. This Note is entitled 'Sanitation without Sewers', by Henry T. Mann, and summarises the available systems.

A more comprehensive study can be found in *Alternative Sanitary Waste Removal Systems for Low-income Urban Areas in Developing Countries* by Jens Aage Hansen and Henning Therkelsen. This report was funded by a research grant from the Danish International Development Agency and is available from the Department of Sanitary Engineering, Technical University of Denmark, DK 2800, Lyngby, Denmark.

Essentially, the available systems are as follows in increasing order of capital cost:

(1)   pit privy;
(2)   aqua privy;
(3)   shared toilet block with septic tank;
(4)   individual septic tanks;
(5)   individual w.c.s in each house with full sewerage.

A number of other experimental systems such as anaerobic digesters or compost privies are reviewed in the publications referred to above, but these are not in general use in tropical low-income countries, largely owing to cost and maintenance problems.

Notes

1. *Sites and Services Projects*, a World Bank Paper (Washington, April 1974), pp. 10-11.
2. Robin Best, *Land for New Towns: a Study of Land-use Densities and Agricultural Displacement* (TCPA, London, 1964), p. 17.
3. Texeira de Sampaya *et al.*, *Habitação Social em Angola* (Secretaria Provincial de Obras Publicas e Communicações, Luanda, 1968), p. 185.
4. Shankland Cox Partnership, *Site and Service Housing in Jamaica* (Ministry of Housing, Government of Jamaica, 1973), pp. 31-3. In this instance the population was multiplied by 1.5.
5. See the Dudley Report, *Design of Dwellings* (HMSO, London, 1944).
6. Margaret Willis, 'Sociological Aspects of Urban Structure' in Gwen Bell and Jacqueline Tyrwhitt (eds.), *Human Identity in the Urban Environment* (Penguin Books, Harmondsworth, 1972).
7. Peter Willmott, 'Housing Density and Town Design in a New Town', *Town Planning Review* (Liverpool) (July 1962), pp. 115-27.
8. Willis, 'Sociological Aspects', p. 271.
9. P.H. Levin and A.J. Bruce, 'The Location of Primary Schools; Some Planning Implications', *Journal of the Town Planning Institute* (London) (February 1968), pp. 56-66.
10. H. Caminos, J. Turner and J. Steffian, *Urban Dwelling Environments* (Massachusetts Institute of Technology, Cambridge, Massachusetts, 1969).

11. Max Lock and Partners, *A Survey and Plan of the Capital Territory for the Government of Nigeria* (Kaduna, Nigeria, 1967).

12. *Etude de Typologie des Zonas Residentielles Futures a Luanda* (Formulation Preliminaire, OTAM, Luanda, Angola, 1972).

13. *Programa do Formento do Habitação e Reordenamento Urbano no Lobito*, Ano II, no. 15 (Camara Municipal do Lobito (undated)).

14. Private land is sometimes referred to as 'saleable' land and is the net area of lots. It is this which generates a return on investment in the form of rents or mortgage repayments. The other land uses (roads, open space, etc.) are not revenue-generating.

Selected Bibliography

USAID, Division of International Affairs, *Proposed Minimum Standards for Permanent Low-cost Housing and for the Improvement of Existing Substandard Areas* (Washington, May 1976).

van Huyck, A. *Planning for Sites and Services Programs* (USAID, Washington, 1971).

World Bank, *Site and Services Projects: Survey and Analysis of Urbanization Standards and On-site Infrastructure* (Divisional Paper, preliminary draft, Washington, August, 1974).

—— *Services projects* (edited by Horacio Caminos and Reinhard Goethert, Urban Projects Department Washington, October 1976).

9 LOW-INCOME HOUSING

Alan Turner

9.1 Housing Policy

In order to improve the living conditions of the poorest people in the developing world it is essential to use limited resources in the most cost-effective way and only policies which aim to do this are likely to have any impact on the 'gargantuan task – the appalling prospect' referred to by the World Bank. It is abundantly clear that the solution does not lie in 'housing', if this is conceived as the provision of conventionally designed and built physical shelter by a paternalistic authority. It simply will not suffice to 'house' a poor person (even if we subsidise his house) if, at the same time, we do not make it possible for him to improve his earning capacity and thereby his access to many other benefits of community life. If we look at it in this way, the word 'housing' becomes synonymous with 'planning' and interrelationships become the foremost consideration. To avoid over-sophistication these can be reduced to those which seem to be irrevocably interdependent: for 'housing' these are employment, transportation and the provision of major infrastructure and social facilities.

Without new employment (which a house-building programme can help to stimulate), people will not be able to afford improvements to their houses, whether they are built conventionally or by self-help methods. Subsidised public housing usually turns out to be too expensive for the poorest people and in the end the occupants may not be those for whom it was intended. Heavy subsidies make it impossible for governments to recycle funds and to repeat the projects; cost recovery becomes vital. (This is dealt with in detail in Chapters 6 and 10). Where resources are severely limited the priority must lie with the creation of new jobs – people can and do build their own houses but they cannot build new industrial estates or create new agricultural programmes. Public transport is absolutely integral with this; the location of house and job is obviously important where family budgets allow little for transportation costs, but often this elementary fact is ignored by well intentioned housing authorities.

After employment the next priority is to achieve some improvement in physical infrastructure – essentially water supply, drainage and sanitation, but including other elements such as access and street lighting. Once again, it is true to say that ordinary people can build themselves a house, but they cannot provide themselves with the service networks which, in urban conditions, are essential to the health and welfare of a community. This concept is the basis of the slum-upgrading and sites-and-services projects which will be discussed later.

With jobs, transportation and infrastructure in reasonable balance the need for major social services is paramount. Without schools, clinics, shops and many other commercial facilities, including entertainment, large new housing areas will be barren places unloved by the people unfortunate enough to have been 'relocated'. Again, this may seem quite obvious, but is given little attention by many housing authorities, to whose officials the term 'social facilities' means only the government-provided school or clinic and excludes, say, shops or cafés which must be legislated against on the grounds that they are not part of 'housing'. There is now ample evidence of the social problems caused in developed or developing countries by the single-minded approach to building huge unrelieved housing projects. Because of the scale of the problem in urban areas it will not be possible to 'solve' it in a neat and tidy way. No flight of the imagination can visualise all the poorest inhabitants of Rio de Janeiro or Madras housed in rows of industrialised concrete boxes, served by paved roads and connected to all the urban services. Nor, on the other hand, is the *unaided* ability of people to house themselves likely to produce anything but vast urban slums of the kind that are already so familiar. It is absolutely essential to make as much use as possible of people's efforts through self-help and sites-and-services programmes; their energy and initiative is a country's greatest housing resource. But programmes should also aim to improve the supply of housing through many forms of conventionally built public housing for the slightly better-off and, for the higher-income groups, through the normal market mechanisms. It is clear that self-help housing in all its forms is absolutely vital, but we must not fall into the trap of thinking that because so much public housing has been ineffective, *all* public housing is necessarily bad and should not even form a part of an overall housing policy. This, however, is the position which some housing policy-makers have adopted, apparently forgetting that the rich mix of incomes, abilities and aspirations in any society (even a poor one) demands an equally rich mix of solutions. However, as the emphasis of this book is on the poorest groups, the emphasis of this chapter is on upgrading and sites and services which, today, offer the best chance of success.

People in 'shanty towns' are often located fairly near to available work. By a combination of walking, bicycles, motor cycles, shared taxis, cars and buses, they manage one way or another to solve their collective problem of mobility at a price they can just afford. However, over-zealous politicians and officials anxious to improve the 'image' of their city may often consider (or even worse, implement) new housing projects on the periphery of the city where land is cheaper and available, without, at the same time, improving public transport facilities or providing new employment facilities within easy access of the new areas.

In rural areas one of the most severe problems is dispersal; where people are scattered over wide areas there is no economic means of providing them with the same degree of access to jobs or facilities as in the towns. Yet it is precisely the lack of these which causes people to migrate to the cities in the hope of a better life. At the lowest level, that of the scattered settlement, agricultural extension programmes should be coupled with the provision of mobile services (which in themselves would provide new job opportunities for drivers, medical auxiliaries, teachers, etc.).

At the next level, programmes should aim at the planned expansion of strategically placed 'central villages' where a range of services can be provided and where the primary processing of agricultural produce can begin. This, in my opinion, is vital in order to bring to rural areas some of the simple forms of industry implied by intensified agricultural programmes. The undue concentration of new industry into large developments is perhaps more 'efficient' in the terms of the industrial economist but may, in the end, be counter-productive. This is not to minimise the difficulties of achieving small-scale developments, which are discussed in Chapter 5, but suggests that decisions should be based where possible on a wider view of costs and benefits.

The phenomenon of the primate city exists in many developing countries and in almost all there is a considerable regional imbalance, leading to migration to only a few major centres. Thoughtful economic and physical planning at the national level can lead (as in Malaysia) to the establishment of new regional centres, based on agricultural or perhaps extractive industry which, over time, will help to reduce pressure on the existing cities by providing 'counter-magnets' to migration.

Finally, we must learn from the people themselves some elementary but easily overlooked lessons about the relation of houses to their environment. A Malay village (or kampung) is a close adaptation to external conditions which has taken centuries to evolve. The simple wood houses are perfectly suited to the climate, which is itself modified by the tall palm trees which provide shade and are an integral part of the village. But large-scale public housing has its own false economies and these do not allow trees to be retained. In Malaysia (and nearly everywhere else) the result can be treeless deserts of red laterite and severe erosion. This can lead to hidden expenses in drainage and water management, which never form part of the balance sheet. An essential factor in housing is to get back to a real understanding of habitat and to find ways of giving people access to employment, services and shelter without, at the same time, destroying their environment.

9.1.1 A Balanced Policy

A balanced policy for lowest-income housing should contain at least the following elements:

Upgrading Existing Slum Areas. This will concentrate on the provision of affordable infrastructure and facilities rather than improving the houses; the latter can be left to the residents. In addition to physical improvements, upgrading must include social and economic development programmes.

An Adequate Supply of Land for New Settlements. Given existing rates of natural growth and in-migration, new slum areas will be created faster than the old ones can be upgraded, unless a related programme of sites-and-services projects is sustained. This implies forward planning in the sense of a structure plan for urban growth and an ongoing land assembly programme with all the attendant problems of acquisition by negotiation or expropriation. The latter activities usually take so long that the necessary legal action may need to be initiated several years before the land is required.

Security of Tenure for the Residents. In both slum areas and new projects, security of tenure is a vital incentive to self-help housing improvements. Families are understandably reluctant to invest in building if they fear that, at any time, they may be moved. The form of tenure may be either freehold or leasehold, but without security there will be little progress.

Access to Finance. Where lots are offered for sale or where self-build housing is to be encouraged, it is vital to ensure that even very low-income families have access to small loans for purchase of materials and other expenses of improvement.

Social and Economic Development. Physical improvements need to be supported by innovative social and economic development, including job creation, training programmes, small business loans and other programmes aimed essentially at some degree of income redistribution.

Appropriate Technology. Although most families will use traditional building methods, many will need instruction and technical assistance. Research and development can often improve local building methods without radically changing them or substituting new materials.

Legislation. Most countries will need new appropriate legislation to be drafted and this, in itself, is a difficult and time-consuming task; the legislation has to be practical and easy to apply or it will be unused. Often the acquisition of sites can be interminably delayed owing to inadequate cadastral maps, and arguments over ownership can seriously delay urgently needed housing programmes.

9.2 Slum-upgrading

This section deals with the physical aspects of the improvement of existing slums; the residents may or may not be squatters in the legal sense, but it is assumed that some regularisation of land tenure will be necessary.

There are two basic physical alternatives:

(1) equalisation and 'squaring up' of lots, producing a regular layout but giving rise to considerable upheaval and the destruction of many houses;

(2) minimum movement of houses, which may produce an irregular layout with unequal-sized lots but which is generally found to be much more acceptable socially and economically. .

The type of solution must inevitably vary from country to country; in parts of Asia, lightweight bamboo- (or timber-) framed houses are the norm and these can easily be picked up by twenty or thirty men and moved to a new lot or adjusted by a few metres, as shown in Figure 3.6 (p. 86). Community self-help has been common for generations and moving a house is quite acceptable; it is known as 'gotong-royong' in Malaysia or 'bayanihan' in the Philippines. In other countries or regions, houses may be built of brick, stone or mud and are immovable without demolition. In these cases there is clearly little flexibility and minimum movement solutions are essential.

9.2.1 Public Participation

The type of solution and the new layout must be discussed with the residents to ensure that the project will succeed. Ideally this should be done at two levels:

(1)   when an overall layout showing roads, footpaths and facilities is prepared for a wide area, general meetings for all residents should be held;

(2)   when, as part of the overall scheme, a block is to be upgraded, specific details of movement, lot subdivision, etc. should be discussed with the families who live on the block.

It must be emphasised that there can be no possibility of successful upgrading if the participation process is not taken seriously. If it is not, there is a danger that the community may be antagonised to the extent that they will refuse to co-operate and may even sabotage the project because they feel threatened. (In so many communities the arrival of a government jeep spells trouble and threatens eviction. Perhaps success can be measured by the achievement of a situation where the government jeep is received with friendly smiles.)

9.2.2 Minimum Lot Sizes

This is discussed in general terms in Chapter 8 with particular reference to new layouts. In existing slums the queston of minimum lot size is extremely difficult to resolve with reasonable balance being given to fairness among the residents, affordability, sanitation, public health and fire risks. In some places, lots are as small as $10m^2$ and huts are jammed together leaving no room for pit latrines and with a severe risk of rapid fire spread over a large area. Stipulating an arbitrary minimum lot size may cause so many houses to be demolished and may require so much new land for relocation that a project would be quite impossible, without heavy subsidies. Inevitably there must be compromise and although there are no generally applicable rules, it should be possible to devise a set of guidelines to suit a particular place. If the examples given in Figure 8.7 are used as a guide then the basic lot size would be about $40m^2$-$50m^2$ for a single-storey house. This could serve as a target which would be aimed at in the first sketch layouts, but if an unacceptable amount of relocation and disturbance were caused, this could be reduced to give better overall results. In very closely built areas the lot size will be only slightly larger than the houses. However, this takes no account of the method of sanitary disposal. If pit latrines are necessary, the lots will have to be increased in size to allow sufficient space for two pits (to allow a new one to be dug when the first is full) and to take account of the spacing between pits in certain soil conditions. Where pits cannot be used (for example, where there is a danger of polluting the water supply) piped systems of various kinds must be considered and these will enable smaller lots to be used without health risks. Although piped systems will be more expensive, they may have a beneficial effect where land costs are high; higher densities can be achieved and there may be a point at which it is more cost-effective to accept a high density with a sewerage system rather than to reduce densities and rely on pit latrines.

9.2.3 Identification of Eligible Households

An informal slum is often quite difficult to define with regard to its physical extent, the ownership of the land or the status of the families who live there. The first steps are usually to carry out physical surveys, research land ownership and register the resident families at a particular point in time. Once it becomes known that a project is in hand, where tenure will be awarded, there may be a rapid influx of families trying to qualify for inclusion, and this may cause some conflict with the interests of the longer-term residents who feel, quite rightly, that they should have priority. If it is possible to have fairly low-level aerial photographs flown, these can speed up the process enormously by making it fairly easy to define each house and the extent of the appropriate lot. To achieve the same by normal land-survey methods can be technically very difficult (owing to the congestion of the houses and the problem of obtaining sight lines) and time-consuming. The registered households will usually be the owners of the houses; whether renters are allowed to become beneficiaries will be a matter for local policy, but it should be borne in mind that, with the extra costs of upgrading, the owner-households will find it even more necessary to rent out part of their houses. However, as sites-and-services schemes will be an essential adjunct to the upgrading process, it may be felt that renters should be offered lots if they wish to move.

9.2.4 Selecting a Layout Plan

When discussions are held with residents about the details of the layout, there will be many difficult questions. If a few houses have to be demolished to make way for a new road or path, how will the route be chosen? How much adjustment should there be to existing houses to achieve a more regular layout? (In some instances families have perceived a desirable 'middle-class' virtue in rectangular lots — they think that they may be easier to sell.) At this stage it is essential to have rough cost estimates available so that residents can be told the implications of their decisions. It is one thing to ask people whether they prefer A to B, but quite another to say that if they choose B it will cost them more in rent or mortgage payments. Most projects will produce 'trade-offs'. For instance, in a densely packed slum it may be possible to provide shared toilets to serve groups of houses, where this is socially acceptable. An alternative might be to relocate more families and increase lot sizes so that pit latrines could be incorporated. The different costs must be carefully evaluated.

A great deal of difficulty may be encountered when trying to explain a plan to people who cannot read drawings and where possible, models made of wood or cardboard should be used, combined with actual on-site inspections. In many cases, although there are no marked boundaries, householders know where their lots begin and end and there is an unwritten agreement to respect a neighbour's land. It may be possible in some cases to supply residents with pegs and invite them to draw up their own boundaries in agreement with their neighbours.

9.2.5 An Illustrated Example

Figures 9.1 to 9.6 show an example of a slum-upgrading project based on an actual site in Manila. The site is not part of an official programme and does not necessarily reflect government policy; the scheme for upgrading was worked out specifically as an illustration for this book and the principles are based on those which emerged during studies carried out in the Philippines by a team led by the author. The description of the site has been modified and includes many of the typical conditions found in slum and squatter settlements in the region.

The site is flat with the general ground level slightly below that of the unsurfaced roads; there is no drainage and during the wet season there is local flooding made worse by the raised roads. The houses are mostly built of lightweight materials (timber, palm thatch or nipa leaves) on a timber frame with the floor level raised off the ground on stilts. If necessary, the houses can be moved by a group of men who lift the house and carry it to its new position. This is a traditional form of mutual assistance known as 'bayanihan' (see Figure 3.6, p. 86).

Some of the houses are built of more solid materials such as concrete
blocks and these, of course, cannot be moved without demolition.

There is no sewerage system but a proportion of the houses have
pit latrines, some of which are used by neighbours for a small fee.
Other families use a system known locally as 'wrap and throw' (an
accurate description) which, needless to say, is a severe health hazard
and causes very unpleasant local conditions. There is no water supply
to the house and residents carry water in five-gallon cans from various
places where it is sold by middlemen at many times the cost of metered
water.[1] Although there are narrow paths through the block, these are
not paved and are often very muddy and contaminated with human and
animal faeces.

The socio-economic status of the residents varies considerably and
some of the families are relatively well off. However, the vast majority
are extremely poor and the median income is about 380 pesos (US $50)
per month. Most of the employment is in casual unskilled labour and
there is a high level of underemployment, especially among women and
young people. Sanitary conditions and poor nutrition are responsible
for severe health hazards and such diseases as broncho-pneumonia,
influenza, gastro-enteritis, dysentery, pulmonary tuberculosis, and
amoebiasis are common.

Figure 9.1 shows the existing conditions with a haphazard
arrangement of houses and no defined lots. The land belongs to the
government and all the families are squatters with no legal rights to the
land they occupy. However, each family knows the limits of its private
space and generally this is respected by others.

Figure 9.2 shows a rationalisation of this pattern with a reasonable
circulation system introduced with only a small loss of houses – 18.6
per cent slightly moved and 11 per cent demolished. The layout is still
informal and the lots are different shapes and sizes, but any attempt to
impose regular road layouts and equal-sized rectangular lots would
result in much greater movement and dislocation. This, in turn, would
throw a much greater load on the associated sites-and-services
programme.

Figure 9.3 records the houses demolished and moved. In this
example movement has been kept to a minimum. In a real situation the
plan would have to be discussed with the residents and worked out
carefully with their full collaboration to achieve minimum disruption,
damage and social friction.

Figure 9.4 shows the site development plan with small communal
open spaces, some planting and reasonable access to the centre of the

Figure 9.1: Slum-upgrading; the Existing Site

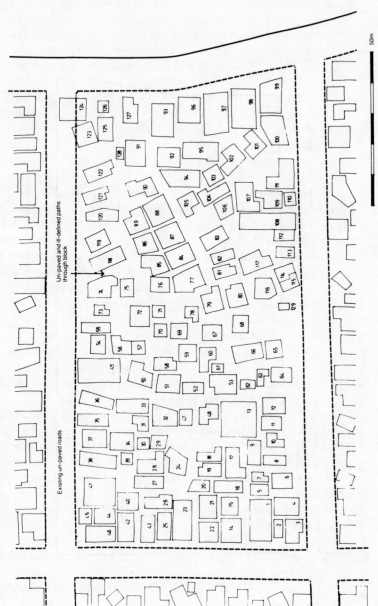

Un-paved and ill-defined paths through block

Existing un-paved roads

50m

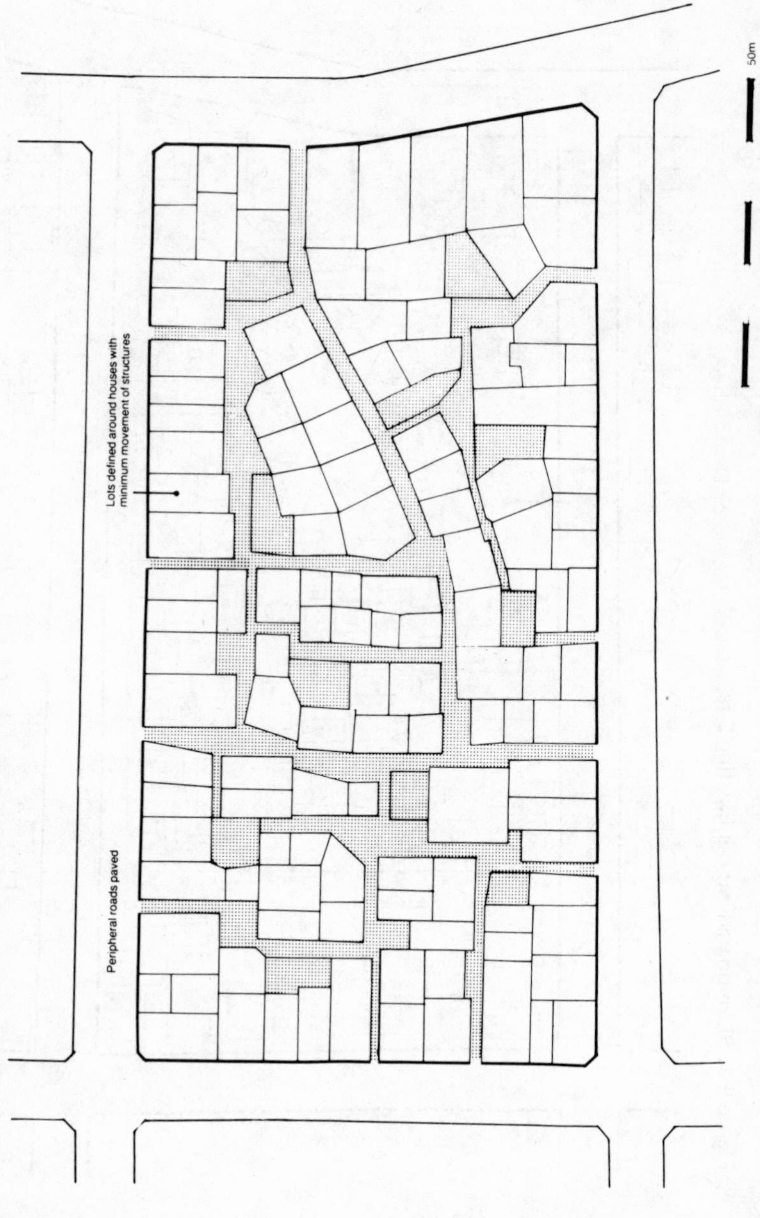

Figure 9.2: Slum-upgrading; Layout of Lots and Paths

Lots defined around houses with minimum movement of structures

Peripheral roads paved

50m

Figure 9.3: Slum-upgrading; Houses Moved or Demolished

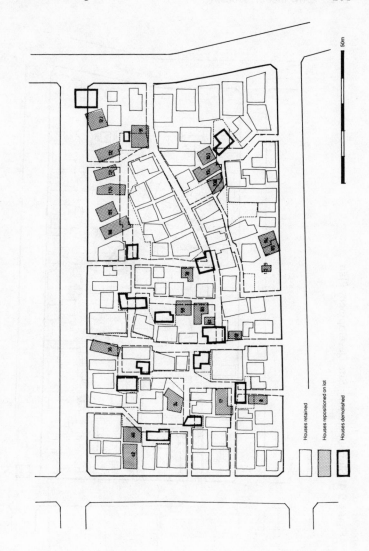

Houses retained

Houses repositioned on lot

Houses demolished

50m

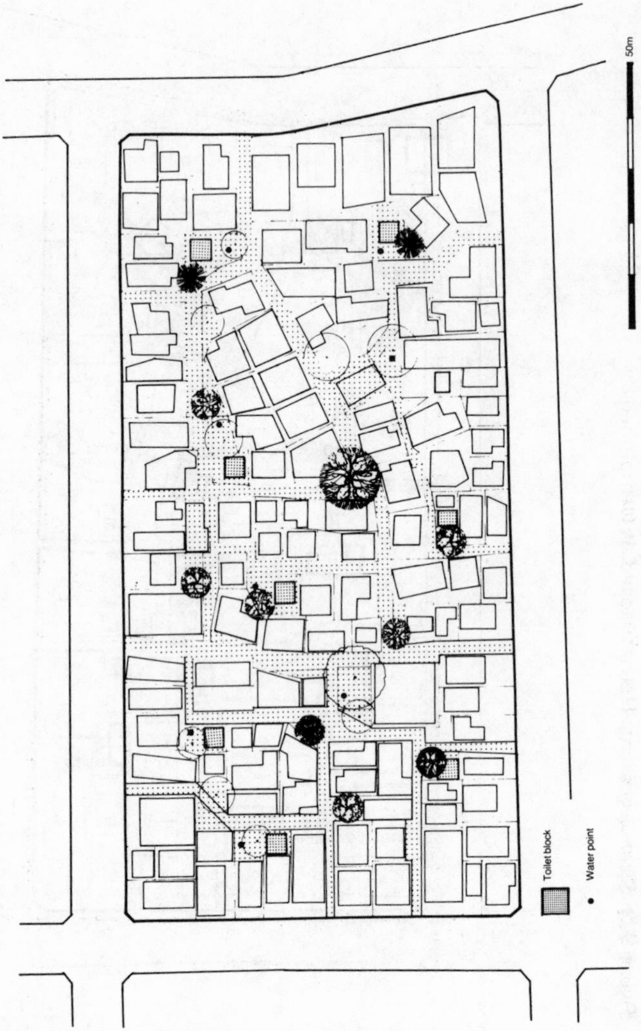

Figure 9.4: Slum-upgrading; Site Development Plan

Toilet block

• Water point

50m

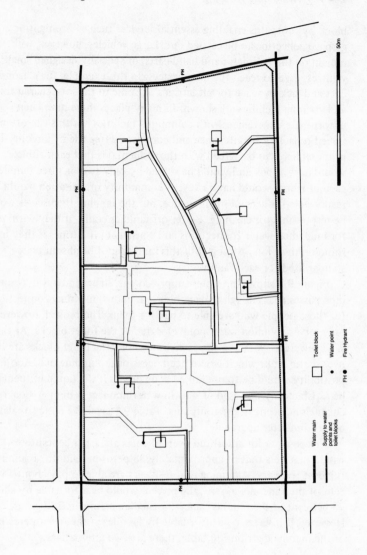

Figure 9.5: Slum-upgrading: Water Supply Layout

Water main

Supply to water
points and
toilet blocks

☐ Toilet block

• Water point

FH ● Fire Hydrant

50m

block by footpaths enabling essential services such as fire-fighting and garbage collection to be carried out. Large vehicles, however, will remain on the perimeter and hand-carts, or specially designed small vehicles, used to reach the inner spaces. In this example, for reasons of cost and lack of space for pit latrines on some of the lots, shared toilet and washing facilities are shown. In many places there have been unfortunate experiences with communal facilities but this can often be traced to lack of maintenance and completely free use by anyone. The proposal here (to be agreed with the residents) is that each cubicle would have a lock and would be shared by only two or three families, each of whom would have a key. A community organisation would be responsible for general maintenance, but the families themselves would be responsible for cleaning. Better-off families could, if they wish, pay for individual water connections and construct pit latrines if they have room on their lots. A project of this kind cannot be absolutely standardised for each family.

Figure 9.5 shows the water-supply layout. In general a water-supply pipe passes near enough to each house to allow individual connections for those people who are able to pay for them. The project, however, only serves common water-points located at the toilet blocks. As there is no sewerage system in the town as a whole, the toilet blocks are built over septic tanks which would need occasional pumping out. Another possibility would be to use linked aqua privies if the liquid effluent can be satisfactorily disposed of. Storm-water drainage is in open concrete channels adjacent to the footpaths. Table 9.1 gives the basic site data before and after upgrading.

This cost per lot amortised over 20 years at 11 per cent interest would require a rent of approximately 38 pesos per month, assuming full cost recovery. Assuming that residents are able to pay about 15 per cent of their income in rent, the project would be affordable by about 75 per cent of the families, since the median income is 380 pesos. However, if it were to be affordable by families at the lower percentiles of the income distribution table, there are two alternatives:

(1)   the standards (already low) of the new services would have to be reduced to whatever level is affordable; or

(2)   the poorest families would need to be subsidised either directly by the government or by cross-subsidy from higher-income lots or commercial development in another part of the project (which could be on a separate site).

Table 9.1: Upgrading Example: Basic Data

Site Data; Existing Situation

	m^2	Percentage of total
Total area of block	11,268	100
Total area of buildings	5,251	46.6
Open areas, including footpaths	6,017	53.4
Average ground floor area of house	41	—
Total number of houses	128	
Density: houses per ha.	114	
persons per ha.	795	— assuming 7 persons per lot

Site Data; Proposed Layout

	m^2	Percentage of total
Houses retained	91	70.6
Houses repositioned on lot	24	18.6
Houses demolished	14[a]	10.8
Total number of lots in new layout:		
residential	126	
used for shared toilets	9	
Total	135	

Average area of lot 68 m^2

Note: a. As there are 126 lots in the new layout, only two of these have to be relocated to another site.

The costs (excluding land) for this hypothetical example were estimated at 1978 costs in the Philippines, and are shown in Table 9.2.

Table 9.2: Upgrading Example; Estimated Costs

Item	Standard	Costs per lot Pesos	US $
Footpaths	2-3m wide, rubble and gravel	450	60
Paving peripheral roads	Asphalt (½ width of road allocated to block)	1,000	133
Sanitation	9 shared blocks, septic tanks	1,000	133
Water supply	9 common points; individual connections paid for separately by residents	180	24
Drainage	Open concrete channels	850	113
Street lighting	1 per 100m	70	9
Surveying and pegging lots		60	8
Moving houses/demolition		170	22
Total		3,780	502

Figure 9.6: An Upgraded Project

The visual quality of an upgraded area may be very similar to the original and it
may lack the photogenic character which appeals to politicians. However, there is little
doubt that the appearance of the neighbourhood will improve over time as the residents
make gradual improvements to their properties.

9.3 Sites-and-Services Projects

Within the last decade this term has become the generic title of a wide array of projects and has acquired an almost talismanic quality of being a cure-all for the housing problems of the poor. However, the essential nature of a sites-and-services approach is constantly misunderstood by both politicians and professionals, and it seems useful at this stage to sharpen up the focus a little. The World Bank has attempted a definition:

> Site and services [*sic*] is the sub-division of urban land and its servicing with varying combinations and levels of public utilities and community facilities for residential and commercial use. Generally the objective of site and services is to provide an economically accessible physical framework to a specific target low income population for their shelter and related employment needs. Site and services schemes normally rely heavily on the efforts of community residents with or without outside assistance, to attain their objectives.[2]

Quite rightly, this definition emphasises the need for related employment needs; sites and services housing alone may not make much improvement to people's lives.

There seem to be two distinct schools of thought; one is that government intervention should be minimal and restricted to subdivisions and basic infrastructure, and the other is that a considerable amount of organisation is necessary to make the best use of opportunities.[3] This leads to a very wide variation in standards and costs, from simple land subdivision to what is almost conventional public housing. The following are variously considered to be 'sites and services' by housing authorities in different parts of the world:

(1) pegged-out lots, unpaved roads and paths, common water-taps and pit latrines;

(2) as above, but with main service connections (water and sewer) to each lot;

(3) as (2) above, but with paved roads and footpaths;

(4) paved roads, footpaths, main service connections and a sanitary core;

(5) any of the above with one or more walls or in some cases with a partly finished house, including roof covering.

Clearly the target income group for (1) would be very different from that for (5), but there is no reason why a large project should not include all these levels. The World Bank suggests that generally the target group should represent the middle stratum of the poor and that this will reduce the pressure on the very poor remaining in the slum areas.[4] This seems to be very doubtful, as more very poor (or even moderately poor) people would rush into the gaps without draconian measures to restrain them. Furthermore, a policy which tends to 'cream off' the slightly more affluent will probably create polarisation between the new areas where people will be aspiring towards middle-class values and the very underprivileged original slums. For this, and many other reasons, a sites-and-services area should be accessible to the very poor, with minimum services, even though opportunities are made for better-off families to improve their standards, perhaps by paying for their own water connections and so on. What must be understood is that the level of public subsidy (and, therefore, standards) must be kept down to allow the project to be repeated on a large scale. (The term 'replicability' is often used, which may confuse foreign readers. It will not be found in a dictionary but is a word coined to denote projects whose costs are low enough to allow a high percentage to be recovered from rents and sales, thus allowing funds to be recycled and projects repeated.)

9.3.1 Site Selection

A great deal of care must be given to locational analysis. There are projects in many parts of the world where the recipients of government aid in badly located areas have abandoned (or sold) their lots and moved back to the inner city to be nearer to their work. The primary reason usually given for selecting sites which may be as much as 20km from the city on hilly land is that the cost is low or that the land is in government ownership. This is completely false thinking, as only the middle classes, who can easily pay for transport costs, can afford to live so far from their work.

In most cases there will be a number of possible sites from which one or more must be selected, and it is useful to have a set of criteria on which to base a decision. It is likely that there will be particular local criteria (possibly cultural constraints), but generally a chart such as that shown in Figure 9.7 can be used. At the simplest level each site can be checked off to ensure that it at least possesses the basic qualities required. A more sophisticated analysis could be made by allotting weighted scores to each quality and totalling the results. For instance,

Figure 9.7: A Site Evaluation Chart

CRITERIA		SITES				
		A	B	C	D	etc.
ACCESSIBILITY	Less than 500m from existing transport route	●				
	Less than 3 km from major employment centre	●				
	Less than 3 km from existing market or shops		●			
	Less than 5km from existing secondary school	●				
ENVIRONMENT AND TOPOGRAPHY	General environment suitable for housing	●	●			
	Convenient shape for housing	●				
	Absence of steep slopes	●				
	Absence of physical constraints (rock, marshy ground etc.)	●	●			
	No danger of flooding	●	●			
INFRASTRUCTURE	Local water supply with reserve capacity	●				
	Existing access road(s)	●	●			
	Existing sewers nearby					
	Existing electricity nearby					
COSTS	Acquisition — low		●			
	moderate	●				
	high					
	Development — low					
	moderate	●				
	high		●			
OTHER SPECIFIC QUALITIES						
	Total (if numerical scores allotted)					

Actual distances should be adjusted to
be appropriate to specific regions

proximity to employment may be thought to be more important (and, therefore, have a higher score) than proximity to shops, or the existence of roads may score higher than an existing electricity supply.

The two hypothetical sites recorded on the chart are not untypical. I have seen a site such as B selected even though it was far from employment and had steep slopes, simply because the cost of acquisition was very low. However attractive low acquisition costs may be, if insufficient attention is given at this stage to the subsequent high costs of development and transport, the result may be a project which is unaffordable by the prospective occupiers and not feasible when subjected to detailed financial analysis.

In addition to the selection criteria referred to here, more detailed environmental criteria are defined in Chapter 7.

9.3.2 Layout

In practice it is extremely difficult to produce attractive well landscaped layouts when standards must be kept very low. If a typical example of an 'attractive' layout with public open spaces and trees is analysed, it will almost certainly be found that there is too high a percentage in public land or that the shapes of lots and lengths of roads and services produce an uneconomic, or at least unaffordable, result. However, there are some basic rules which may help and these may be summarised as follows:

Lot Size. Ensure that there is a wide variety to accommodate different income groups; serried ranks of similar-sized lots tend to produce an ugly environment and give little opportunity for a mix of income groups. The distribution of lot sizes should relate to the need, but in practice it may be found that perhaps 20 per cent of very small lots for poor (or small) families, 60 per cent of moderate lots and 20 per cent of large lots (some of which may be used for small business enterprises) will be reasonable. As pointed out earlier, the size of lots is influenced by methods of sanitary disposal and preliminary financial calculations will be necessary to provide a guide to the designers.

Lot Shape. There is no compelling reason for all lots to be the same shape, although the need to keep frontages narrow will be a constraint. Wedge-shaped or irregular lots may be necessary when planning clusters and these can be a great help in avoiding monotony.

Clusters and Footpath Access. To avoid long roads which may be visually dull and financially unsound, houses should be clustered into groups served by narrow footpaths. Car ownership will be very low and it will usually suffice to ensure that all houses are within reasonable distance of a road.

Relationship to Topography. The influence of climate and topography on layout has been extensively discussed in Chapter 7, but it cannot be over-emphasised that layouts which respect topography are not only more attractive but are usually cheaper than those which ignore it. The reasons may not be obvious, but if the hidden costs of damage to natural drainage systems, erosion and possible flooding elsewhere were added to the initial project costs, what appear to be economical layouts may prove to be just the opposite.

9.3.3 An Illustrated Example

Figures 9.8-9.11 show sites-and-services layouts for the same site of 4.8 ha. The site is intended to be part of a much larger site which would contain commercial activities, community facilities and other land uses. The major variables are density, the proportion of private (saleable) land to non-revenue producing land and the standard of development in terms of physical infrastructure or level of service. To some extent these may form alternatives at the stage of the initial development and costs may be estimated and compared, for example:

low density-low standard;
low density-high standard;
high density-low standard;
high density-high standard.

As the residents will only be able to afford a relatively low level of service in the early stages, it may be more realistic to think of the project as one which can, itself, be upgraded over time. The chosen density will remain the same (or nearly so) but almost everything else can change over a period of years, during which time the residents' incomes will probably improve, allowing them to spend more on their accommodation.

Figure 9.8 shows a low density (35 lots per ha.) layout with minimum development standards. Only the main roads are surfaced, the rest being rolled rubble or gravel; lots are pegged out and a pit latrine is constructed on each. Water is taken to several common points, although the supply network will allow later individual connections to

Figure 9.8: Sites and Services A; Low Density/Low Standard

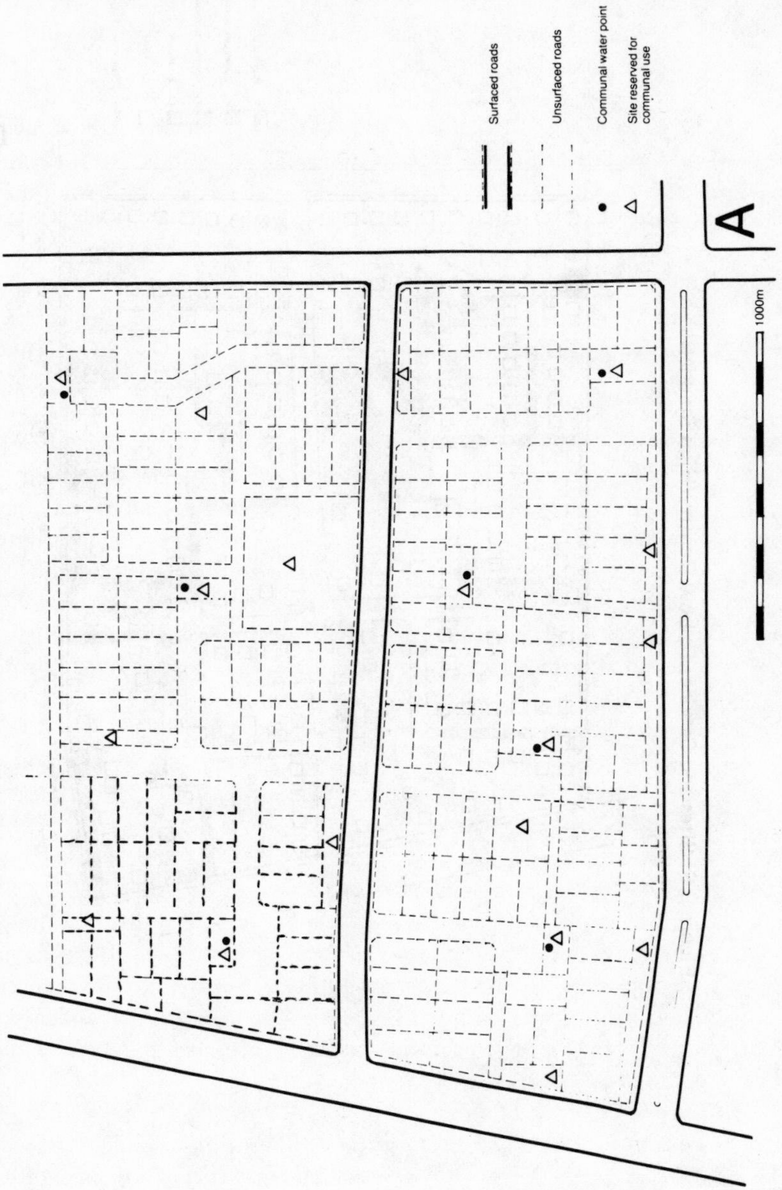

Surfaced roads

Unsurfaced roads

Communal water point •

Site reserved for
communal use △

A

1000m

Figure 9.9: Sites and Services B; Low Density/High Standard

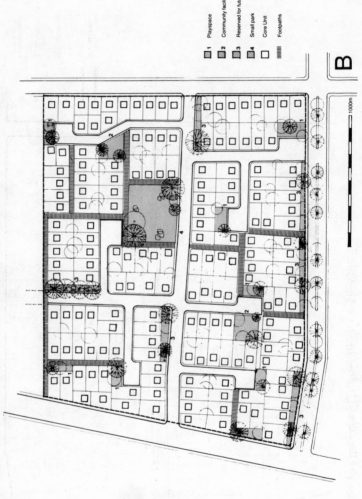

1   Playspace
2   Community facility
3   Reserved for future parking
4   Small park
    Core Unit
||||| Footpaths

B

1000m

Figure 9.10: Sites and Services C; High Density/Low Standard

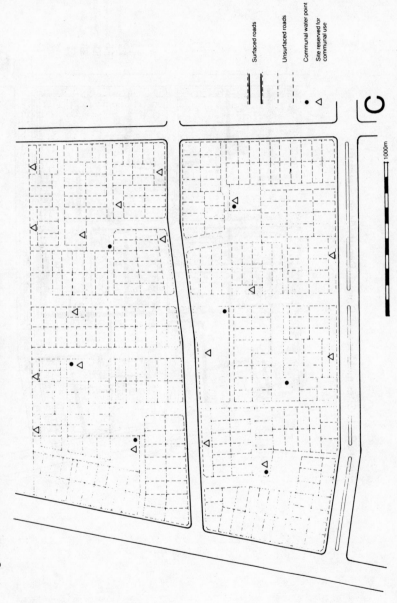

Surfaced roads

Unsurfaced roads

Communal water point

Site reserved for
communal use

C

1000m

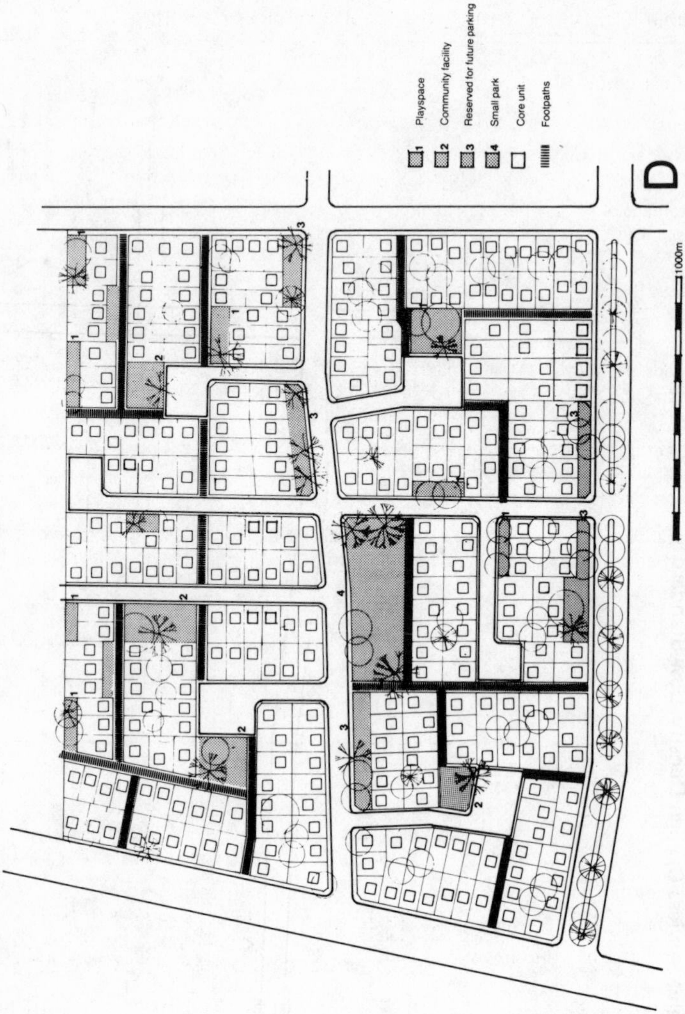

Figure 9.11: Sites and Services D; High Density/High Standard

Playspace

Community facility

Reserved for future parking

Small park

Core unit

Footpaths

1000m

D

Table 9.3: Data Relating to Sites-and-Services Examples

Infrastructure Standards

Item	Low Standard	High Standard
Water supply	Common point within 75m of all lots	Individual connections to each lot
Drainage	Open channels, concrete-lined where roads or paths are paved, otherwise unlined	Concrete channels and pipes
Sanitation	1 pit latrine per lot	Sanitary core for each lot with septic tanks serving groups of houses
Roads and paths	Main roads: asphalt Access roads: rolled rubble Footpaths: gravel	: asphalt : asphalt : concrete paving
Street lighting	1 light per 100m of road	1 light per 100m of road

Land Use and Density

Total Area 4.8 ha.	Schemes A and B Low Density. 170 Lots	Schemes C and D High Density. 312 Lots
Density lots/ha.	35.4	65
Average lot size m^2	200	100
Private area (per cent)	70.8	65
Public area (per cent)	9.4	13.1
Roads and paths (per cent)	19.8	21.9

Lengths of Roads, Paths and Pipes per House

	Scheme			
	Low Density		High Density	
	A	B	C	D
Paved road per lot m	3.11	6.3	1.76	3.49
Unpaved road per lot m	3.19	—	1.73	—
Footpaths m	2.23	2.23	2.22	2.22
Water pipe (inc. connections) m	5.39	19.28	2.93	15.39

be made.

Figure 9.9 can be considered to represent either:

(1) a high standard initial layout with all roads and paths paved and with a core unit for each house containing water and sanitary services; or

(2) the same scheme as 9.8, say 5 or 10 years later, by which time

roads have been paved, various other services have been introduced and houses have been built and improved by the residents.

Several lots have been set aside for community facilities (which may not be affordable at the outset), and one or two spaces have been earmarked for further parking as vehicle ownership increases over time.

Figures 9.10 and 9.11 show the same site developed at a higher density (65 lots per ha.) and with similar differences in time or standards. An indication of the different levels of service (and, therefore, costs) is given in Table 9.3. Obviously the combinations of standard and density are very numerous and these examples can only serve to give a rough guide. In general, however, the greatest cost savings are to be made by keeping infrastructure lengths as short as possible (per lot or per hectare) and by minimising the amount of land devoted to circulation and facilities. This applies whether the development standards are high or low. The order of costs for the schemes illustrated are as follows (taking the lowest cost as 100):

Scheme C (high density-low standard)	100
Scheme A (low density-low standard)	129
Scheme D (high density-high standard)	198
Scheme B (low density-high standard)	291

These figures exclude land costs.

Notes

1. It is common for drinking-water to be sold for 5 centavos a gallon, which is equivalent to 13.20 pesos per cubic metre. A person with an individual supply may pay as little as 1 peso per cubic metre after paying a small standing charge. The difference is one of the costs of being poor and represents a considerable portion of family income which could be much better used in paying rent or a mortgage.

2. *Site and Services Projects: Survey and Analysis of Urbanization Standards and On-site Infrastructure*, divisional paper – preliminary draft (IBRD, Washington, August 1974), p. 3.

3. *Sites and Services Projects*, a World Bank paper (Washington, April 1974), p. 22.

4. *Ibid.*, pp. 4 and 5.

10 FINANCIAL APPRAISAL OF THE PROJECT

Kenneth Wren

10.1 Pre-feasibility Results

We are concerned here, essentially, with a low-income housing
development, but where some ancillary development of commercial
and industrial sites, and provision of schools, health and welfare
facilities form a necessary part of the overall development plan. The
detailed financial appraisal of any development project will normally
be undertaken within the context of an overall feasibility study which
examines all the issues of the project. A pre-feasibility study should
have determined that the target group's affordability rating is broadly
sufficient to meet the costs of new development after allowing for
known contributions from government and likely allocations to
national and local agencies with specific responsibility for components
of the development.

The first task will be to determine the income distribution of the
target group and their affordable level of monthly payment relative
to the specific benefits to be received. Generally speaking, one would
expect the lowest income levels to pay a lower percentage of their
income than those in the higher levels of the target group. There is
also the question of the allowance to be made from the beneficiary's
income towards the cost of maintenance of the urban fabric and the
running costs of the key social services in the calculation of the
affordable level of payments for specific benefits.

Essentially, there are three key elements in total costs to be
recovered from project beneficiaries: land, infrastructure and
superstructures, leaving aside the question of maintenance and
management of the new development. The cost of the land is probably
predetermined and will vary from very little in the more rural areas to
very expensive in major cities.

After allowing for the capital cost of land amortised on the basis
of say 20 to 25 years at the rate of interest currently applied to the
project, the residual amount of income can also be capitalised to
determine the level of investment affordable for the other two
components, infrastructure and superstructure.

Table 10.1 demonstrates the calculations necessary to arrive at the

Table 10.1: Affordability of Target Group in Terms of Investment Level

Target group income distribution	Monthly income	Monthly affordability				Land costs[a]		Balance of monthly charge available[b]	Allocation of residual costs and equipment monthly[c]			
									Infrastructure		Superstructures	
(Percentile group)		10%	15%	20%	25%	Capital	Monthly charge		Capital	Monthly charge	Capital	Monthly charge
10%												
15%												
20%												
25%												
30%												
40%												
50%												
60%												
70%												
80%												

Notes: The following assumptions, though not sacrosanct, may be applied reasonably to most developments.
a. Assumed land costs represent 5 per cent of earnings in terms of monthly charges.
b. In this example assume 30 per cent for superstructure and 70 per cent for infrastructure; monthly charge represents 15 per cent of earnings.
c. Assume 20 per cent affordability in this example.

indicative levels of investment for the two categories, infrastructure and superstructure.

10.2 Costs and their Allocation

Costs to be included in each project will consist of:

(1)   cost of land acquisition where land is already in government ownership. Such land will be transferred to the project at a cost which reasonably reflects market conditions in that particular locality. Cost will include legal and survey fees and associated administrative expenses;

(2)   the cost of infrastructure including:
        off-site costs (where attributable);
        site reticulation costs;
        land reclamation;
        cost of communal toilets (if any).

(3)   on-plot development costs including:
        service connections;
        sanitary disposal cores;
        pit latrines;
        fire walls;
        superstructures;

(4)   the cost of planning, design and supervision of contracts including surveys and cost of reproduction of reports, plans, etc.;

(5)   operational costs including interest during construction; financing charges; cost of collecting revenues from beneficiaries and other project revenues;

(6)   adequate provision against default in payment by project beneficiaries and for depreciation of assets acquired for project execution;

(7)   the cost of providing schools, health centres and other social and cultural facilities.

Additionally, expenditure will be incurred in the development of industrial and commercial activities to enable a cross-subsidy to be made to residents, particularly at the lower-income end of the target population group. These possibilities are detailed in following sections.

10.2.1 Affordable Level of Development

Given a fixed amount of monthly income available for housing purposes, the rate of interest chargeable for accommodation provided has a strong influence on the affordable level of investment; the lower the rate, the higher the level of investment possible.

10.2.2 Rate of Interest

The charges to beneficiaries for the amortisation of capital costs will reflect the average rate of interest on funds raised by the project agency. It is likely that loans raised by the project agency will be a mixture of multilateral agency loans (e.g. World Bank), bilateral loans (e.g. Ministry of Overseas Development UK) and loans by the indigenous government. These will vary in accordance with market conditions prevailing at the time of the loan negotiations and mixture of components in the development. However, the average rate is usually much lower than commercial rates charged for loans for housing development purposes.

10.2.3 Amortisation Periods

Equally, the period over which investment is amortised (or in other words the period over which a loan to the beneficiary is recovered) also influences the affordable level of investment. Clearly if a loan to the beneficiary is to be repaid by him over a period of 5 years the resultant monthly charge would be far in excess of that if the loan were spread over 25 years (Table 10.2).

Periods of between 15 and 25 years are quite normal and generally reflect the periods over which the project agency raises its own funds. For example World Bank loans for low-cost housing are currently spread over 20 years, with a short grace period before repayments are due to begin.

10.2.4 Subsidies Available to Beneficiaries

Following the principles already specified earlier in terms of allocating costs of components to those agencies who traditionally have responsibility for their provision, an indirect subsidy has already been afforded to the development. It is important, however, to recognise that these agencies must themselves be funded from either government sources, probably through taxation levies, or through user charges, for example electricity and water. In other words, somebody must pay eventually for services provided. Uncontrolled subsidies usually result in the eventual breakdown of community development programmes and therefore must be avoided. For the purposes of this description it is assumed that agencies accepting responsibility for these various components have adequate resources available.

Table 10.2: Loan Repayment Impact Comparisons

Principal Sum: 100,000. 5, 15 and 25 Years Repayment Period.
8% and 12% Interest.

Year	5 Years		15 Years		25 Years	
	8%	12%	8%	12%	8%	12%
1	25,046	27,741	11,683	14,682	9,368	12,750
2	25,046	27,741	11,683	14,682	9,368	12,750
3	25,046	27,741	11,683	14,682	9,368	12,750
4	25,046	27,741	11,683	14,682	9,368	12,750
5	25,046	27,741	11,683	14,682	9,368	12,750
6			11,683	14,682	9,368	12,750
7			11,683	14,682	9,368	12,750
8			11,683	14,682	9,368	12,750
9			11,683	14,682	9,368	12,750
10			11,683	14,682	9,368	12,750
11			11,683	14,682	9,368	12,750
12			11,683	14,682	9,368	12,750
13			11,683	14,682	9,368	12,750
14			11,683	14,682	9,368	12,750
15			11,683	14,682	9,368	12,750
16					9,368	12,750
17					9,368	12,750
18					9,368	12,750
19					9,368	12,750
20					9,368	12,750
21					9,368	12,750
22					9,368	12,750
23					9,368	12,750
24					9,368	12,750
25					9,368	12,750
Total	125,230	138,705	175,245	220,230	234,200	318,750

N.B. Principal and interest combined: yearly rests.

10.2.5 Profit-making Developments

However, there are further possibilities available usually for relieving the beneficiaries of the total impact of the investment cost, through the introduction of revenue-generating land uses alongside the housing development.

The introduction of commercial/industrial development into the project not only enables a cross-subsidy to be generated but has the additional advantage of creating employment opportunities.

But the amount of industrial and commercial development is conditioned by the market demand, in terms of the overall allocation of land for this purpose and its forecast rate of absorption.

Having ascertained what the market will bear, then the likely surpluses from this form of development can be ascertained. Table 10.3 demonstrates the basis for calculation of sales of land for both industry and commerce and these revenues are included in Table 10.4, which determines the net present value of surpluses generated by these forms of development. The discount rate used should reflect the average borrowing rate of the funds raised for the project.

10.2.6 Differential Cost Allocations to Residents

In addition, it may be possible to allocate costs per residential lot to facilitate a reduction of costs to be charged against the lowest-income end of target group beneficiaries. Internal cross-subsidies of this nature are possible where there exists a fairly wide income distribution among the settlers, the better-off subsidising those who can only meet the cost of minimum standards with difficulty. This possibility is referred to later in the analysis.

10.2.7 Cost Recovery from Beneficiaries and Calculation of Monthly Charges

It is now necessary to analyse total project costs between components and beneficiaries, including those costs to be borne by other agencies. Table 10.5 shows this analysis. It is important to make adequate provision in this cost schedule for design and supervision of the contract, usually around 10 per cent and, apart from a physical contingency of say 10 per cent, a price contingency based on the current movement in prices and materials should also be added for each year of the construction period. Finally, to ensure that all costs are fully recovered, 'financing charges' should be added to cover interest

Table 10.3: Pricing/Phasing of Commercial and Industrial Land

(a) Commercial   US $

  (1) Selling price per square metre (freehold)   275

  (2) Leasehold price per square metre[a]   –

  (3) Absorption rate of development   5 years

				Years				
Item	Total	1	2	3	4	5	6	7
Sq. metres	96,000	10,000	10,000	20,000	30,000	26,000	–	–
Price/m²[b]		$90	$100	$110	$120	$127	–	–
Yearly revenues	$11 m	$0.9m	$1.0m	$2.2m	$3.6m	$3.3m	–	–

Notes:

a. In this example the sale of freehold land has been adopted to assist early recovery of investment and therefore the cash flow position. Only if a system of leasehold which provides for large initial premiums is adopted, equating broadly to the freehold price, will it be more advantageous to adopt leasehold rather than freehold sales policy. Urgent cash requirements in early years dictate this policy.

b. To take account of inflationary changes and changes in real values over time the price per square metre has been escalated on the basis of 10 per cent per annum from the base date.

(b) Industrial   US$

  (1) Selling price per hectare of land (freehold)   1.65 million

  (2) Leasehold price per square metre[a]   –

  (3) Absorption rate of development   7 years

				Years				
Item	Total	1	2	3	4	5	6	7
Hectares	70	3	9	11	12	16	10	9
Price per hectare[b]		$1.65m	$1.8m	$2.1m	$2.2m	$2.4m	$2.6m	$2.9m
Yearly revenues	$161.2m	$5.0m	$16.2m	$23.1m	$26.4m	$38.4m	$26.0m	$26.1m

Notes:

a. As for Commercial.

b. As for Commercial.

(These revenue forecasts will be used in Table 10.4 in order to ascertain profitability.)

Table 10.4: Calculation of Commercial/Industrial Profitability (i.e. surpluses from development)

US $ Million

		Totals	Years 1	2	3	4	5	6	7
1 Commercial development									
(a) Development costs:									
Land acquisition	0.27								
Land reclamation	1.70								
Land infrastructure	1.70	3.67	2.00	0.60	0.50	0.27	0.30	—	—
Design and supervision (12%)	0.20								
Contingencies									
Physical (10%)	0.17								
Price (10% p.a.)	0.57	0.94	0.51	0.15	0.10	0.11	0.07	—	—
Total development costs		4.61	2.51	0.75	0.60	0.38	0.37	—	—
(b) Revenues (see Table 10.3)									
Freehold sales		11.00	0.90	1.00	2.20	3.60	3.30	—	—
Leasehold sales		—	—	—	—	—	—	—	—
Total net revenues		11.00	0.90	1.00	2.20	3.60	3.30	—	—
Less: Selling and admin. costs		0.55	0.05	0.05	0.11	0.18	0.16	—	—
Total net revenues		10.45	0.85	0.95	2.09	3.42	3.14	—	—
(c) Surplus (deficit) (a)–(b)		5.84	(1.66)	0.20	1.49	3.04	2.77	—	—
(d) Net present value (12%)		3.86	(1.66)	0.19	1.21	2.20	1.92	—	—
2 Industrial development (similar layout)									
(a) Development costs		39.02	17.45	5.75	6.31	3.94	3.71	0.76	1.10
(b) Revenues (see Table 10.3)		161.20	5.00	16.20	23.10	26.40	38.40	26.00	26.10
(c) Surplus (deficits) (a)–(b)		122.18	(12.45)	10.45	16.79	22.46	34.69	25.24	25.00
(d) Net present values (12%)[a]		75.59	(12.45)	9.32	13.4	16.00	22.05	14.32	12.95

Note: ... calculated on the basis of 12 per cent discount factor, equivalent to loan rate ... to take account of time ...

Table 10.5: Allocation of Total Project Costs

Component	Total cost	Residential beneficiaries	Commercial industrial	National and local agencies			
				1	2	3	4
1 Land acquisition/reclamation							
2 Off-site infrastructure							
3 On-site infrastructure							
Site preparation							
Drainage							
Roads							
Footpaths							
Street lighting							
Water reticulation							
Sewerage. Reticulation treatment							
4 On-plot development							
5 Community facilities							
Sub-total							
6 Project design/supervision							
7 Contingencies — physical — price							
8 Interest during construction period							
Total cost							
Percentage of total cost	100 per cent						

accruing during the period of construction. The analysis can now concentrate on 'residential beneficiaries', the elements of cost that will be recovered from them, and the pricing implications of lots to be disposed to each beneficiary.

10.2.8 Calculation of Monthly Incomes

The distribution of income of the target group will have been ascertained from recently published data or from social security material. An important task will be the updating of this data to reflect trends in income since the information was collected. Projects are likely to be spread over a year or two and it is important that movements in income are properly taken into account, even during the project implementation period. For project feasibility study purposes it would be appropriate to project incomes to the mid-point of the construction period to reflect possible income changes and thereby improve the standards of development possible.

In the allocation of costs to each lot it is usual initially to calculate basic infrastructure costs on a square metre basis, using an average cost of infrastructure per square metre. Particular on-plot development costs are normally individually allocated.

On-plot development options may be various, and therefore need separate tabulation. Table 10.6 shows an example of plot distribution costs in terms of size and number, and the various options calculated for each lot. In choosing the distribution of on-plot development options which are to be added to general infrastructure cost allocations, the overall investment range of affordability as expressed in Table 10.1 must be observed. General infrastructure costs per square metre of lot are aggregated with the chosen distribution of on-plot development options to arrive at total allocated costs per plot.

The allocation of a particular percentile group to a particular lot size, while possible perhaps in a new development project, becomes much more difficult when dealing with an upgrading project, a feature of many community development projects. It is therefore appropriate to examine the implications of cost allocations per lot across the full range of the target group. Although there is unlikely to be an exact correlation between one plot size and one percentile income group, it would be preferable to locate the lower end of the percentile range in the smaller and less expensive plots, in order to increase the chances of affordability.

From Table 10.7 it will be possible to conclude whether the largest majority of beneficiaries will be able to meet monthly charges without undue difficulty. Should a reasonable interpretation of this schedule in

Table 10.6: On-plot Development Options

Key: On-plot developments
1 Service connections
2 Sanitary core
3 Shared firewall
4 Posts and roof
5 Walls

| Plot Size/Distribution | | | On-plot Development | | | | | | | | | | Total | |
Area m²	Number	%	Option 'A' No.	%	Option 'B' No.	%	Option 'C' No.	%	Option 'D' No.	%	Option 'E' No.	%	No.	%
49	900	5	–	–	–	–	630	70	180	20	90	10	900	100
60	6,300	35	–	–	–	–	4,410	70	1,260	20	630	10	6,300	100
72	5,400	30	–	–	–	–	3,780	70	1,080	20	540	10	5,400	100
84	1,800	10	–	–	1,800	100	–	–	–	–	–	–	1,800	100
98	1,800	10	–	–	1,800	100	–	–	–	–	–	–	1,800	100
112	720	4	360	50	360	50	–	–	–	–	–	–	720	100
120	720	4	720	100	–	–	–	–	–	–	–	–	720	100
120+	360	2	360	100	–	–	–	–	–	–	–	–	360	100
Totals	18,000	100	1,440	–	3,960	–	8,820	–	2,520	–	1,260	–	18,000	–
Percentage of options			8		22		49		14		7		100	

Options
A 1
B 1+2
C 1+2+3
D 1+2+3+4
E 1+2+3+4+5

Notes:
a. In this example, a number of options are offered to settlers in respect of on-plot development standards, in addition to the basic plot the cost of which is common to all, subject to size.
b. Thus the larger size plots 120/120+ simply have a service connection — after that they will arrange to have on-plot developments to a standard they can afford but not provided by the project agency.
c. Plot sizes 84 and 98 are assumed to be provided with the service connection plus a sanitary core; after that households will be responsible for further building work, perhaps with a building materials loan.
d. The smaller plots have options ranging from C to D depending on a household's needs and resources.

Table 10.7: Affordability Comparisons — Related to Lot Sizes and Options

Area m²		48			60			72			54	98	112		120
1 Options		'C'	'D'	'E'	'C'	'D'	'E'	'C'	'D'	'E'	'B'	'B'	'A'	'B'	'A'
2 Initially allocated costs $		2,844	3,814	4,165	3,209	4,179	4,530	3,574	4,544	4,895	3,682	4,108	3,649	4,534	3,892
3 Monthly payment (12% – 25 years) $		30	40	44	34	44	46	36	46	48	37	43	36	46	41

Percentage of Monthly Income Represented by Monthly Payment

Percentage

Monthly income	Percentile grouping	48 'C'	48 'D'	48 'E'	60 'C'	60 'D'	60 'E'	72 'C'	72 'D'	72 'E'	54 'B'	98 'B'	112 'A'	112 'B'	120 'A'
118	15	25.5	34.0	37.1	28.6	37.4	40.5	32.0	40.5	43.6	32.9	36.8	32.6	40.5	34.8
129	20	23.2	30.9	33.8	26.0	34.0	36.9	29.1	36.9	39.7	29.9	33.5	29.6	36.9	31.7
140	25	21.3	28.4	31.0	23.9	31.3	33.9	26.8	33.9	36.5	27.5	30.8	27.2	33.9	29.1
156	30	19.3	25.7	28.0	21.6	28.3	30.6	24.2	30.6	33.0	24.8	27.8	24.6	30.6	26.3
169	35	17.7	23.7	25.8	19.9	26.0	28.2	22.3	28.2	30.4	22.5	25.6	22.7	28.2	24.3
182	40	16.4	21.9	23.9	18.5	24.1	26.1	20.6	26.1	28.1	21.2	23.8	21.0	26.1	22.5
205	45	14.6	19.5	21.3	16.4	21.4	23.2	18.3	23.2	25.0	18.8	21.1	18.7	23.2	20.0
253	55	11.9	15.8	17.3	13.3	17.4	18.9	14.9	18.9	20.3	15.3	17.1	15.2	18.9	16.2
277	60	10.8	14.4	15.7	12.1	15.9	17.2	13.6	17.2	18.5	13.9	15.6	13.8	17.2	14.8
342	70	8.8	11.7	12.8	9.8	12.9	13.9	11.0	13.9	15.0	11.3	12.7	11.2	13.9	12.0
467	80	6.4	8.6	9.3	7.2	9.4	10.2	8.1	10.2	11.0	8.3	9.3	8.2	10.2	8.8
541	85	5.5	7.4	8.1	6.2	8.1	8.8	7.0	8.8	9.5	7.1	8.0	7.1	8.8	7.6
616	90	4.9	6.5	7.1	5.5	7.1	7.7	6.1	7.7	8.3	6.3	7.0	6.2	7.7	6.7
688	92.5	4.4	5.8	6.4	4.9	6.4	6.9	5.5	6.9	7.5	5.6	6.3	5.6	6.9	6.0

respect of percentile range/plot size relationship suggest that monthly charges to beneficiaries will fall within the range of earnings adopted (say 10-25 per cent), then one can broadly assume that the standards adopted are appropriate. Should the reverse be true, further analysis is called for. These results might suggest that the infrastructure standards adopted may be too high, having regard to the affordability of the beneficiaries; therefore adjustments should be made. On the other hand, difficult site conditions may have caused the costs to rise, notwithstanding a standard of infrastructure which generally reflects the reasonableness of the benefits when compared with similar developments in the locality.

10.2.9 Cross-subsidy Facility within Residential Areas

It is now appropriate to calculate the subsidy which would be required to bring the cost of these benefits within the affordable range of the beneficiaries. The results from Table 10.7 indicate that a particular group within the percentile range enjoys a level of affordability which is in excess of the benefits being provided. This suggests the possibility of internal cross-subsidies, the more favoured groups assisting those where the impact on earnings is much greater. This levelling-up process for those beneficiaries who are better able to afford the benefits being provided should not, however, be undertaken without care. Inequitable comparisons between benefits provided and charges being made must be avoided, notwithstanding the need to assist the lowest-income groups. The process described emphasises the need from the very start to determine the broad level of investment affordable by all members of the target group — across the full percentile range. Failure to do so could at best lead to a delay in the design of the project as changes are found to be required, but, even worse, create a development that either requires extensive subsidies or results in a high level of default in payments by beneficiaries.

Table 10.8, therefore, calculates the subsidy required if 15 per cent of earnings is the maximum rent payable for general infrastructure and on-plot options. It will be seen that the higher-income group in the percentile range can be charged slightly more than originally allocated costs to assist the lower-income groups. The justification for not charging 15 per cent of earnings first reflects the 'comparative benefits' principle where to do so would impose a burden on these beneficiaries relatively out of line with the benefits being received. Second, allowance is made for the additional on-plot investment required on the larger plots which the smaller plots, in this particular example,

Table 10.8: Calculation of Monthly Charges and Subsidy per Unit

Plot size m²	On-plot option	Target income level $	Percentile group	Monthly affordability (say 15%) $	Capital equivalent $	Allocated cost $	Capital difference $	Percentage subsidy on capital difference	Actual subsidy $	Cost recovered	Monthly charge	Percentage of income
48	C	118	15	18	1,651	2,843	1,192	100	1,192	1,651	18	15
	D	129	20	19	1,841	3,814	1,973	100	1,973	1,841	19	15
	E	140	25	21	2,032	4,165	2,133	100	2,133	2,032	21	15
60	C	156	30	23	2,190	3,208	1,018	100	1,018	2,190	23	15
	D	169	35	25	2,413	4,179	1,766	100	1,766	2,413	25	15
	E	182	40	27	2,603	4,530	1,927	100	1,927	2,603	27	15
72	C	205	45	31	2,920	3,573	653	100	653	2,920	31	15
	D	253	55	38	3,619	4,544	925	100	925	3,619	38	15
	E	277	60	42	3,968	4,895	927	100	927	3,968	42	15
84	A	342	70	51	4,857	3,682	(1,175)	Nil	Nil	3,682	39	11
98	B	467	80	70	6,667	4,108	(2,559)	−20	(412)	4,520	49	10
112	A	541	85	81	7,747	3,649	(4,098)	−50	(2,049)	5,698	60	11
	B	616	90	92	8,794	4,534	(4,260)	−50	(2,130)	6,664	70	11
120	A	688	92.5	103	9,810	3,893	(5,917)	−50	(2,953)	6,846	72	10

Notes: a. This table indicates the amount of subsidy required if only 15 per cent income is reckoned to be available for monthly payments. For example on a 48m² plot size the subsidy would range from $1,192 to $2,133, depending on options, but in practice, where possible, the more expensive options might be unavailable to the lower percentile groups. This must depend on availability of overall subsidy based on internal cross-subsidies. b. It is suggested in this schedule that 100 per cent of the difference between allocated cost and 'affordable' cost should be available for occupiers of plot sizes 48, 60 and 72m² within 15 to 60th percentile groups. Occupiers of plots 98 to 120m² will provide cross-subsidies ranging from 20 per cent to 50 per cent of difference between initially allocated costs and what they can afford. Bearing in mind that additional costs will be incurred by these groups in completing the development of their plots, between 10/11 per cent only of earnings have been reckoned as available for monthly rental.

already possess. ·

10.2.10 Cross-subsidy from Commercial/Industrial Development

The financial appraisal has so far determined the level of subsidy likely to be required by various beneficiaries after taking into account relevant standards of infrastructure and basic land acquisition costs. The pre-feasibility study and earlier assessments in this appraisal should have ensured that the aggregate of all subsidy requirements can be met by surpluses created by the presence of commercial/industrial development in this project.

10.2.11 External Government Subsidies

All previous evidence of development programmes in developing countries tends to suggest that heavy reliance on external forms of subsidy will ultimately lead to a failure of the programme. It follows, therefore, that the programme for creation of a new community should objectively be developed within a broadly self-financing framework. There is, however, evidence to suggest that land acquisition costs in and around the major cities may be destructive of viable projects, based on the philosophy so far outlined in this chapter. As a country's programme develops, it will become clear how constraining an influence the price of land will become on the continued development of the programme. It will be for each government to monitor progress. The possibility may have to be faced of earmarking some form of assistance to ensure the programme's continuity.

10.3 Cash Flow Analysis

10.3.1 Sources and Application

In preparation of the cash flow it is suggested that the order of items to be classified should be as follows:

(1)   Sources:
       government capitalisation or loans
       loans from bilateral or multilateral agencies
       line agency contributions
       income from residents
       income from other revenue-producing developments
       less allowance for uncollected rentals
(2)   Uses/application:
       land acquisition and reclamation

construction costs:
    infrastructure (on-site/off-site)
    on-plot developments
    building materials loans
    community development costs
design and supervision costs
administration and overhead costs
loan repayments:
    government)
    other agencies) principal and interest
working capital
net inflow (outflow)
cumulative cash balance (deficit)
discounted net present value

These are embodied in Table 10.9, entitled Projected Cash Flow, to which the following comments relate.

Sources of Funds. The basis for recovery of costs of the project, either by national line agency or other public sector contributions, should enable the government's capital investment in the project to be treated as a loan to the project and therefore recoverable over time. Normally the basis one might reasonably assume is for recovery of such loans to be spread over 25 years at the prevailing rate of interest.

In practice, however, it may be possible to recover government funds invested in the project at an accelerated rate, especially where profitable elements such as commercial/industrial developments are part of the plan, and freehold disposal is chosen as the basis for land disposal.

Loans from Bilateral and Multilateral Agencies. Loans intended to fund foreign exchange costs of approved projects may be planned to run the full term, for example twenty years with a grace period of five years. Interest during the grace period can either be capitalised (i.e. added to the original capital sum) or if preferred and feasible, paid independently of the principal sum over the first five years.

National and other Agency Contributions. These may be planned to be received within the year in which expenditure is incurred. The financial and administrative arrangements proposed for their recovery should be facilitated by the suggestions outlined. Broadly, therefore, the sources of funds — government loans, loans from international agencies, and national and other agency contributions (items 1, 2 and 3 of the cash flow statement) — should equate to the costs of land acquisition and construction (items 8 and 9) under the category of 'uses'. The timing of the commencement of residential monthly payments will depend on the phasing programme adopted and the schedule of completion of the lots. Every attempt should be made to release lots to the chosen beneficiaries at the earliest point consistent with the requirements of a continuous implementation programme, in order to assist the recovery process.

Disposal of Commercial/Industrial Lots. The appropriate marketing investigation for disposal of commercial/industrial lots will determine the price and absorption rate possible. The terms of both freehold or leasehold disposal will also have been ascertained and it is a matter of simple arithmetic which is to be preferred on a strict net present value basis. But there are other considerations that are dealt with elsewhere.

Default of Beneficiaries. An allowance needs to be made for future default of beneficiaries. This will vary from city to city, but experience dictates that between 8 and 10 per cent of monthly charges should be allowed. There is, however, no substitute for an efficient and effective collection system.

Land Acquisition Costs. In all projects land costs are inevitably weighted towards the front end of the phasing of development and therefore have an early impact on project-funding. The construction costs, however, can be so phased as to limit front-end costs to an absolute minimum consistent with efficient contracting arrangements and the need to generate productive land use in the early part of the programme.

Administrative and Overhead Expenses. Adequate provision must be made for administrative and overhead expenses likely to be associated with the project. The effect of future inflation should be taken into account in forecasting such costs over the longer term.

10.3.2 Results of the Cash Flow

From the tabulation of resources and their utilisation a net inflow (or outflow) of funds can be ascertained on a year by year basis and cumulatively. Viability of the project should already be assured, based on the procedures for recovery adopted. In practice minor cash flow

Table 10.9: Projected Cash Flow Statement, 1978-2002 (Million US $)

	1978	1979	1980	1981	1982	1983	1984	1985	1986	1987	1988-2002	Total
Sources												
Government loan	40.2	10.1	9.6	12.9	9.9							82.7
Loan: international agency	12.1	13.1	12.0	10.5	5.2							52.9
Line agencies — contributions	44.0	38.8	33.1	22.3	8.2							146.4
Residential charges	0.1	1.4	3.3	5.2	7.0	8.1	8.7	9.5	10.1	10.6	161.6	225.6
Commercial/industrial sale of plots	6.2	17.3	24.2	30.0	42.2	26.6	26.3					172.8
Less: uncollected rentals — residential		(0.1)	(0.3)	(0.4)	(0.5)	(0.6)	(0.6)	(0.6)	(0.6)	(0.6)	(8.8)	(13.1)
Total inflow	102.6	80.6	81.9	80.5	72.0	34.1	34.4	8.9	9.5	10.0	152.8	667.3
Uses												
Land acquisition and reclamation	45.3	2.6										47.9
Construction	51.0	59.3	54.7	45.7	23.3							234.0
Administration and overhead expenses		0.1	0.2	0.3	0.5	0.5	0.6	0.8	0.9	1.0	24.0	28.9
Loan repayments												
(International agency)												
Principal						2.0	2.2	2.3	2.5	2.7	41.2	52.9
Interest						3.9	3.8	3.6	3.4	3.2	18.1	36.0
Interest during grace period	1.5	3.4	4.1	5.0	5.8							19.8
Interest on government loan	2.4	5.3	5.3	4.6	3.0							20.6
Working capital	0.6	0.5	0.5	0.3	0.3	0.3	0.3	0.3	0.3	0.3	0.3	4.0
Total	100.8	71.2	64.8	55.9	32.9	6.7	6.9	7.0	7.1	7.2	83.6	444.1
Net inflow (outflow)	1.8	9.4	17.1	24.6	39.1	27.4	27.5	1.9	2.4	2.8	69.2	223.2
Repayment of government loan	1.8	9.4	17.1	24.6	30.1							83.0
Cumulative surplus available for re-investment					9.0	36.4	63.9	65.8	68.2	71.0	140.2	140.2

Note: Capital expenditure includes the expenditure of central government agencies in the sum and time scale shown for contributions.

problems might occur, particularly in the earliest part of the programme where revenues from commercial/industrial sales and residential leases lag slightly behind interest and amortisation payments and recovery of contributions from line agencies are delayed. The projected cash flow, however, is unlikely to show other than minor net outflows on a year by year basis and cumulatively should indicate a growing surplus of funds for re-investment. To complete the analysis, the year by year net flow of funds should be discounted to a positive net present value (NPV). A negative NPV would require investigation and probably suggests inadequacies in the analysis rather than the doubtful viability of the project (Table 10.9).

10.3.3 Sensitivity Analysis

The projected cash-flow statement is based on a series of assumptions ranging from the phasing of construction costs to the realisation of surplus funds from commercial/industrial development; and from the timing of line agency contributions to the speed at which options to purchase land are exercised by beneficiaries. Such assumptions are naturally based on the best information available at the time of the analysis. Some of the assumptions made may be critical to the long-term viability of the project; therefore, the effect of possible changes in those assumptions should be tested and the impact on the cash flow demonstrated.

10.3.4 Project Financial Analysis Flow Chart

The flow chart shown in Figure 10.1 describes the process from initial establishment of the target group and funding of the project to the cash-flow results and viability tests.

10.4 Land Tenure Arrangements for the Housing Programme

Security of land tenure is not only one of the most important goals of the average beneficiary, but is also a stimulus to their investment of both time and money on constructing dwelling units on land they occupy. Although within this context freehold ownership is generally considered to give the greatest security of tenure, this is not to say that leasehold is considered unattractive, particularly where granted over a period of 25 to 30 years. It also has the added attraction of giving the implementing agency greater flexibility for subsequent redevelopment of the project site if future patterns of urban growth change.

The granting of a legal freehold title to existing squatter settlements, a feature which is becoming common in many developing countries,

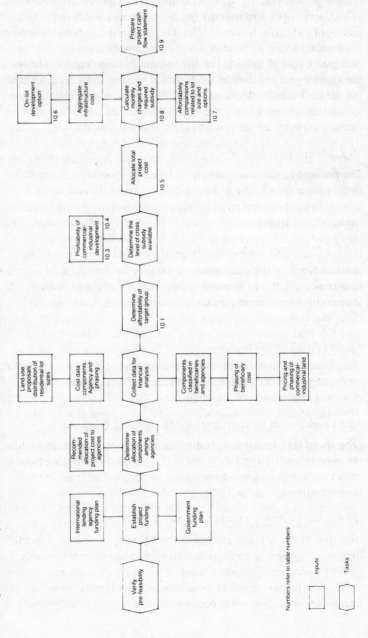

Figure 10.1: Operational Flow Chart for Project Financial Analysis

Numbers refer to table numbers

Inputs

Tasks

Verify pre-feasibility

Establish project funding

International lending agency funding plan

Government funding plan

Determine allocation of components among agencies

Recommended allocation of project cost to agencies

Collect data for financial analysis

Land use proposals distribution of residential lot sizes

Cost data components. Agency and phasing

Components classified in beneficiaries and agencies

Phasing of beneficiary cost

Pricing and phasing of commercial-industrial land

Determine affordability of target group   10.1

Determine the level of cross subsidy available

Profitability of commercial-industrial development   10.3   10.4

Allocate total project cost   10.5

On-lot development option   10.6

Aggregate infrastructure cost

Calculate monthly charges and required subsidy   10.8

Affordability comparisons related to lot size and options   10.7

Prepare project cash flow statement   10.9

raises other issues concerning illegal invasion of privately or publicly owned lands as, if it is continued without control, it may encourage further invasions to the detriment of required urban growth patterns. This is quite separate from the question of equity as far as the original landowner is concerned and is essentially a political question. Leaving this aside, there is little doubt that, taking existing squatter settlements, the granting of a legal title is clearly a basic consideration in obtaining community support for the upgrading of the site and acts as a stimulus to self-help improvements necessary for the successful rehabilitation of those neighbourhoods. It is clear, though, that this policy must be accompanied by an equal emphasis on new community programmes (including sites-and-services areas) to reduce the prospect of continuing abuse of the legal rights of existing landowners. A positive effort in the provision of new development would have the twofold effect of meeting the overspill from the upgraded sites, at the same time removing the pressures and scarcities that initially created the problem of squatter settlements.

10.4.1 Preferred Policy – Residential Lots

On balance it can be argued that land tenure for beneficiaries awarded residential lots in government projects should be largely freehold ownership. However, in a situation where freehold status is offered from the outset, the possibility of exploitation must always be present and this leads to the suggestion that although freehold ownership should be the ultimate goal, safeguards may be necessary initially to avoid the kind of speculation that has occurred in the past. There have been many instances where unencumbered lots are put up to the highest bidder by the initial beneficiary; the eventual beneficiary is from the middle-upper-income range and is probably able to afford other forms of shelter not available to the lower-income group. Therefore, initial tenure might be offered on a leasehold basis, with an option to purchase after a period of continued and uninterrupted occupancy, and faithful and complete compliance of leasehold rules and regulations.

10.4.2 Land Tenure – Conditions and Regulations

It is usually necessary to introduce some form of regulation relating tenure to the development of the lot. Regulations normally would cover two separate problems; those of controlling quality and density of plot development, and of avoiding speculation or exploitation. The regulations would prescribe conditions which must be fulfilled before the right of option can be exercised. For example, that the building on the lot is of reasonable standard in terms of construction materials and layout and does not constitute any statutory nuisance, nor generally present a health hazard to the neighbourhood.

10.4.3 Right of Option to Purchase – Safeguards

The right of option will naturally only be exercised by the original beneficiary of the lease, unless any transfer of lease has prior approval of the managing agency. Any lessee, prior to approval of the purchase option, must have paid all dues and demands under the lease and have a reasonable record of payment. All other conditions having been fulfilled, it may often be recommended that a period of at least one year should elapse before such rights of purchase are accepted, in order to allow adequate time for assessment of the lessee and to avoid exploitation. But otherwise in the majority of projects every encouragement should be given to the beneficiary to take up rights of purchase.

10.4.4 Sale by Beneficiary to Third Party

In the event that beneficiaries may wish to sell their lots at some time in the future, it is important to introduce adequate safeguards to avoid speculation. One measure that may be considered for adoption is a period of grace, once ownership is established, before sales are permitted to third parties. It might be considered that a period of between 3 and 5 years would be appropriate; any desire by the beneficiary to sell within the chosen period could be satisfied by the executing agency purchasing the lot at cost plus inflation, or the agency's approval being sought for sales to third parties at an agreed price. Local circumstances might suggest a number of alternative safeguards which may differ from location to location.

10.4.5 Outright Purchase of Lots

Implementing agencies may wish to consider that, when the right of option to purchase is exercised, any beneficiary choosing to pay for the lot outright may do so, rather than continue on the basis of monthly amortisation. This would assist the project cash flow and should be encouraged, subject to the rigorous enforcement of the safeguards on possible resale to a third party, as previously suggested.

10.4.6 Use of Local Co-operative Group

Enforcement of all the regulations and conditions outlined above would greatly benefit from the participation of a co-operative group, representative of the residential beneficiaries. This community approach is essential in achieving the co-operation of would-be beneficiaries and in the ongoing management and regulation of the newly enfranchised community. The co-operative could be involved in the development of the lots through the organisation of self-help building operations, regulation of on-plot structural standards, management and maintenance of communal facilities and could assist in the day-to-day management of the project, including the collection and recovery of rentals and amortisation payments. The co-operative would also ensure that exploitation is kept to an absolute minimum.

10.4.7 Marketing Policy for Disposal of Commercial Industrial Land

The inclusion of an element of commercial/industrial development in a sites-and-services or upgrading project has a twofold objective. First, as a means of providing a cross-subsidy for residents in meeting development costs, and second, in the creation of employment opportunities. It is important therefore in determining the market policy to have these two objectives in mind.

The appropriate marketing investigation for disposal of commercial/ industrial lots will have determined the prices likely to be realised if sold either leasehold or freehold. It is therefore a matter of discussion which is the more attractive in strict financial terms. Arguments can be mounted in favour of freehold or leasehold disposal. The case for the executing agency retaining the freehold, thereby retaining control over the development and gaining the benefit of future inflationary increases in addition to 'real' growth in values of land as the pace of development proceeds has some merit. But this must be balanced by the pressure for early recovery of capital investment, which on occasions is critical to the project being undertaken.

Clearly, there will be local circumstances that influence the decision, but the cash-flow argument becomes so compelling that freehold disposal should usually be the policy that is adopted for general application. The freehold price for land must be so arranged as to achieve a reasonable pace of development. Prices must be reviewed from time to time; must be competitive and will probably escalate, even over the period of implementation. If leasehold of sites becomes a necessity, the terms of the lease should allow maximum flexibility for future development, should certainly include provision for periodic rental reviews, and might also include an option to purchase after a period of years. A positive and aggressive marketing policy is necessary to maximise the potential of this element of the development programme.

GLOSSARY

Most of the terms in this glossary have been used in the book. Some which have not been used have been included where they have specific relevance to developing countries.

Action Plan: A detailed proposal setting out the action which must be taken to implement the proposals of a development plan. It includes programming and fiscal and administrative proposals.

Affordability: Normally referred to in relation to the level of investment or standards affordable by target beneficiaries in a low-cost housing project.

Amortisation Period: The period over which loans are repaid or assets written down.

Aquifer: A water-bearing geologic stratum.

Betterment: The increment in the value of land owing to public expenditure, or action.

Bilateral Aid Agreement: An agreement to provide assistance (financial, technical) made between two parties — usually government to government.

Core Unit: A small building usually containing sanitary facilities (or at least connections) provided by the developers of a sites-and-services project. It serves as the core of the completed dwelling.

Cost Recovery: The process by which project costs are recovered from the beneficiaries. Low-cost recovery results in high subsidies and leads to poor 'replicability'.

Cost Threshold: The point at which the cost of providing a service or facilities increases substantially due to the need for a major increase in an associated service or facilities, e.g. where the provision of water for expanding residential development would require an additional reservoir or a new main trunk supply.

Cross-subsidy: The use of revenues from profitable elements of a development project to subsidise non-profitable elements.

Draw-down Funds: Those funds which are drawn down from the lending agency for the financing of a project in accordance with the pace of development.

Environmental Area: An area having no extraneous traffic and within which considerations of environment predominate over the use of vehicles.

Freehold: Tenure of property or land on the basis of ownership of title.

Gross Area: The total area (including all uses) of land within a specified boundary. Gross residential area includes the net residential area together with the sites of primary schools, local shops and facilities, workshops and open spaces not included in the net area. It is usual to include half the width of any road on the perimeter of the area.

Gross Density: The total number of units of a particular category (persons, dwellings, industrial workers etc.) divided by the gross area.

Habitable Room: A room which is normally used for living or sleeping in. A kitchen is regarded as a habitable room when it is also used as a living-room.

Household: Usually taken as a group of people who eat together and may include members of more than one family. Often the terms family and household are used indiscriminately and this can be misleading. In some countries a household is taken to be the people who live in a house, but in practice there are usually more households than dwelling units.

Informal Sector: In most poor countries a large proportion of activity is in small businesses making and selling things, and offering a variety of services. These operations are usually unrecorded and may not form part of employment statistics. In other words, they are outside the formal economy.

Infrastructure: The basic system of services and facilities which enables an area to function; it refers to both physical structure such as sewers and roads and social facilities such as educational and health care systems.

Internal Rate of Return: The percentage of the revenue return on capital investment, calculated by reference to the incidence of such investment and the time scale over which the revenues are received. In the calculation the value of each year's revenues would be 'discounted'; the discounting factor used increasing as the years progress. The IRR is the equated figure of such discounted annual rates of return.

Land Use: The use to which land is put. For purposes of measurement the whole curtilage of a site is considered to be used for the purpose to which the buildings within that curtilage are used. Thus the whole area of a garden attached to a house is recorded as residential.

Leasehold: Tenure of property or land for a specified period on the basis of rent paid to an owner (freeholder).

Line Agency: National or regional agency responsible for provision of a particular service to a community.

Lithosol: An extensively distributed group of tropical and sub-tropical soils, freshly and imperfectly weathered without a clearly expressed morphology.

Multilateral Aid Agreement: An agreement to provide assistance (financial, technical) made between three parties or more — usually international funding agencies to government.

Multiplier Effect: The degree to which a job, and the income derived from it, can generate other jobs through spending and associated activities.

Net Area: The total area of a particular land use, exclusive of all other major uses, within a specified boundary. Net residential area normally includes (in addition to housing lots) any small public or private open spaces. It does not include roads. (See also Saleable Area.)

Net Density: The total number of units of a particular category (persons, dwellings, industrial workers etc.) divided by the net area for the relevant land use.

Net Present Value: The net present value is the present-day value of an investment which allows for time-series differences in the rate of that investment and the corresponding rates of return. Thus each year's investments and returns are 'discounted' by an increasing factor as the time scale of the investment increases.

Node: A point of increased intensity; a point of interaction between two systems such as a pedestrian route and a bus route.

Occupancy Rate: (1) The ratio of occupants to the number of habitable rooms in a dwelling; (2) the average number of occupants in a passenger-carrying vehicle.

On-plot (or On-lot) Development: This refers to the development provided by the authority on a housing lot, as distinct from that provided by the beneficiary. For instance, in a sites-and-services development, a service core would be on-plot development and its cost would need to be recovered from rents.

Overspill (or Spill-over in the USA): A term used to describe the excess of population in a given area over the estimated reasonable capacity of the area. In upgrading projects there is usually an 'overspill' of families who will require to be located elsewhere.

Para-transit: Any of a number of small vehicles, such as auto-rickshaws, jitneys, por-puestos etc. which offer seats at a fixed charge over a fixed route. They are usually privately owned and publicly regulated and provide a necessary adjunct to larger buses and trains.

pH: The negative logarithm of the hydrogen-ion activity of a soil; the degree of acidity or alkalinity of a soil.

Poly-nuclear Development: A city or urban region having several important centres. Most cities have a main centre and sub-centres; the term poly-nuclear is used to indicate a less hierarchical system where the centres are more comparable in importance.

Population: Net migration. Balance of out-migration and in-migration to a city or region. May be positive or negative.

Population of Working Age: Potential labour force. This is not the same as the actual working population which is usually referred to as the economically active population.

Primary Activity: Fishing, farming, mining, similar extractive activity, and first-stage processing, e.g. drying and curing tobacco, oil-refining, steel-making.

Primate City: A term used to define the case where a country has one city which is absolutely predominant, and usually several times larger than the next city.

Replicability: A word coined to describe the process whereby project costs can be recovered from rents and sales, in order to allow funds to be recycled and projects repeated.

Reticulation: A network of pipes in a water supply or drainage layout.

Saleable Area: The net area of residential lots and small commercial lots; the area of land in a project which generates revenue. Similar to Net Residential Area, although the latter often includes small 'incidental' open spaces, which are not revenue-producing.

Secondary Activity: Manufacturing and formal service employment, e.g. buying and selling in a store for which rent is paid.

Sensitivity Analysis: An analysis of the sensitivity of the various assumptions which form part of a financial/economic appraisal. By varying each assumption within a realistic margin, the impact of such changes on the overall result can be calculated.

Service Industries: A term used to define industries which are neither extractive nor manufacturing, such as:
    shopping and financial institutions;
    warehousing and communications;
    construction;
    repair shops;
    utilities;
    transport, etc.

Sites and Services: The subdivision of land for residential use and the provision of services, utilities and social facilities. Generally intended

for low-income families, sites-and-services projects normally leave
the building of houses to the families but in some cases varying
amounts of structures, such as core units or dividing walls, are built.

Slum-upgrading: The provision of services, utilities and social facilities
in an area of existing substandard housing. The emphasis is on
improvements in environmental sanitation and access and the
rehabilitation of the houses is usually left to the occupants.

Structure Plan: A development plan which sets out the strategic
framework of policies for economic, social and physical
development — usually at the regional scale. It should also include
a financial programme, sectoral development programmes and a
timetable for immediate action plans.

Tertiary Activity: Employment of a formal or informal nature which
depends on the existence of secondary activity which it tends to
serve and supplement. It includes small-scale informal crafts and
repairs or irregular work such as street-hawking, messenger services,
cleaning and washing, etc.

NOTES ON CONTRIBUTORS

Alan Turner is an architect and planner and is a director of Alan Turner and Associates, a planning consultancy which specialises in the problems of developing countries. In addition to the UK and the USA, he has worked in Venezuela, the Caribbean, Angola, Malaysia, Iran, the Philippines and India, where his experience has ranged from national and regional development planning to specific slum-upgrading and sites-and-services projects. He has published a number of articles on planning and development and is a contributor to a recent book on international urban growth policies.

David Walton is a planner responsible for the direction of the planning and development activities of Halcrow Fox and Associates. He has had experience of projects in Malaysia, Thailand, the Philippines, Indonesia, Tanzania, Iran, Brazil, the Caribbean, Jordan, Europe and the UK. He was Project Director for the Design of Six New Towns in Malaysia and has a special interest in the socio-economic aspects of planning in the Third World and in low-cost, particularly self-help, development.

Graham Fowler is a specialist at Halcrow Fox and Associates responsible for social research and public participation programmes associated with the firm's work in transport and town-planning. As the basis for the design of Six New Towns in Malaysia, he directed a social investigation into the life-styles of potential migrants and their attitudes, preferences and aspirations for the future.

John Butler is an independent economic consultant with long experience of practical work in the field of developing activities in the Third World countries. In 1978-9 he participated in an industrialisation study in Morocco, and was the economic adviser to an urban planning study in Saudi Arabia. He has also worked extensively in East and West Africa. His published works include works on east-west trade, copper and aluminium, and urbanisation, together with participation on an UNCTAD paper on private investment in developing countries.

Kenneth Wren is a director of Economic Development Unit, a consultancy specialising in financial and economic aspects of urban

308

development. Following a career in municipal finance — he was Borough Treasurer for the town of Banbury, Oxfordshire — he held the post of Finance Director and subsequently Deputy General Manager of Milton Keynes Development Corporation. Between the years 1974 and 1979 he was a partner in the consultancy firm of Roger Tym & Partners. He has experience of a large number of developing countries including Thailand, Jamaica, Malaysia, Indonesia, Liberia, The Gambia, Jordan, the Philippines and India.

Richard Westmacott is a landscape planning consultant who specialises in problems arising in developing rural areas due to the effects of urbanisation or of more intensive and changing land use. This work has included assignments in several developing countries, as well as in the UK and USA, and two research studies, one for the US Office of Water Research and Technology, the other for the US Office of Surface Mining. He teaches in the School of Environmental Design at the University of Georgia.

Christopher Blandford is a landscape architect who specialises in ecological planning as an independent consultant. He has worked in the UK, the USA and the Middle East. He is a visiting lecturer at the Department of Architecture, Bristol University.

INDEX

Abrams, Charles 26, 32
action plan 303
administration 148-56; changes in
149; control by 151; costs 150,
295; delegation of 148;
employment in 126-7; local 148-
9; of completed development
165-6; relations with private
sector 150; unit size 149-50, *see
also* finance *and* management
team
aerial photographs 41, 77-8, 256
affordability 80, 88, 253, 264, 279,
281-2, 303; comparisons 290;
increasing 288; investment level
and 280, 291; standards and 218-
19, 229, 264
Africa 23
agricultural industries 28, 56, 123-4,
139
agriculture 21; employment in 133;
importance of 127; in rain forests
177-8; yields 28, 29, 54
aid 16, 71, 128, 156, 282, 303, 305;
institutions 128, 140; recovery of
loans 294-5
alternative plans 89; evaluation of 90
amortisation period 282, 283, 303
Angola 24, 54, 58; land use in 223
aquifers 181-199, 200, 202, 265,
303; yield 213
architects 70
Asia 23
assistance, types of 43

banks 137; government support for
136; rent collection and 152
Basaldua, Raul 24
berm 207-8
Best, R. 221-2
betterment 303
bicycling 56
birth rate 133
Blandford, C.J. 217n
block-making 137-8
Bogota 56, 57, 60; Development
Plan 27
bread making 125

building industry: capacity of 88,
91; in small communities 137-8
building materials 88, 175;
manufacture of 131
buildings: cost of 161, 279, *see also*
housing
bureaucracy 28, 32

capital *see* investment
cash crops 123-4, 139
cash flow 160-2, 301, 293-7;
projections 90, 296
central villages 252
China, People's Republic of 127
cigarette manufacture 125
cities: growth of 21-2; over-
concentration on 21, 252; large
free standing 50; new
communities within 51, 52, 57;
resource based 50-1
Ciudad Guayana 54, 55
climate 36, 90, 178-81, 205;
amelioration of 89; importance of
37-9; categories of 62n, *see also*
desert, rain forest *and* savannah
clothing industry 131-2
Cloudsley-Thompson, J.L. 216n
Clouston, B. 216n
Colombia 56, 57, 60
community 16; concepts of 224,
225-7; opinions 42; participation
in decisions 81-2; role in
administration 149; size of 25,
see also new town and
communities
community centres 245-6
community development 35-64, 91
community facilities *see* social
facilities
conservation areas 89
constraints, development 193, 195;
controls and 205; ranking of 200;
seasonal 215
consultants and consultancy 11-15;
medical analogy for 14; role of
11-12, 75
contracts: choice of contractor 12;
supervision costs 281, 284

310

312   *Index*